FEB   2017

INFERNO

INFERNO

A Doctor's Ebola Story

Steven Hatch, M.D.

ST. MARTIN'S PRESS
NEW YORK

www.stmartins.com

The Library of Congress Cataloging-in-Publication Data is available upon request.

ISBN 978-1-250-08513-9 (hardcover)
ISBN 978-1-250-08514-6 (e-book)

Our books may be purchased in bulk for promotional, educational, or business use. Please contact your local bookseller or the Macmillan Corporate and Premium Sales Department at 1-800-221-7945, extension 5442, or by e-mail at MacmillanSpecial Markets@macmillan.com.

First Edition: March 2017

10 9 8 7 6 5 4 3 2 1

APPROPRIATELY, FOR MARK

Author's Note

When doctors, nurses, and other health-care professionals write about their experiences, they face a particular challenge in how to describe their experiences with patients. On the one hand, I believe that it is critically important to tell the story of the Bong County Ebola Treatment Unit, in no small part so that readers who have not been to Africa can know something about how Ebola affected real people there. On the other hand, patients are entitled to privacy, and should not have to worry about whether their doctor will inappropriately expose their lives for the world to see.

I have tried to walk this fine line by leaving out of this story identifying details about the lives of the patients described in the following pages. In many cases, I have provided pseudonyms and altered superficial aspects of patients' lives so that they are not identifiable. Patients whom I describe from, say, Nimba County may have actually come from Lofa or Margibi counties instead; a man with a daughter may have actually had a son; and so on.

However, a number of the patients from the Bong County ETU had previously been interviewed by local Liberian media as well as a variety of international news organizations. I have not changed the names of those patients who had consented to such interviews, and also of some others whose names were already publicly known. Even as to those, however, I have avoided adding further details about their stays in the ETU beyond what is already a matter of public record.

Contents

How I wish I was in a dream, and I'm waking up, and
I discover, "Oh, that's a dream."

— Joshua Blahyi, formerly known as
"General Butt Naked," circa 2013

INFERNO

INTRODUCTION: THE ABANDONMENT OF UNWHOLESOME THOUGHTS

I think we're never going to agree, for our disagreement is
one between sensibilities. I'd designate them as, on the one
hand, the ironic and ambiguous (or even the tragic, if you
like), and, on the other, the certain. The one complicates
problems, leaving them messier than before and making you
feel terrible. The other solves problems and cleans up the
place, making you feel tidy and satisfied. I'd call the one
sensibility the literary-artistic-historical; I'd call the other
the social-scientific-political. To expect them to agree, or even
to perceive the same data, would be expecting too much.
—Paul Fussell, "Thank God for the Atom Bomb"

Not long after I submitted the first draft of this book to St. Martin's
Press, I found myself sitting in a lecture hall at the medical school
listening to a group of students who had won prizes for writing in
medicine. Over the next hour and change, the prizewinning students
read aloud their essays or poems to the crowd. For the most part, they
told stories about the patients whom they encountered as they began
their formal training. The patients one meets at the beginning of training tend to form an indelible impression, and these students wanted
to preserve those memories for posterity.

After listening to a few readings, I was struck by the similarities
among the pieces, even though the writing styles differed from one another, sometimes starkly so. Virtually every student's musings, whether
in verse or prose, were preoccupied with what the process of learning
medicine was doing to them as individuals. It was clear they feared losing
an essential quality of themselves as the riptide of medical knowledge

and the jargon of physicians pulled them away from the shores of some perceived humanity. You could practically hear all of them shout that they didn't want their capacity for caring and empathy to abandon them, dreading that the system was grinding them into soulless automatons as they learned how to reduce their patients' lives and hopes and dreams to a few terse lines summarizing their "history of present illness" and "past medical history" and culminated in some efficient medical plan. There was a shared poignancy to their laments.

One particular student's words caught my ear. The piece was written by a young student doctor named Haley Newman, someone whom I had known peripherally while she was doing her internal medicine rotation. Her essay described her relationship with a veteran who had been given an unexpected diagnosis of a devastating illness, a cancer with which he would have long and unpleasant battles. She had a gift for words and was able to paint a picture with a carefully selected image: "His Vietnam Veterans of America hat was always sitting on his bedside table, along with a bag of Lays potato chips and a Snickers bar" was but one image that struck me as coming from someone destined to write a weekly column, or a book, on medicine.

Haley's essay was an exercise in enumerating the misgivings that to some extent plague the lives of everyone who takes up the stethoscope as a calling. "Regardless of everything dehumanizing in the hospital—the blue johnnies, the tubes and IV lines, the meals on trays and red help buttons—these individuals are not just patients," she wrote. "They are unique people with powerful stories, and their identities should not be erased by their illnesses." To my ears, her eloquence masks a quiet rage against all the degrading aspects of medicine, a process she can sense is already changing her, hardening her in ways such that she may not even be able to recognize herself a few years hence.

It's even worse than she knows, for some of that learned insensitivity to suffering is pretty much required for us to care for our patients, and it constitutes one of the central paradoxes of being a doctor or nurse. The good news, I want to tell her, is that it really *is* possible to maintain the human element in medicine, although it takes some conscious effort. The bad news is that one almost never stops fighting this rearguard battle to preserve that element every day of one's professional life, and even the finest physicians will have a career littered with defeats.

These student essays also underscored another feature of how we medical professionals cope with that kind of paradox: We simply bear witness to what happens to our patients. All of the essays told stories of sadness and loss, and that kind of activity continues well beyond medical school. We tell these stories to one another in conference rooms, quick conversations in hallways, longer rap sessions with spouses or friends, and for some of us, in formal writing. They provide our way not only of coping but of reaffirming why we chose the work of caring for total strangers in the first place. Nearly all great literature is an affirmation of humanity, and the act of bearing witness is what the best writers have done for millennia. But doctors' stories are our special means by which we can say to the world that the lives of our patients matter and the practice of medicine is essential to humanity. We tell these stories by using the technical language of anatomy and physiology, as we elaborate upon the privileged access we are granted to our patients' bodies and, on occasion, souls.

At its core, this book is no different than Haley's essay and those of her classmates whose work illuminated that day; it possesses the same structure, with the same goals in mind. As the title proclaims, *Inferno* is a *doctor's* story of the Ebola outbreak. It is an attempt to use my experiences as a physician working before, during, and after the West African outbreak of 2014 and 2015 to provide readers with an understanding of something beyond much of the news coverage at the time—especially the television news, which so greedily chewed up and spat out images of workers in space suits moving alongside dying Africans.

The West African outbreak, an unprecedented biological catastrophe that killed tens of thousands, completely shut down the three countries of Guinea, Sierra Leone, and Liberia, along with the twenty-two million people who live there. During that time, Ebola's tendrils reached far beyond this small patch of African soil. The virus itself managed to find its way to ten countries in all, although the fear it engendered caused governments around the world to hastily alter travel policies and infection control procedures. An Ebola story simply focused on what took place in air travel could easily fill a volume; a different story about what happened to the world stockpiles of, say, latex gloves (a rudimentary yet critical piece of Ebola protective gear) could, in the hands of a good writer, make for gripping reading. But this is a doctor's story, one that focuses its gaze on the destruction of the body as part of a doctor's daily work.

My goal, in writing this story, is to ask a few simple questions. Why did this Ebola outbreak kill so many, when twenty prior outbreaks never infected more than a few hundred? How does the virus spread, and ultimately kill, with such ruthless efficiency? What impact did it have on the lives of the people who lived through the epidemic—those never infected, as well as the survivors? And what could have been done differently so that there was less aggregate misery once the virus jumped into its first human host? My experiences—what happened to me in real time—are what I use to frame these questions.

Answers of a sort can be found in the pages that follow. However, I am less interested in providing the reader nice, clearly defined solutions to these questions, as if they were a kind of mathematical equation, than I am in wanting to impart a *sensibility* about the meaning that the story of the West African outbreak holds for readers everywhere. If after reading the final page you have a distressing sense of the depth of the problems the Ebola outbreak unmasked and just how fragile the idea of optimism is in this troubled part of the world, then I have achieved at least one of my aims in writing this.

In the late 1980s, the essayist, literary critic, and political commentator Paul Fussell wrote a provocative essay with the even more provocative title "Thank God for the Atom Bomb," which, as advertised, offered an explanation of why he was thankful for that act of ultimate aggression. It appeared in the pages of *The New Republic*; after its publication, Michael Walzer, the author of *Just and Unjust Wars*, took Fussell to task for what he perceived was the defense of a morally indefensible act.

Far from being a far-right-wing nationalist screed about extremism in the defense of liberty not being a vice, Fussell's reply to Walzer's critique sketched out the importance of experience in shaping one's thoughts about the world and how the further away from a complicated and contradictory situation one gets, the easier and more tidily such ambiguities get resolved in the minds of those who did not live through it. His objective was, in some sense, to scramble the debate about the ethics of dropping the atom bomb since it presupposed a clarity of moral choice, yea-or-nay, that was far foggier in the moment.

Fussell's quote that opens this introduction encapsulates his philosophy: an explanation that demands we cradle a sense of tragedy and irony when we encounter history, and not simply banish it to the far reaches of our consciousness. Since the tragic sensibility is, almost by definition, so painful to maintain, it is asking a lot of readers, and it is understandable why so many social scientists and other commentators can hold forth on a variety of historical horrors with a sense of happy certainty. *If only X hadn't taken place, then Y wouldn't have happened*, you hear the arguments go, and suddenly history transforms into a series of easily correctable mistakes, instead of an appalling slog of frequently stupid, inane, and self-mutilating events as we collectively slouch toward Bethlehem.

I'm not here to relitigate arguments about the ethics of the atomic bomb but only to note that this book takes its cues from Fussell and attempts to locate itself in that literary-artistic-historical tradition of which he writes. And I partly follow his lead in thinking that experience can shape perspective. Not everyone could experience the Ebola outbreak in order to arrive at such a sensibility; this book is an attempt to help translate that experience for readers.

Despite coverage from news organizations that exhibited a wide range of depth and quality, the media portrayal of the Ebola outbreak was surprisingly uniform in terms of how it portrayed the "bigger picture." By my reckoning, it could be summarized thus: Ebola was a major catastrophe that was stopped through the heroic efforts of aid organizations working in conjunction with local governments, with significant help from several countries outside Africa. *That* is the social-scientific-political way of understanding the events of the largest Ebola outbreak in history. There is a certain truth to it. But *Inferno* tries to add a deep sense of disquiet to that mostly upbeat, but largely shallow, narrative. Yes, the outbreak was brought to heel, and people's lives are better in West Africa today as a consequence. But to provide a more complete perspective on what took place, it is necessary to lace a good deal of despair around a tenuous thread of hope, and the stories I tell in the following pages have that objective in mind. I would like to think *Inferno* isn't oppressive in its outlook, for I do mean to try to convey a kind of hope. Nevertheless, reading it may well make you feel terrible, at least for a time.

Anyone who has read Richard Preston's work of horror *The Hot Zone* knows that Ebola stories center on the virus's astonishing lethality and the grisly manner by which people die—namely, bleeding from every orifice. That story has been written, however, and *Inferno* tries to offer a different perspective (and, on occasion, correct some misunderstandings that Preston created) so that the word Ebola conjures up more than mere fear but rather a tragedy created by the virus, one that affected real humans whose lives have been thrown into chaos because of the contagion. In *The Hot Zone*, the central character is the virus itself, while the people it infects are mere props. Most of the news coverage of the outbreak, especially the television news coverage, followed Preston's lead in this respect.

Inferno by contrast puts the spotlight on people: principally the Liberians infected by the virus but also others who worked to see it halted. I'm not interested in engendering fear but, instead, a sense of loss, for there was much of that as a result of the epidemic. To understand the contours of that loss, to *feel* that loss, is to veer away from the vicarious thrills that much of the news coverage encouraged, even if it was mostly subconscious.

I have studied lethal viruses and bacteria for most of my adult life, and I can assure you there are a good many other infections whose reputations should be equally notorious as Ebola's. The Nippah and Hendra viruses, for instance, cause encephalitis (infection of the brain), can be lethal in up to one-third of cases, and have been associated with person-to-person transmission; the movie *Contagion* was based on an imagined version of an easily transmissible Nippah variant. Plague still continues to plague civilization, as it were, and we may well hover on the verge of a massive outbreak of plague's agent, *Yersinia pestis*; the last episode of airborne plague occurred in Surat, India, a city of four million people, in 1994. Then there is SARS, perhaps the one virus that I find truly frightening, as it is about as lethal as Ebola but spreads much more efficiently, since it is a respiratory virus whose transmission dynamics are not much different from those of the common cold. I could go on like this quite happily for some time, and you would lose sleep for a night or two.

The question, then, is *why* does Ebola occupy the starring role among the cast of lethal viruses? I would argue that the features that make Ebola so terrifying are plainly visible in the news coverage devoted to outbreaks over the years, as well as nonfiction books like *The Hot Zone*, and even fictional accounts based on the virus, like the 1995 box-office hit *Outbreak*. They revolve around three basic themes: blood, facelessness, and, of course, Africa—a region about which Westerners in particular have much angst and guilt.

In short, it is the legacy of slavery that lurks beneath the surface of the anxieties unleashed by Ebola. The profound otherness of Africa and its people is a direct consequence of European government policies that lasted generations on end, which led to unspeakable acts that debased the humanity of all the participants. But the termination of slavery as an institution did not end the mutual mistrust, and the iniquities of our European forebears have been visited upon us in countless ways. (They need not be *literal* forebears, either, for we have all inherited their model of government, as well as their notions about liberty, despite the concept of "liberty" resting on the backs of the millions of African slaves without whom the building of the modern world might not have taken place.) The sins of slavery have been ingrained into our consciousness, even without our consent, and continue to make discussions of race so discomfiting today. Richard Preston described Ebola in one metaphorical fugue as "the revenge of the rainforest," but what makes *The Hot Zone* in part so disturbing is that the virus is just as easily understood as *Africa's* revenge, and all the baggage that goes with it, the ultimate payback for five hundred years of barbarity.

Inferno starts with the assumption that one must rob the virus of its metaphorical power, which requires calling attention to the institution of sub-Saharan African slavery and the changes it wrought on at least three continents. While I am not writing a book *about* slavery, one cannot truly grasp something essential about the outbreak unless one begins to come to terms with it, and in particular how slavery has seeped into the American worldview in ways about which we are often only dimly aware. To talk about the "meaning" of the outbreak is to shine a flashlight on the nearly imperceptible threads that link Westerners, West Africans, and a good many other people to the decisions made by, say, ministers who lived in London or Amsterdam four hundred years ago.

Since this is a doctor's story, but also a story by a white American doctor in the midst of African patients, I have tried to be acutely aware of the need not only to bear witness to their stories but to note the special circumstances in which I am obligated to bear witness to them. A century ago, Joseph Conrad, who was not a doctor, did a good deal of bearing witness to the shocking cruelty taking place in the Belgian Congo, and he turned that experience into the classic work of fiction *Heart of Darkness*. Marlow's travels up the Congo would become required reading for generations of students in the West, and in some sense set the standard by which we measured this kind of literature. If *Inferno* shares Paul Fussell's notions of literary tragedy, it follows Conrad's form.

Yet in a lecture given in 1975, the great author Chinua Achebe reappraised Conrad's work, and the critique that resulted is scathing. Achebe alleges that *Heart of Darkness* represents a "desire—one might indeed say the need—in Western psychology to set Africa up as a foil of Europe, as a place of negotiations at once remote and vaguely familiar, in comparison with which Europe's own state of spiritual grace will be manifest." He charges that Conrad's novel projects the image of Africa as "other," a savage place where "man's vaunted intelligence and refinement are finally mocked by triumphant bestiality." That is, Achebe alleges *Heart of Darkness* is just idealized claptrap about Africa; what makes it supposedly great literature is that Conrad happened to be a remarkable English prose stylist.

Achebe wrote those words while living in Massachusetts, the place I now call home, and I suspect that by "Europe" he meant not just the physical place where Europeans live but a mental space where a good many people of European descent locate themselves no matter where they find themselves on a map. The problem with *Heart of Darkness*, he argues, is that whatever its earnest contempt for human enslavement, it nevertheless manages to hold fast to this duality of civilization/primitiveness and doesn't appear to be especially interested in doing the hard work required to move beyond it. The *actual* Africans are just window dressing.

He ponders all of this as he completes his analysis of Conrad, saying that the West's goal should be "to look at Africa not through a haze of distortions and cheap mystifications but quite simply as a continent of people—not angels, but not rudimentary souls either—just people, often highly gifted people and often strikingly successful in their enterprise with life and society." It's a relentlessly downbeat evisceration of a work that even Achebe agrees is deserving of attention. By the end, the reader might dare to hope for a silver lining, but his dissection of Conrad doesn't end on a buoyant note. He concludes by writing, "I realized that no easy optimism was possible. And there was, in any case, something totally wrong in offering bribes to the West in return for its good opinion of Africa. Ultimately the abandonment of unwholesome thoughts must be its own and only reward."

If we, as Americans, or Europeans, or even Africans, are to find a way past the degrading binary of civilized-versus-savage—a binary that was subtly reinforced in the vast amount of news coverage devoted to the West African Ebola outbreak, even though it took place one hundred years after Joseph Conrad's tale and nearly forty after Chinua Achebe's prescient diagnosis of its shortcomings—then it's high time we made some effort at demystifying our larger narratives about events in Africa that have a major impact on the West. *The Hot Zone*, for all of its spine-tingling excitement, not only fails to take part in this demystifying process but largely perpetuates the dualities that so incensed Achebe in the first place.

What I have tried to do here, in telling my Ebola story, is to remove the haze of distortions and cheap mystifications as best I can. I cannot say whether the effort is clumsy, nor whether it is any less racist than Conrad's well-meaning and lyrical work. I send this work out into the world mindful, even perhaps fearful, of a sharp reprimand from the spirit of Achebe as well as his intellectual descendants that

I have repeated Conrad's mistakes, substituting my own distortions for his, having gotten no further in understanding the place a century later. I can only note that I have tried to do something different in writing about Ebola, which is to be conscious of the virus as a metaphor and the power that metaphor holds in so many people's thinking. I have done what I can to meet Africa on its own terms.

The patients my colleagues and I treated weren't *Ebola victims:* They were farmers, miners, and nurses; they were husbands, wives, and children; they were the aged who had lived through so much suffering in the lives of their countries and still were there. The words of Haley Newman, the med student I listened to that day, are right: Patients *are* unique people with powerful stories, and their identities should not be erased by their illnesses. No more, no less. If their identities, their stories, become part of the larger Ebola narrative as understood in the West, then the virus won't simply serve as a stand-in for all that is "savage" or "primitive" or all the other nonsensical things ever written or thought about Africa by a Westerner. Ebola is just a *virus*. That fact should not by any means distract from just how deadly that virus could be, however.

Since I mean to keep the focus of this story on my experience as a physician working through the outbreak, I have largely kept my personal and family life out of the narrative. Readers may wonder at various points about how my departure or return affected my family and find it a bit of a shock when they finally are mentioned more than two hundred pages into the book, thinking that I have removed a critical piece of a narrative puzzle, or perhaps have revealed myself to be a disembodied or heartless professional with no personal attachments in the world.

For better or worse, I deliberately chose not to include extensive passages about my family or personal life, for I mean to keep the spotlight on Africa, since I believe *this* is the story that needs telling. Already much is known about the personal experience of Ebola volunteers through the experiences of such brave and remarkable people as Craig Spencer, Kent Brantly, and Kaci Hickox, so writing about my own life would describe already-covered ground. The major exception is the chapter "Purgatory," which covers the period immediately following my return home. In that instance, I thought it important to explain what it felt like to be a returning volunteer, so that people could have some understanding of the effect of the many policies being implemented by various states at the time and how those policies played an important role in national politics during that stretch.

A word as to the title. Dante's masterpiece serves as the starting point for many reasons: Africa is hot, working in protective gear is hotter still, and *inferno* aptly describes the almost unending raging fever of Ebola, a phenomenon that I have only rarely seen in an acute viral illness. But other parallels justify borrowing his title as well. *Inferno* calls attention to the time during which the work made its appearance in the 1320s, for Dante finished it a little more than a generation before one of the greatest plagues, the Black Death, decimated Europe. There were definitely moments when even the most seasoned epidemiologists wondered whether the West African outbreak might reach similar proportions.

The title *Inferno* also underscores that the Ebola outbreak was experienced by the vast majority of people living in the affected countries, to varying degrees, as a religious experience in which God's judgment was unleashed on the world and people were being asked to journey through a literal hell on earth. In Liberia, where I worked, this spiritual dimension was broadly understood through a Christian frame of reference, as Christians constitute nearly 90 percent of the population. I meditate on the relationship between Ebola and Christianity in Liberia at greater length in the chapter "Behold, a Pale Horse."

When I began writing *Inferno*, I had a more concrete notion of how the book would pay homage to the original by incorporating nine circles, each one descending further toward some final, unspeakable horror that encapsulated the entire episode. After a few attempts at drafting an outline like this, I realized I was being too literal. However, the nine chapters of the *Inferno* you find before you are, I hope, not entirely unlike Dante's poem: stops on an unplanned pilgrimage that consumed nearly two years of my life and altered me in ways with which I am still coming to terms.

Along this journey I have encountered not only patients but hundreds of professionals from all walks of life and dozens of countries. They, too, were in the midst of their own journeys, and I have tried to capture a shared quality of the collective experience.

I pray that I have done right by all of them.

1

THE VESTIBULE

A screaming comes across the sky. It has happened before, but there is nothing to compare it to now.

—Thomas Pynchon, *Gravity's Rainbow*

This is a horror story. And as if someone from central casting were pulling the strings, this horror story begins with a small child happily playing right outside his home.

Meliandou is a small village of a few hundred inhabitants living in approximately thirty rustic dwellings in the hinterlands of Guinea, a satellite of the city of Guéckédou, a place to which the villagers, mostly farmers, come to sell their produce in the Nzérékoré Region, the easternmost province of a country shaped almost like an apostrophe that lost its footing in the middle of a sentence and was falling forward. Meliandou's North American equivalent would be described as "sleepy" and perhaps "idyllic." Although it would be naïve to think that Meliandou's people have lived a content, pastoral existence for centuries or even decades, as of the early twenty-first century, a quiet kind of peacefulness could be found there.

Emile Ouamouno was the beneficiary of this relative prosperity. The child of Etienne and Sia, Emile was growing up as children do in a relatively sheltered environment, exploring the natural world around him, which in the depths of the West African rain forest provided no end of wonders for a curious two-year-old. A picture of the three of them can be found on the Internet. Although they aren't smiling, one gets the sense that they are satisfied with their lives. They're an unmistakably beautiful family. Sia is on the right, her left hand on her hip, wearing an abstract-patterned light dress, with long white earrings and a yellow bead necklace. Her hair is close cropped. Etienne occupies the center, wearing a red-and-black soccer jersey. And Emile sits upright, staring into the camera, held in the crook of his father's right arm, eyes wide, the chubby cheeks of toddlerhood not yet dissipated. The graininess of the picture makes it look like it could have been taken in the 1960s, but it is from 2013.

Along with other children, Emile used to frequent a large tree at the periphery of the village. The tree was a natural jungle gym, with a hollow at its center large enough for a grown man to walk inside and even climb up into. By the news reports, the kids used to love playing around the tree. Again, you can find pictures of this tree in a few seconds with a Google search. It provided a natural setting for children to spend their afternoons doing what kids should do, especially a child of Emile's age.

It wasn't only children who utilized the tree for its size and the protection it offered. Farther up in the hollow, a nest of Angolan free-tailed bats had quietly taken up residence. The bats belong to the insect-feeding species *Mops condylurus*, and they are extremely common throughout much of sub-Saharan Africa. Their droppings would fall to the ground and mingle with the soil. With the heat of the jungle in the dry season, you would hardly have noticed the guano at all. And nobody did. Certainly the children didn't, focused as they were on the joys of playing. But it was this interface of child-bat-guano that may have led to Emile Ouamouno becoming Patient Zero of the West African Ebola outbreak in December 2013, the first spark in a fire that would rage for months and then years, a child who became the nexus of a tragedy in which thousands would die, thousands more would be maimed, and tens of thousands of others would feel its shockwaves without ever coming near the agent that transmitted such suffering.

The screaming first came across the sky in 1976. Quite remarkably, *two* simultaneous outbreaks took place hundreds of miles apart, one in the southern part of Sudan, the other in Zaire, the country we now call the Democratic Republic of the Congo, or DRC. The Sudan outbreak led to nearly three hundred infections, and half of the patients died. The Zaire epidemic led to about the same number of infections, but in this outbreak nine of every ten patients died. The identification of this strange and very deadly new virus would take place in state-of-the-art facilities designed to deal with the most lethal pathogens on the planet—so-called Biosafety Level 4 laboratories. In short order Ebola would develop a reputation among the scientists who studied it as the most fearsome of a small group of truly terrifying infectious agents.

Ebola became one of a number of viruses that would earn the moniker of "emerging infectious diseases," although the term itself indicates the hubris by which *Homo sapiens* sometimes regard our world. The virus had hardly "emerged"; it's just that we finally happened to stumble upon it and identify it for what it was. What we now call Ebola has without any doubt been around for thousands of years, probably tens of thousands. Although much of what we know about Ebola is provisional and therefore subject to wide ranges of interpretation, we're reasonably sure that the virus has circulated among fruit bats for millennia in much the same way that cold viruses circulate among humans—that is, it might make them sick, but not ever sick enough to do any real harm. A virus has an interest in not making its host too sick, because then it can survive in a happy equilibrium by making copies of itself and continuing to survive as long as it has plenty of hosts to which it can spread. It has no interest in killing its primary host—or at least killing it quickly—since then it can't spread and will ensure its own demise. But when a virus jumps a species, and it happens to be deadly to that other animal, all bets are off.

The fruit bat may be Ebola's "natural reservoir"—the creature in which the virus finds its primary home—although, again, nobody is completely certain of that. Unlike many other viruses, whose place in nature scientists have been able to deduce from careful field studies, Ebola for all its ferocity has been something of a shy predator, disappearing back into the jungle as quickly as it materializes, making itself seemingly invisible despite decades of animal testing conducted on the creatures who live at the site of the outbreaks. It wasn't until 2005—after nearly three decades of seriously funded, high-level research—that scientists were able to spot the genetic signature of Ebola in the blood of fruit bats, which provided indirect evidence that the bats were its natural home. Four years later, Ebola's sibling, the Marburg virus, was isolated in fruit bats. Thus far, three species have been proven to possess the virus: the hammer-head bat, or *Hypsignathus monstrosus*; the little collared fruit bat, or *Myonycteris torquata*; and finally, the elaborately named Franquet's epauletted fruit bat, or *Epomops franqueti*. Fruit bats are fairly endearing creatures, with humanlike faces and a soft fur on all but their wings. They are commonly called "flying foxes" based on their resemblance. But the bats believed to be nesting in the tree in Meliandou were not fruit bats at all and aren't especially cute. Yet the close proximity of *Mops condylurus* to Emile Ouamouno seemed suggestive, although subsequent research on bats captured in the area found no evidence of current or prior infection. The bat-origin hypothesis could not be confirmed, becoming another tantalizing clue in a complex puzzle, and much about how the virus behaves in its natural environment remains completely unknown.

Ebola got its name by a slight bending of the rules of virus nomenclature on the part of the scientists who discovered it. The Zaire outbreak in 1976 began in a Catholic mission hospital in a village known as Yambuku. The hospital saw the first patients of this distinct and novel disease, more than twenty in all. Nearly all of them died, which led the staff doctor to alert the Zairean Ministry of Health, who sent a team to investigate and found the hospital closed because the staff themselves had become sick. The medical staff too nearly all died. This was what prompted the government of Zaire to call for the international response that led to the collection of blood samples and eventual isolation of the virus. Traditionally, viruses such as these are named based on the location where the first cases are identified. Marburg's natural reservoir, for instance, is in Africa, but it is named after the German town where the first known human cases of the disease occurred, in animal workers handling African green monkeys. Similarly, at nearly the same time the patients in Yambuku were dying, a group of teenagers in a small town in Connecticut had become moderately ill with a disease that would eventually be proven to be bacterial in origin, but the scientists applied the same "viral" rule of naming it after the site of its discovery. The town's name is Lyme.

There were, however, some downsides to following the custom of naming this particular virus Yambuku, especially in a place like rural Africa. Stigmatization was a serious problem. A virus discovered in the late 1960s in a small Nigerian town led to its christening as the Lassa virus, with the consequence that the inhabitants of that place were treated with suspicion and hostility for years afterward. Of the international team, Dr. Karl Johnson, who served as the head of the Centers for Disease Control's Special Pathogens Branch, had proposed sidestepping this problem by naming the virus after a local river. He had done the same the decade before with a deadly virus that caused a disease known as Bolivian Hemorrhagic Fever, giving it the name of Machupo—a tributary of the Amazon. The team favored this approach. They looked on a map, saw a tributary of the Congo known as Ebola, and the name thus took. The name Ebola is from a local Bantu language, Lingala, and means "black river." It was hard to come up with a better name for it than that.*

Ebola required another name as well—the class to which it belonged. Viewed under the scanning electron microscope, both Marburg and Ebola had a shape that was completely unlike that of any virus seen before. Most human viruses are roughly spherical in shape, whether HIV, measles, the Hepatitis A, B, and C viruses, and so on. One partial exception is rabies, which if contracted and left untreated is nearly 100 percent lethal, and is thus, along with untreated HIV, technically humankind's most deadly virus. Rabies has a shape that looks almost exactly like a bullet. But Ebola and Marburg have a long, tube-like structure that folds over on itself in erratic ways, each copy of the virus appearing to be slightly different from the next. Not long after Ebola's discovery, a group of scientists proposed the family name of *tuburnavirus*, from the Latin meaning "tubular virus." Instead, in the early 1980s, a symposium on Ebola and Marburg naming was held by the International Committee on Taxonomy of Viruses, the body in charge of providing names and classifications not only to Ebola and

---

* While the above etymology is from Peter Piot's memoirs, an alternate explanation is that Ebola is a corruption of the French colonial *l'eau blanche*, which means "white water." Given the behavior of the French, Belgians, Germans, and British in the Congo River Basin in centuries past, it may be harder to come up with a better name for the virus than *that*, on second thought. The articles explaining both versions are cited in the bibliography.

Marburg but to all viruses discovered in the world, so that there is some uniformity of nomenclature in the scientific literature. Shortly thereafter, a new proposal to call the family *filovirus* (from the Latin for "filamentous virus") was submitted to the committee. The concept was the same as that of the name tuburnavirus but was less of a mouthful, and the name stuck.

The mystery deepened. The Sudan outbreak of 1976 would prove to be an Ebolavirus, but although its behavior in humans was roughly similar to that of the Zaire strain—it was, indeed, a little less lethal—its structure was not identical. While the basic internal machinery of the virus was the same, the proteins that coated the surface of the virion were shaped differently. In the laboratory, antibodies that were highly specific for the virus from the Yambuku patients could not latch on to the virus from the Sudanese patients. However, less specific antibodies cross-reacted with both types. Thus, two strains of Ebola had been discovered that year: the Sudan Ebolavirus and the Zaire Ebolavirus. It was the latter that would reappear in Meliandou.

But in 1976, just as quickly as it had begun, the screaming abruptly halted. In 1979, a small outbreak occurred in the town of Nzara, the same location as the original Sudan outbreak. Nearly three dozen people were infected, and two-thirds of them died. After that, however, human Ebola would not be heard from again for more than fifteen years. Then, starting in the mid-1990s, the virus would burst back in terrifying paroxysms that would affect not only Sudan and the now newly named DRC, but also Gabon, Uganda, and the Republic of the Congo. The outbreaks would return almost yearly up to the present day, and these governments in Central Africa would learn to maintain extreme vigilance against the disease.

The screaming then took an even more ominous turn. In 1989, an animal quarantine facility in Reston, Virginia, noticed some crab-eating macaques from the Philippine island of Mindanao—more than seven thousand miles away from Sudan or the DRC—had come down with an unexplained serious illness. Under the eyes of the electron microscope, it had the hallmark spaghetti-like appearance of a filovirus, and the nonspecific antibodies against Ebola lit up, which must have come as a serious shock to the scientists involved. Moreover, the disease was spreading inside the facility, as macaques from different shipments began to fall ill. This strongly implicated that the pathogen wasn't transmitting through direct creature-to-creature contact, as had all previous accounts of Ebola transmission.

You couldn't have scripted a more unsettling scenario: Not only had one of the world's deadliest viruses nestled itself into the United States, it was an *airborne* strain of the disease. And it was within a half hour's drive of the nation's capital. Because of this, several years later, when Richard Preston penned *The Hot Zone* in 1995, very little needed to be exaggerated for the book to live up to its subtitle: *A Terrifying True Story*. The core story of the Reston outbreak in the hands of a masterful writer such as Preston quickly turned *The Hot Zone* into an international best seller, and Ebola captured the popular imagination. At almost the same time, a more comprehensive and scholarly consideration of the subject of emerging infectious diseases (of which Ebola was one small chapter) had come out, and Laurie Garrett's *The Coming Plague* also catapulted to fame.

The only good news from the 1989 Reston outbreak was that it appeared *not* to cause disease in humans, as a half dozen of the workers involved in the incident were found to have antibody responses to the virus, even though they never became ill. The more sobering news, which wasn't much emphasized in *The Hot Zone*, was that the Reston Ebolavirus could be found almost halfway around the world from the previous outbreaks, and in a place where the citizenry travels much farther and with much greater frequency. It indicated there were biological threats out there of which we were only dimly aware, and they were capable of exploiting ways in which humanity was organized in the late twentieth century that might, at its worst, threaten civilization itself.

The release of *The Hot Zone* and *The Coming Plague* in 1995 couldn't have been more serendipitous, for in that year perhaps the scariest of Ebola outbreaks until then took place, when the virus made its first truly urban appearance in Kikwit, a city of around two hundred thousand people in the country then called Zaire. As with the initial outbreaks, more than three hundred people became infected; the case fatality rate was 80 percent. But the Kikwit outbreak did more than just boost sales and make publishers happy, for it got people thinking about what might happen if Ebola was discovered in a truly large African city—say, of one or two million people. Those cities, of course, have airports with international destinations. And by the late 1990s Africans were traveling more and more, and to every corner of the world.

Emile Ouamouno fell ill in late December 2013.* Nobody knows what his precise symptoms were because hardly anyone who cared for him is left alive. He had a fever and may have had a headache. He reportedly had bloody diarrhea. Of course, dozens of diseases can cause bloody diarrhea, all of them considerably more common than Ebola, which had not been seen before in Guinea. This is a book about Ebola, but it is worth pointing out that infectious diarrhea remains among the biggest killers of children under the age of five in this part of the world. Baby Emile was much more likely to have rotavirus, enterohemorrhagic *E. coli*, non-typhoidal *Salmonella*, or *Campylobacter*, among many other organisms, than anything so exotic as Ebola. The global health community has made considerable progress in preventing such deaths, cutting the mortality rate in half over the past fifteen years. It's actually a great story that should be told to the public. Yet, despite this uplifting advance, more than half a million children annually still die of this largely preventable and treatable condition, which is virtually unheard of in the West.

Emile, of course, did have Ebola. He died on December 28. The death of a child in this setting is not all that uncommon; on average, nearly one out of every ten children born in sub-Saharan Africa does

---

* I am following the timeline supplied by the World Health Organization. On August 9, 2014, *The New York Times* reported Emile Ouamouno as having died in early December 2013, although in a later story in the *Times* entitled "How Ebola Roared Back" (December 30, 2014), a picture of a list of the victims transcribed by one of the villagers of Meliandou showed the dates consistent with the WHO timeline. Likewise, the BBC reported that it was a midwife in Meliandou who sought care in Guéckédou rather than Koumba Ouamouno, but WHO's flowchart indicated otherwise. Moreover, it is also worth mentioning that Emile was sometimes identified as a one-year-old in the news reports by these organizations. All of these minor discrepancies highlight the difficulties of recording accurate information in the midst of this fast-moving epidemic in a place as remote as the rain forests of West Africa, especially given the potential for misunderstandings between Western reporters working on tight deadlines and rural African villagers. (NB: "How Ebola Roared Back" is essential reading for anyone wishing to understand more details about the problems in the early global health response, of which I relate only a small amount here.)

not live to see their sixth birthday. But the despair of the Ouamouno family would not end there. On New Year's Day 2014, Emile's three-year-old sister Philomène became ill and would follow Emile to the grave by January 5. Both were cared for by Sia, who was then seven months pregnant with her third child. The fever hit her the day after Philomène died. Sia had a miscarriage on January 11 and died that same day. Emile and Philomène's grandmother, Koumba Ouamouno, cared for all of them. Her symptoms started the same day Sia miscarried, which meant that she had been incubating the virus for at least a few days, perhaps more.

Koumba sought care in a hospital in Guéckédou, and from there the linear chain of the West African outbreak starts to expand in multiple directions. A midwife became ill at the hospital; one of her close relatives traveled north from Guéckédou to a village known as Damdou-Pombo, and a half-dozen people there were killed. Another staff member at the hospital traveled east to Macenta, a city of nearly a hundred thousand people, and a chain of transmission started there. A doctor in Macenta died and was transported back to his ancestral home in Kissidougou, a city of about the same size. His brothers prepared his body for the funeral, and they became infected and started an epidemic there. Another person carried the virus from Guéckédou to a different village called Dawa. By then, several weeks had passed, and the outbreak had quietly begun to creep outward. The virus was edging along, as if to test its boundaries.

The Zaire Ebolavirus had several advantages in its ability to cause destruction in West Africa that an identical copy of it would have lacked in Central Africa. First, it had never been seen before in any of these countries, so local health officials were slow to recognize what was happening. One of the initial beliefs was that it was cholera, and since cholera was largely a regional concern rather than an international crisis, time was lost in the initial diagnosis.

Second, there wasn't much of a health infrastructure in place for local officials to even *see* the data. To track an outbreak of any kind, from the most feared, like Ebola, to the most mundane, like a diarrheal outbreak in Iowa following a family reunion one August afternoon, cases have to be carefully tracked and recorded. For that to happen, there needs to be someone paid to do this—typically this is a function of government—and there needs to be a centralized bureaucracy to collect and process the information. But Guinea was not only poor; its southeastern corner had felt the ripples from Liberia's Civil War, as tribal alliances brought Guineans into the conflict, with the result that an already impoverished corner of the world had damaged what tenuous infrastructure was in place. Of the three countries of Guinea, Sierra Leone, and Liberia, Guinea *might* have been in the best shape in this respect, but that wasn't saying much.

Third, there was a new technology that permitted the virus to travel vast distances in a fairly short time. It wasn't cars or airplanes, which were luxuries far too costly for poor agrarian communities in this part of the world. But it was at some level the underprivileged person's solution to achieving mobility: the motorcycle. Cheap, relatively easy to maintain, far more gas efficient than cars, and much more versatile in narrow and muddy country jungle roads than buses, motorcycles provided the perfect answer for remote villagers needing cheap transportation to sell their wares and engage in trade. One or two generations before, travel from a place like Meliandou to Guinea's capital of Conakry could take many days and be exorbitant. With motorcycles, one could travel not only to Conakry but to Sierra Leone's capital of Freetown or Liberia's capital of Monrovia in less than a day. Whole fleets of motorcycles could be found in the regional centers, and ferrying passengers around became an important part of the local economy. Riding on a motorcycle also requires close contact with the driver, which provided another chance for the virus to spread beyond normal traditional family or tribal routes.

In short, it was an ideal place for a killer virus that moved at a Goldilocks pace—not too fast for people to recognize immediately that something was dangerously amiss, and not too slow for it to easily hitch a ride on its human host to make more copies of itself, but just the right speed to stay out of reach of local, regional, and eventually, world health authorities.

Touch was how the virus spread. Any direct, skin-to-skin contact with an infected person, or the virus-filled fluids that issued from them, provided a chance for spread. Fortuitously for the virus, West

Africans, whether Christian or Muslim, observe a funereal custom by which acquaintances pay their respects to the dead by touching the body directly and handling it as part of the burial rites. To decline to perform this action—something that public health authorities would soon advise—was tantamount to refusing to shake someone's hand in the West for no apparent reason. It would have been regarded as obnoxious in the extreme, an affront to traditional values. The more funerals that took place, the farther the virus would spread.

The recognition that this was an Ebola epidemic would not come until nearly the end of March 2014. At that time, blood samples had been taken by staff members of Médecins Sans Frontières, or MSF, the group known better to Americans as Doctors Without Borders, and were sent to Europe for testing. MSF had an inkling that something wasn't right in the weeks before, and eventually the blood samples proved it. The WHO was informed and sounded the alarm.

But other events were taking place in the world that had stretched the WHO thin. At the time, a virus known as MERS-CoV—the Middle Eastern Respiratory Syndrome Coronavirus—had generated a fair amount of alarm and was occupying the efforts of WHO officials day and night. And that was only the beginning. Dr. Robert Fowler, a physician working with the WHO at the time, said that the discovery of an Ebola outbreak in West Africa with everything else happening at that time was like "a plane crashes in the Hudson in the morning, and there's a snowstorm in the afternoon and floods in the subways in the evening, and then you have two planes hit the World Trade Center in the middle of the night." Moreover, the cash-strapped WHO was tasked with responding to the outbreak with a regional staff whose budget had been cut in half over the span of several years. To expand Fowler's analogy, it was as if the calamities befalling New York were met with a response from a police and fire department working something very close to a skeleton crew.

To make matters worse, politics got in the way. Ebola experts from the CDC and WHO's headquarters in Geneva were initially stiff-armed by local African WHO officials, who wanted to "prove they could handle this one without help." As guiding principles, self-sufficiency and self-reliance were the recipe for Africa's future success. In an Ebola outbreak, however, that strategy backfired, and although no media reports can explain exactly how much of a delay these back-channel arguments caused, precious time may well have been lost in the early days.

Then came what almost any impartial observer would regard as a moment of pure farce, perhaps the most darkly comic moment of the entire epidemic: A Twitter war broke out between public health organizations, as if one group had just dissed the other's wardrobe. The WHO administrators appeared to regard the outbreak relatively lightly. "There has never been an #Ebola outbreak larger than a couple hundred cases," wrote WHO spokesperson Gregory Härtl in the days following the announcement of the outbreak, later saying Ebola "has always remained a very localised event." By this time, about fifty cases had been documented, in keeping with the size of many of the outbreaks that occurred during the 2000s.

But MSF, whose ground intel was reporting a different story, reacted with incredulity, noting in a press release that "we are facing an epidemic of a magnitude never before seen in terms of the distribution of cases in the country."

Härtl's tweet in response was nonchalant: "No need to overblow something which is already bad enough."

MSF took another turn, pointing out that it was hard to "overblow" the Zaire Ebolavirus, as it had now been identified: "This is the most deadly strain of the Ebola virus. It kills 9 out of 10 patients."

Almost immediately Härtl shot back, tweeting, "Don't exaggerate. #Ebola can kill up to 90% of those infected and in this particular outbreak fatality rate is less than 67%."

MSF's view of the matter would ultimately prove to be the more prescient of the two. However, Härtl's final statistic of the case fatality rate for the West African outbreak did basically hold, which must have provided him some comfort in retrospect.

What MSF had sensed, and what at least some of the people at WHO were oblivious to, was that this particular outbreak found itself in the perfect storm of destitute local governments, shoddy surveillance infrastructures, byzantine international bureaucracies, and societal observances such that it could be silently moving through the countryside unbeknownst to these groups, waiting for its chance to deliver a blow with crushing force. Yet that isn't how it played out initially. March turned into April, and with it came a decline in cases. Guinea, which hit a peak in the first weeks of April, started to trend down. Liberia, which had seen a case or two in a village called Foya in the northwestern corner of Lofa County, could find nothing else. Sierra Leone still hadn't registered a case at all. Härtl was on his way to being vindicated.

Then came May, and Ebola did indeed roar back. The second wave, which would continue on through the next several months, was on a trajectory that had never been seen before. In a way, Härtl's original statement was, strictly speaking, still correct: There never *had* been an outbreak larger than a couple hundred cases. What was happening in West Africa would be an *n* of 1.

This was unprecedented. Sierra Leone saw its first case, and almost immediately those cases multiplied with frightening speed. Liberia's previous flirtation with Ebola in March and April looked like a tremor before the real earthquake. And, of course, Guinea's tally increased at the same rate. Ebola always *had* remained a localized event, but now it threatened to engulf three countries with a total population of about twenty-two million people simultaneously, with cases breaking out hundreds of miles from one another. This was no longer a *single* outbreak by previous definitions but had instead become a meta-outbreak where *dozens* of local outbreaks were taking place, and all in one of the least-prepared areas that could be imagined. Yet hardly anyone in the outside world was fully aware of this, even by late May. By contrast, the Kikwit outbreak of 1995, primed as it was by the popularity of Preston's and Garrett's books, had become front-page news much more rapidly.

Emile's father, Etienne Ouamouno, bore witness to the loss of his family, never having been infected despite having lived and breathed and slept right next to the virus for days on end, only belatedly aware of the danger it had posed to him. Whether the fact that he escaped its clutches makes him feel lucky or the opposite is a question I suspect he ponders often. A few brave souls from the international media came to Meliandou in the midst of the outbreak to interview him, and he spoke of how the events of the previous year had affected his outlook.

"When I think about them, I feel very sad," he said to the BBC in a video recorded in late 2014. "The pain is too much. I just can't bear it. But then, I have to say to myself, 'they've gone.' I just have to accept it and move on." He says this and then quickly looks away into the distance.

Even before Ebola roared back, the villagers of Meliandou had realized that their neighboring communities looked at them, however unjustly, as the source of this scourge. The same effect that had been seen two generations ago in Lassa was again playing out in West Africa, as the farmers of Meliandou were unable to sell their produce on account of hailing from the outbreak's Ground Zero. In an attempt to exorcise the evil they believed was in their midst, and perhaps to make some kind of a symbolic atonement for a wrong they didn't commit, on March 24, 2014, they took torches to the tree in and around which Emile Ouamouno had joyfully played only a few months before. The tree, a living, being creature that would also become collateral damage just the same as Etienne Ouamouno and his fellow villagers, finally caught fire.

According to Michelle Roberts, a reporter working for the BBC, the villagers said that a "rain of bats" then issued from the tree.

And the screaming flew back across the sky. But by then, the epidemic was raging on the ground.

2

PREPARING FOR THE END OF THE WORLD

Most of us in the developed world don't pause to think how amazing it is that we drink water from a tap and never once worry about dying forty-eight hours later from cholera.
—Steven Johnson, *How We Got to Now*

My personal connection to the outbreak was through Liberia, which was soon to feel Ebola's full force. Guinea was regarded the epicenter of the outbreak in the spring of 2014. That would soon change, and the names Ebola and Liberia soon became practically synonymous throughout the world.

Before I had ever set foot there, I knew almost nothing about it beyond the fact that it was a tiny little country on the elbow of West Africa and was originally an American colony, our only colonial imprint on the continent, founded by former slaves.

My impression would turn out not to be true. Or it was at most a half-truth, for many of the first colonists were actually freedmen. They were highly skilled and reasonably literate people, the forerunners to today's middle class. Brickmasons, carpenters, and merchants filled their ranks. When the first settlers landed their ship, the *Elizabeth*, on the shores of what would become Sierra Leone and Liberia in 1824, they had enough practical knowledge to build themselves a society in much the same way that the Pilgrims did in Massachusetts Bay two hundred years before.

That they came with a white American overseer who went by the euphemistic description of "agent" must have rankled these colonists no end. Unskilled former slaves, which was the picture I conjured up when imagining the African-American founders, mostly came to

Liberia in subsequent waves of immigration during the mid-nineteenth century. But the true founders, those who would eventually demand their sovereignty from an overseas government that had infuriated them with its condescension and aloofness, were people who could articulate their notions of freedom in a way that John Locke would instantly recognize. They certainly weren't "slaves" in the way we normally understand the term.

However, it's true that these founders, whether they came direct from the plantation or had been freed upon their master's death, were still bound up by the legacy of slavery in much the same way. Yet I think it's important to note the dissimilarities among those making their way in the world at the dawn of Liberia. For one thing, the idea that a bunch of unskilled and uneducated slaves just showing up on the western African shoreline, where they commence in the cheery building of a country, demonstrates the lengths to which Americans like to tell Mickey Mouse stories to avoid the unsettling implications such stories might have for the present. Only when one really stares at the Liberia origin myths does one realize that they are patently absurd—not unlike our own founding myths—and the absurdity may be designed to make us Americans feel better not only about the Liberia of here and now, but the legacy of slavery as well, and our country's role in it.

Consider, for instance, the predicament of the Liberian founders who were most well off before Africa. The majority lived in Virginia, Maryland, and southern Pennsylvania. They had every advantage a field slave would have, quite literally, killed for: nutrition, education, literacy, and, of course, freedom. They sold goods and contracted their work just like anyone in the middle class of the early Republic. Only their skin was dark, at a time when attitudes about the inseparability of Africanness and slavery were hardening in these border states.

If slaves could observe that there were free Americans who had dark skin and African features, why should they regard their own lifetime bondage, to say nothing of the bondage of their children and children's children, as legitimate? Had not the colonists just risen in armed revolution to secure their own freedom using a similar rationale? Having free blacks in the midst of an indefensible system created practical problems for that very system. Moreover, the economic incentives of antebellum slavery put these people at risk of being kidnapped for resale. They were a threat if they remained free, and they also presented a lucrative opportunity for those who weren't troubled by taking away that freedom.

In short, it was not an enticing position for a free black person in the 1820s and 1830s in the mid-Atlantic states; thus, the "fact" that Liberia was founded by former slaves completely inverts the narrative. The story as I initially thought of it goes like this: *Here is Liberia, Africa's first independent country, founded by some plucky former slaves with a helping hand from its big brother, the United States.* I was left with the sense of these people as being *happy* in their liberation, sailing to distant shores with the same kind of hopes and ambitions as George Washington.

Yet the reality was that these people were embittered by their unwinnable quandary and headed to Liberia not elated but filled with a grim determination to eke out something better than what they left, even if it meant going to their deaths—or subjecting others to a similar fate. Elijah Johnson, one of the original settlers and its first true leader, emerged from the *Elizabeth* onto the tiny island that would eventually be named, apparently without intentional irony, Providence. Following a brief reconnaissance of the island, Johnson's words made his resolve clear: "I have been two years searching a home in Africa and I have found it, and here I will remain."

Later, when the settlers teetered on the brink of collapse, threatened with annihilation by the natives, the British navy offered protection on the condition that they subjugate themselves to the Crown. Johnson would have none of that, even if it meant certain death, responding to the British offer, "We want no flagstaff put up here that it will cost us more to get down than it will to whip the natives!" Both of these sayings of Elijah Johnson have been recounted for more than one hundred years on Liberia's Pioneers' Day in the same way that Americans quote Jefferson on July 4. Pioneers' Day, which celebrated military victories of the colonists over the native populations, has unsurprisingly fallen out of favor over the past generation or two. From time to time I think about the softball question sometimes asked during a job interview: *If you could have dinner with anyone, whom would you choose?* Back in college I answered Freud, sometimes Einstein. They still seem like fine choices, but if I had to pick one person to have an evening meal with now, I think I would pick Elijah Johnson. There would be much to talk about.

Another voice from Liberia's past for me summarizes the eloquent rage of these early settlers. By the 1850s Liberia had become a full-fledged nation. A pair of brothers had grown disillusioned with the shitty living conditions of Liberia, frustrated by high prices and a material existence that didn't live up to its utopian billing. They resolved to go back home to the United States as soon as the next available ship would bear them. Upon learning of this, the Liberian Reverend James Wilson quipped in retort, "As for my part I do not know what [these brothers] return for unless it was for the whip. It cannot be for something to eat, for we have a variety of foods too tedious to mention. I cannot see what a man of color wants to go back to the United States to live for unless he has no soul in him, for where there is a sign of a soul within a man it pants for freedom, in this life and the life to come."*

The other subtlety missed by the slaves-happily-founded-Liberia nugget is that, much like our own country's creation myths, it sidesteps the rather uncomfortable fact that there happened to be a native population on site who had no say in its foundation and mostly rejected it on principle. "The Love of Liberty Brought Us Here" is Liberia's national motto, found on official stationery and various other government paraphernalia, but that motto raises the question of who constitutes "us" and glosses over the fact that most of the people who inhabited early Liberia weren't *brought* by anything but were *here* from the start. The unpleasant relations between the group that would come to be known as the Americoes (or "Americo-Liberians") and the native Africans would go on to define the history of this place.† Maybe

---

* I modernized the English, lest the crude spelling distract from the searing message.
† The Americoes were also commonly referred to as Congos by the natives. The origin of the term is not fully clear, as the Congos may originally have been slaves from the Congo Basin who never made it to the West but were repatriated to what is now Liberia by the British navy, and thus constituted a distinct group from the American immigrants. Whatever the truth, the people referred to by these names eventually became the ruling elite, whether their origin was a village near modern-day Washington or modern-day Kinshasa.

it was *Liberty* for the American settlers. The natives had a different perspective.

Once you come to terms with how a simple fact about a country can be misleading in ways that are designed to pacify by deliberately avoiding troubling matters, then can you start to appreciate the peculiarly cruel ironies of Liberia's history.

First is the entire purpose of the African Colonization Society, the organization founded mostly by white "progressives" that funded most of the early settlement missions. It was an operation aimed at getting as many people as possible of African descent off the North American continent. A policy that was little more than a benign form of ethnic cleansing through mass deportation, the enthusiasm for African colonization was a by-product of an impulse toward racial purity not altogether indistinguishable from Nazi philosophy.

The whole idea was harebrained to begin with, based on the flimsy logic that one should "return" a people to a place because their skin happened to look more like an African's than a European's. That makes about as much sense as the U.S. government returning me to Warsaw simply by virtue of the fact that my great-great-grandparents lived in Poland. After all, I don't speak Polish and know nothing of the local customs. Basically, I am about as Polish as these Liberian settlers were African. Moreover, sending these African-Americans to one spot on the shores of West Africa ignores the fact that *their* African ancestors could easily have come from places on the continent as distant from Liberia, in both physical space as well as language and custom, as Guatemala is from Boston. Yet all the white power brokers could see was the common denominator of dark skin.

But if you *were* going to pick a place in Africa to return these people—and it is worth noting here that Africa is a *big* continent, so there was not exactly a dearth of choices—you probably couldn't have picked a worse place to deposit them than this section of coastline. First, the original colonization attempt was bungled because Great Britain, in the midst of its own colonization experiment in what would become Sierra Leone, had already taken the region's prime settlement spot on Sherbro Island, forcing the American colonists hundreds of miles east to the mouth of the Mesurado River, the area that would eventually become Monrovia. Regardless, the natives that awaited these colonists weren't merely displeased with the idea of being displaced; they also relied on an economic model that was sure to encourage violent conflict and set in motion generations of ill will, for their main cash crop was human chattel. Slavery *was* their business.

But the most delicious irony was to come over the next few generations, as the descendants of the Americoes created a society based on subjugation and co-optation of these natives—the members of the Kru, the Bassa, the Vai, the Kpelle, the Grebo, and a dozen other tribes that always constituted the vast majority of the Liberian populace. For well over one hundred years, the Americoes dominated a country that resembled in critical ways the very society that its own founders so thoroughly detested, and although the economy of Liberia wasn't formally based on slavery, the power wielded by the Americoes and the manner by which justice was administered was close enough. Liberia nominally had a democracy, one dominated by the True Whig Party. The True Whigs were nearly all descendants of the original settlers, or those lucky enough to marry into Americo families. The true natives, by contrast, had little power.

Elijah Johnson and his comrades, whose rage at the injustice of slavery could not have been more profound, would likely have cringed at what became of Liberia. He put his life in extreme peril to get as far away from slavery as possible, and the country he helped found recreated precisely that system, with the exception that white people were no longer running it. The cynical view is that he needn't have bothered. But offstage in this little drama, white Americans were still busy profiting, mainly in the form of American corporate interests that coddled the Americoes and insured their ongoing control of Liberia at the expense of the tribal populations.

This was the society that had been at one of the slowest, most prolonged boils in history when the structure finally imploded in the late 1970s and the True Whigs were wiped away. It happened under the watch of President William Tolbert, who had been in office since 1971. As if there weren't enough ironies in Liberia's history, it turned out that Tolbert was Liberia's most progressive president ever. Despite charges of nepotism and corruption that were almost certainly true to some degree, he was nevertheless making a legitimate attempt to right some historical wrongs through the power of policy. Only the second Liberian president fluent in one of the tribal languages, his connections to the indigenous populations led to policies designed to encourage their increased representation in government.

The final months of Tolbert's presidency were chaotic, with much of the chaos initially created by hard-leaning conservative Americoes in the True Whig Party who refused to go along with his reforms. The resulting instability culminated in a major episode of rioting in Monrovia when the government raised the price of a one-hundred-pound bag of rice from twenty-two to twenty-six dollars. It was a putative effort to maintain what Liberian self-sufficiency there was by encouraging rural Liberians to continue farming rice and not abandon their villages for jobs harvesting rubber or doing associated industrial work in Monrovia. However misguided the rice policy was from the standpoint of economic theory, its intentions at first blush seem noble enough, although it didn't hurt that the majority of the windfall from the increased revenues generated by the price hike fell to members of Tolbert's own family. Whatever reformist impulses guided Tolbert, the Rice Riots created a dangerous level of instability. The turmoil forced him to crack down on the protesters, as well as the progressives who were encouraging dissent.

Into this chaos stepped a member of the Liberian military, Master Sergeant Samuel Doe, who led a group of commandos into the presidential palace and eviscerated Tolbert in his sleep in April 1980. A member of the Krahn tribe, Doe was exactly the kind of person Tolbert had in mind when he attempted to promote civil servants whose pedigree was primarily tribal. Doe set in motion a coup that would culminate in the killings of thirteen Cabinet members following Tolbert's assassination. The coup led directly to the end of the Americoes as a unified, organized force in Liberian politics, and for a time anyone from the ruling class was in danger of reprisals ranging from rape to murder.

Doe did not prove to be an adept leader. He understood little of governance, nor did those with whom he surrounded himself. He was quick to use violence as a form of political discourse. Tribal conflicts that had not existed during the rule of the Americoes started to surface, ultimately culminating in the rise to power of a man named Charles Taylor.

More on him later, but this is how the stage was set for the Liberian Civil War. The details are complex, but the gist is simple: Doe obliterated the Americoes but subsequently bungled the chance for Liberia to become a more just place, the consequence of which was prolonged, armed intertribal conflict. The Civil War lasted nearly a generation and wiped out perhaps 10 percent of Liberia's population. It was bloody, it was unspeakably savage, and it was stupid. Unlike the American Civil War, which for all its tragedy was at least tied to some higher purpose, the Liberian Civil War was senseless from start to finish. It is better described as autophagy: the consumption of one's own flesh.

Other than having a nodding familiarity with the name of Charles Taylor and the Civil War, and my not-quite-right view that this was a country founded by some former slaves who were content with their newfound freedom, I didn't know any of this when I found myself in Monrovia in November 2013, staring at what had once been a beautiful white building and trying to figure out why it had become little more than a shell and why I was watching so many people die within its walls.

I had come to Monrovia after my annual review with my division chief, Doug Golenbock. I told Doug that I wanted to get involved in doing some work in sub-Saharan Africa, which had long been a career goal, but I had gotten sidetracked by various opportunities and roadblocks. The logical place to start, I told him, was to go to Ghana. The University of Massachusetts medical campus is in Worcester, Massachusetts, a town with one of the largest populations of Ghanaians in the Western Hemisphere. Go figure. Moreover, Ghana was on a virtually vertical rise in its standard of living; understanding why that is and how that relates to my specialty of infectious disease, seemed to me a question worthy of exploration. So I suggested to Doug that we leverage what we've got right here in Worcester, which is a little piece of Ghana itself, and get over there.

"Well, the problem is that I don't know anyone who does work in

Ghana. But Katherine Luzuriaga's group has been going to Liberia for several years now," Doug said. "Why don't I put you in touch with them?"

At the time, that felt like a consolation prize, but in short order I made the acquaintance of Trish McQuilkin, a pediatrician who had been going back and forth to Liberia for several years. The timing was fortuitous because the Liberian Ministry of Health, which had painstakingly been rebuilding the medical system that had been completely decimated by the Civil War, was just about to resume its residency training program. Following the end of the armed conflict and the restoration of civil institutions, the ministry had initially prioritized restarting the medical school and shepherding through new graduates. By 2013 it had produced several classes of full-fledged doctors, and so its attention turned to arranging advanced training for a small number of them in the specialties of surgery, pediatrics, obstetrics and gynecology, and internal medicine. I would have a ringside seat at the foundation of a new program, so as consolation prizes go, that seemed more than good enough.

The program was being run out of John F. Kennedy Hospital in the Sinkor section of Monrovia, on Twenty-first Street and Tubman Boulevard, which is the main thoroughfare running from the city center out to the eastern parts of greater Monrovia. JFK had been built by the Kennedy family following the president's death as a gesture of goodwill between the two nations and in the hope that America's former colony was on its way to being on an equal footing with the rest of the nations of the earth. You can sense the optimism in the modernist, late 1960s architectural style; it must have been magnificent to look at when it was first built. Standing five stories tall—nearly a skyscraper by Monrovia standards—and washed in white, the building faced onto Tubman Boulevard buffered by a huge lawn, the last real uninterrupted spot of urban greenery as one approached the city center, with two enormous fountains on either side of its main, central entrance point. Standing there, picturing what it must have looked like in the late 1960s, you can almost feel the pride that the nation must have taken in such a specimen. JFK was known as the main referral hospital for the country, but it also catered to a good number of West

Africans from other countries. It was a destination hospital, in the same way that I remember the Cleveland Clinic as a child, when the local TV news reported when King Hussein of Jordan had come there for his annual checkup.

But the JFK of 2013 was looking at those glory days through the rearview mirror, like anything else that was once the jewel in the crown of a country that had gone through such terrible suffering. The fountains were just large holes, empty pools with rusting iron-works where the water had been piped. The shining white had gone drab gray, and what had once seemed soaring modern architecture now appeared more nefarious, vaguely Stalinist in its tone. Much of the interior had been shuttered because the hospital's caretaking capacity had been severely reduced; there were entire floors that had been mothballed. During rainstorms, the water seeped through the walls by various leaks. Floor and wall tiles that had fallen off were left unrepaired. Paint peeled from the walls. The treatment bays on the floors housed bed frames older than many of the oldest people in Liberia, with torn-up mattresses and fraying linens. The windowless central hallways on the ground floor, which did not admit much ambient light and whose lightbulbs were not quite up to the task of illumination, were so oppressively dark that it felt like perpetual night. For Americans who have never visited a sub-Saharan African hospital, the JFK of late 2013 would approximate their worst fears.

The one piece of splendor at JFK that remained undiminished was that great front lawn, still pristine in its greenery. But like everything else of what I would come to discover in this country, it too was tinged with the blood of the Civil War. Quite literally, in fact. During the conflict, JFK and many of its staff somehow managed to find a way to soldier on, despite having essentially no resources with which to care for patients, other than their wits. The locals would bring loved ones either sick from some actual disease or from wounds sustained during the violence and put them on the front lawn to be tended by the mostly helpless staff. Given the dearth of equipment, many if not most of these patients died, and the JFK acronym, along with its great lawn, took on a new meaning in Monrovia parlance: "Just for Killing."

One of the interns to whom I took an immediate liking was a man named Phil Ireland. I'm used to referring to residents and interns as *young* men or women, as I am in my mid-forties, dealing with doctors fresh out of medical school who are usually two decades younger than me. I don't describe Phil as *young* now because I did that once when speaking with his classmates, a description that was met with a short burst of laughter. Not getting the joke, I asked what was funny. It turned out that Phil was hardly young—he was, in fact, a year *older* than me, with a family of five children. He certainly didn't look it, standing six feet tall, with a perfectly shiny bald head, wide eyes, and a huge smile that could not always be found among other Liberians, though whether the lack of smiling was due to custom or cautiousness around an outsider is something I don't know.

At any rate, Phil had earned his M.D. as an older student because Dogliotti, Liberia's only medical school, was shuttered during the Civil War, and even after the cessation of hostilities, rebooting the curriculum and reestablishing its courses with the remaining few faculty members left in Monrovia didn't happen for some time. Thus, when I met him, he had just completed his degree and was moving on to the next phase of his career. But there was scant advanced training to be had in Liberia, for similar reasons. He was enthusiastic about Emergency Medicine, which was lacking in Liberia, given the level of trauma caused by car and motorcycle accidents in a country that had almost no traffic laws and hardly any domestic police, to say nothing of workplace injuries due to the lax protective equipment in virtually every industry. We talked about the possibility of him coming to the States for specialty training, but when I learned of his age and his family life, I realized that probably wasn't going to happen given the immense sacrifices that such a plan would entail.

The residents working at JFK were under the supervision of the chief of Internal Medicine, a man named Abraham Borbor. Borbor had come from Lofa County, up in the northwest of the country, the descendant of a tribal chief, and had been working at JFK for decades, through the Civil War, having manned his post in what must have been hellish conditions. In his late fifties or early sixties, Borbor was a big man with a big presence. He had a high, reedy voice and was quick to laugh while teaching his charges. He was feared by the residents but deeply respected as well. He struck me as a natural teacher who loved having an audience; I imagine that the end of the crisis and the ability to train new doctors must have come as a massive breath of fresh air for someone who had practically lived at JFK for years on end with little hope in front of him, watching the best and most productive years of his career being frittered away while his country tore itself to shreds.

He was also among the few Liberian doctors who had been outside the country for stretches, having done some coursework in England. So he knew something about how someone like me might view a place like Liberia, and from the start, he and I spoke about medicine not simply in the narrow terms of this drug or that disease but of how an infrastructure can shape a person's life. One weekend day he picked me up to take me on my first tour of Monrovia, and we drove through some of the most destitute neighborhoods of the city. As I looked around, I noticed some old electricity poles, clearly erected before the Civil War, but sure enough, there *was* electrical wiring running from one to another.

"Dr. Borbor, is there a nationalized power grid in place? I'm seeing these wires, but it's so dark here at night."

He cackled at my suggestion of some Liberian power plant. "Oh, *that* is definitely electrical wiring. It's hooked up to someone in the neighborhood who owns a generator and sells the electricity."

"Oh, I see. And how much does that cost?"

"Probably eight to ten dollars a month." An average working Liberian in 2013 made about two U.S. dollars per day.

"And what does that pay for?"

"It keeps one lightbulb working at night."

Later that afternoon we drove out toward the edge of the city in the Congo Town neighborhood to a popular Liberian haunt known as A La Lagune. We ordered a few drinks and sat talking about our careers, what he had seen during his years in Liberia, and where the country had come. Being November, the dry season was fully underway, and it was hot, so our cold beer and Coca-Cola got warm fairly quickly. As the liquid came to ambient temperature, my enthusiasm for drinking diminished. Borbor took his can of Coke and, as if struck by inspiration, poured it into his glass of Club beer. He looked at the drink and said with that cackle, "Well, it's going the same place anyway," and gulped down the remainder.

I knew from working with him for several days that I admired and respected him, but that's when I realized just how much I *liked* Abraham Borbor.

During the first week I was there I went to help out in the HIV clinic after rounds. We had just finished rounding on the inpatients, twenty in all. The patients presented with a mix of illnesses not too dissimilar from those in an American hospital: a few pneumonias, some strokes, uncontrolled diabetics, a case of heart failure, and some complications of HIV. It was the *severity* of illness that was different, for these patients were much sicker than their American counterparts. Most of the medicines required to care for these people were in good supply. The hospital pharmacy didn't have the newest antibiotics or fanciest insulins or the most expensive beta-blockers, but what they had was enough that their outcomes shouldn't have been completely different. Of the twenty patients on the floor that day, all had been there for some time, and they seemed stable. I felt confident of their plans moving forward, even in as profoundly limited a place as JFK.

On the way down to the HIV clinic, my phone rang. One of the visiting obstetricians, a doctor from the University of Maryland named Kiran Chawla who had spent years in Liberia working for MSF, said there was a patient in the maternity wing of the hospital that she wanted me to take a look at—could I come over right now? I said sure. When I got there, I found a young woman who looked to be mostly baby—that is, the baby she carried inside her—and the rest bones. She was emaciated in the extreme; I doubted that she'd be capable of standing. She was hooked up to an oxygen tank, a huge, clunky apparatus that was probably used in the United States in the 1970s or maybe early '80s, whose pump generated such an insane amount of noise that it was difficult to hear someone speak in its presence. But what impressed me most was how fast she was breathing. A healthy adult typically gets through one minute taking somewhere between eight and twelve breaths. Her respiratory rate was almost *sixty*. I got tired just looking at her.

Kiran looked at me. "She's twenty-four weeks, Steven," she said, referring to the gestational age of the baby. Even in the States, a baby delivered at twenty-four weeks has poor odds of survival, and in Liberia, without the availability of certain drugs to keep a preemie alive, no child could survive being born that young. "There's nothing I can do for her. The procedure would probably kill both of them. I think she needs to go to the medicine service and see if you can stabilize her." It made perfect sense, so I called Ian Wachekwa, a Zimbabwean doctor who was one of the residents in this new medicine residency, and asked him to come over so that we could facilitate getting her to the medicine floor, which was in the adjacent building.* Once he did, we made the arrangements to get her over, and we headed to the clinic.

In the clinic, I saw two young women in quick succession who were obviously quite ill and were going to need to be admitted. One came stumbling in, helped by her father, her body shaking in one prolonged tremor. It was hard to find out anything meaningful from her, and besides getting a blood count, there was nothing we could do until we could get her to the floor and arrange for a spinal tap. So we called to inform the floor resident and sent her upstairs. The next woman had much the same story but was confused and had been losing weight. For her, we added an X-ray, since she had a mild cough, since at least it was something we could do. Both of them had fairly advanced HIV infection which meant that almost *anything* could be wrong with them, and we had virtually no tests by which we could make any meaningful diagnosis. We had blood counts and chemistries and a malaria test. Whatever was going on with these women, malaria would have been only the beginning of their problems.

---

* Ian went to medical school and did his early training in Zimbabwe, where he met his Liberian wife. She convinced him in the late 2000s to come with her back to Liberia. Health care in Zimbabwe is significantly more advanced than in Liberia, which made me wonder about the professional sacrifices that Ian has made for his family life. "Ian, do you ever say to your wife, 'Hey, we could go back to Zimbabwe?' Like, the situation there has *got* to be better, right?" To which Ian dryly responded, "I have that conversation *quite often*, in fact."

By the time we got back upstairs a few hours later at the end of clinic, all three had died. The woman who came from the maternity ward had died even before she made it to the floor. Transporting a patient at JFK involved moving the bed over some bumpy spots, and the physiologic stress of those bumps, along with the general movement of the bed, was too much for her tenuous respiratory status, for she had been holding onto her life by her fingernails. I went back to the dorms on the campus of JFK that night, dejected.

When I returned the next day at the morning meeting, the house officer, a young man named Zoeban Parteh, ran the list, where he reviewed the events of the evening: There was one other admission in addition to these three. Then he went on to note that *four* of the floor patients had passed away, all but one quite unexpectedly, and all under the age of thirty.

That meant, of twenty-four total patients, seven had died in that one-day span.

I'm a doctor, so I'm used to people dying as part of my work. I've worked in Haiti and I've seen hospitals in other parts of Africa as well as South America, and I routinely consult on very sick patients in ICUs in North America, all places with high mortality rates. But I had never before seen that *level* of death, coming in such quick succession, and in so many young people. After I left the hospital that day, I walked a few blocks to the nearby supermarket, a Lebanese-owned bodega called The Exclusive Super Store, bought a large bottle of Johnnie Walker Red, walked back to the dorms, and drank most of it that night by myself, with a little help from Kiran, whose sentiments were, "Welcome to Liberia, Steven."

In the coming days I made inquiries about the mortality rate at JFK, and my mind reeled. "Oh, it's about 40 percent," Ian told me, almost with the casual air of someone who had been following the price of Apple's stock. "The problem is that people know that if you go to JFK, you've got a pretty good chance of dying, so they delay coming when we might be able to make more of a difference, and then they end up coming so far along in their illness that they don't do well, and you have this high mortality rate, which reinforces the sense that you come here to die." The mortality on the surgical service in 2013, according to the residents with whom I spoke, was an astonishing *70 percent*, for much the same reasons.

Most of us in the developed world don't pause to think how amazing it is that we drink water from a tap and never once worry about dying forty-eight hours later from cholera. Spending some time in Liberia might help to reveal just how amazing that really is. In a two-week tour, I saw examples of how the lack of such wonders as running water, the ability to summon light at any moment of a twenty-four-hour cycle, and cheap and efficient transportation all led to people worrying about dying from any number of maladies, even including cholera. Liberia's rudimentary infrastructure underscored how these normally invisible advances that make life so livable elsewhere are crucial to the chances that you'll live to see thirty.

That one night was probably the best preparation I could possibly have for working in an Ebola Treatment Unit, whose mortality rate wasn't appreciably different than that of the combined adult specialties at JFK Hospital.

After I returned to the States from my introduction to Liberia, the early months of 2014 proceeded apace. Trish McQuilkin and I talked about working on a research project in Monrovia, and I schemed to figure out a way to return in the coming year. It wasn't where I had originally envisioned working in Africa, but with the promise of Borbor's company, some very nice residents who seemed genuinely appreciative of my presence, and decent Lebanese food to be had in Monrovia without much effort, I thought it an opportunity worth pursuing. Trish had gotten a small grant funded, the goal of which was to investigate all the potential causes of fever in children: Because there was virtually no laboratory testing available in postwar Liberia, nobody knew with any certainty whether a child presenting with a fever had malaria or typhoid or scarlet fever or any of a dozen other causes. Everything was a guess, and Trish's project was to take out some of the guesswork. As winter turned into spring, we bounced a few e-mails back and forth, and I tried to clear some time to return the following fall.

Then, on March 22, I noticed a headline in *The New York Times* with the title "Guinea Confirms Fever Is Ebola, Has Killed Up to 59."

It seemed odd to me at the time. Ebola had been almost exclusively a Central African problem, so having an Ebola outbreak turn up nearly three thousand miles from there was, to say the least, unusual.

Technically, it wasn't unprecedented: In 1994, one lone case of Ebola turned up when a veterinarian had found a chimpanzee carcass in the Taï Forest National Park of Ivory Coast. She had performed a necropsy on the animal and several weeks later had become so ill that she was flown to Switzerland for care. Specific antibody tests for the Zaire and Sudan strains of Ebola were negative, but the less specific antibody test lit up, indicating there was yet another strain.

To this day, this is the only known human case of what is now called Taï Forest Ebolavirus. The patient survived after a prolonged critical illness, which technically means that as of now, the mortality rate of Taï Forest Ebolavirus is zero. Yet were it not for that single instance, West Africa would have never known Ebola, and even then, the Taï Forest case mainly served as an answer to a trivia question for hemorrhagic fever buffs like me. Eerily, during my time in Liberia the previous November, before the outbreak, I had given a presentation to the residents at JFK about hemorrhagic fever viruses. Most of that hour was devoted to talking about Lassa Fever, the one hemorrhagic fever that they were likely to encounter in their careers, as Liberia has among the highest number of Lassa cases in the world. But when I took a brief detour into Ebola, I pointed out the location of the Taï Forest virus to drive home that Ebola could, in fact, be found in West Africa, then drew a circle around the two adjacent countries of Ivory Coast and Liberia, and flashed the caption "Not Too Far from Monrovia!" I thought it amusing at the time, because I didn't believe they'd ever require this knowledge.

The doctors in Guinea certainly didn't have Ebola on their collective radar screen: The one hemorrhagic fever with which they were familiar was Lassa, and while the worst cases of Lassa are every bit as horrific as Ebola, Lassa is transmitted from rodent to human, but not human to human. Thus, health-care workers finding a bad case of Lassa didn't fear for their own lives unless they were unfortunate enough to suffer a needle-stick injury. Unbeknownst to almost everyone except for a few observant souls working for MSF, by the time the discovery of Ebola in Guinea was announced in late March—more than three full months after baby Emile had so fatefully crept into the tree hollow in Meliandou—several health-care workers already *had* paid, with their lives, for their confusion of Ebola with other diseases.

The Guinea Ebola story at the time struck me as a curiosity and not much more. Although I knew nothing of rural Guinea, I knew that Ebola outbreaks usually were contained within a matter of months, and so I kept tuned to NPR or *The New York Times* for updates, not thinking much about the tiny cluster of cases other than its novelty for that part of Africa.

However, one story at the beginning of April did catch my attention: It noted about a dozen cases in Guinea's capital of Conakry, a city of nearly two million people. That seemed worrisome and unprecedented. The Kikwit episode in 1995 had been until then the only Ebola outbreak in a truly urban area, yet Kikwit was a tenth of the size of Conakry, and it had generated world headlines and substantial alarm at the time.

But the stories only puttered along and so I followed in like manner. April turned into May. Liberia had announced the discovery of two cases up in northwest Lofa County, and since Lofa wasn't far at all from the Guéckédou region where the Guinean cases were reported, it didn't seem too surprising. But then, nothing followed. About this time just by chance I gave the same hemorrhagic fever talk to the internal medicine residents at UMass that I had given to the JFK residents. It was simply an odd coincidence, the date having been set months before. When I talked about Ebola, I made an off-the-cuff mention that there was a current outbreak going on in West Africa, but it would be contained soon enough, for that's how these outbreaks behaved.

The stories never quite went away, though, and throughout June the news seemed to be getting worse by the week. By mid-June I started scanning the headlines on a daily basis to see what was happening. A BBC news item had shown a picture of workers in gear tending to a patient in "northern Liberia," which was later noted to be Lofa County. *Oh my God*, I thought, *what happens if this thing gets to Monrovia?* Even though the news about Conakry should have gotten my full attention, it wasn't quite the same as hearing about Ebola tear through a city I had seen and whose streets I had walked. When I linked Ebola to Monrovia, I suddenly understood that if it took hold there, this outbreak was going to be unlike anything anyone had seen before. A few days later, on June 17, my increasing alarm found form in a piece by the Associated Press, which noted that the first reported cases had reached the capital.

Then I thought of the people I had met.

What I did not know was that chaos had already engulfed JFK and the rest of Monrovia. "Monrovia was upside down," Phil Ireland would later say to me. When I had walked around the Sinkor neighborhood in Monrovia, the main thoroughfare of Tubman Boulevard was bustling with people. Parts of Tubman Boulevard were narrow, as were the sidewalks, so during rush hour cars slowly moved by within arm's length of pedestrians throughout much of the stretch into Monrovia's city center.

In early June, that hadn't changed, although Phil said that paranoia was clearly in the air. "The city didn't shut down. At the early stages of the epidemic, it was just sinking in," he said. "Everybody was taking precautions. I would be driving into work, and there would be a taxi ahead of me, and it would just stop, and somebody would just open the door and just vomit, and suddenly there would be a big periphery, a big crowd would clear. This whole area would just clear. The taxi driver would try to kick that person out. It just got crazier and crazier. It was a bad state."

As June progressed, however, and the outbreak spread across the city, the panic set in. JFK was seeing the results come in through the Emergency Department. "It was like the Twilight Zone. There were lots and lots of cases," Phil said. "Our first case was a guy from Lofa County. He passed all the checkpoints. He had all the cardinal signs of Ebola. It wasn't confirmed. He had fever, injected conjunctiva, scleral redness, very toxic looking. He came in and said he was from Monrovia." But Phil, who by chance happened to have worked on a cocoa plantation in Lofa County years before, recognized the man. "I looked at him and said, 'I know you, you're from Lofa County.' I asked the taxi driver, and he said they had come from Lofa, so I went to Dr. Brisbane and I said to him, 'These guys are coming from Lofa County.' After that I went and washed myself."

Samuel Brisbane, a member of the hospital's senior staff, was skeptical that the Ebola outbreak was really happening, or at least to the extent that was being reported. "Not everybody is an Ebola patient," he would once say to Phil. "We still have to treat patients like we've always treated patients. We have cases of malaria, and we have other diseases." Brisbane was a colleague of Borbor's whom I hadn't met the previous November, though everyone spoke of him in equally glowing terms. When I learned that he doubted Ebola was afoot, I reacted with pure slack-jawed astonishment. Yet when Phil explained how he had arrived at this seemingly preposterous conclusion, I was more muted in my criticism.

Brisbane was suspicious of any pronouncement by the Liberian Ministry of Health. Like Borbor, he had given much of his career to JFK, toiling in a difficult working environment, all the while watching several government officials do very little for the institution, all while enriching themselves through various grifts, often involving donations from wealthier nations, especially the United States and Europe. Brisbane's anger and distrust had been fermenting for years such that Ebola seemed like just another scheme, a ministry shakedown of the international community for more aid with which officials could line their pockets. They had hastily arranged for an Ebola Treatment Unit to be set up on JFK's campus, but one not run by MSF, which was the main group in Liberia with any practical experience in Ebola management. My guess is that to Brisbane, the JFK ETU probably looked like a Potemkin village designed to bilk more dollars out of the World Bank, the International Monetary Fund, or the UN. If his cynicism led him to the ultimate mistake of his career—and indeed, of his life—it certainly was not based on a total departure from careful reasoning and observation.

However, neither Borbor nor Phil shared his views. Indeed, Borbor was furious if the infection control procedures that JFK did have in place, inadequate for Ebola though they were, weren't rigorously followed. "You should know better," he scolded Phil when told of how the staff was handling a suspected case. "If you make one mistake, you guys are going to kill all of us!"

Phil had worked closely with a physician assistant named Vincent. Colleagues and friends, they spent June watching Monrovia slowly come undone. Nevertheless, they both showed up for work without fail. One day in early July, Vincent was working in an area off the Emergency Department informally known as the "Blue Room," so named because of its painted interior. The Blue Room was where patients from the ED were kept while waiting for a bed to open up on the floors. Not originally intended to house patients, it had no ventilation and was therefore unusually hot, even by Monrovia standards—and thus not the best place for patients dehydrated by any infection associated with a fever, whether that was malaria, typhoid, or Ebola. That day, a woman had been sent to the Blue Room by the ED with a fever and malaise. She staggered as she tried to walk to her bed, and Vincent, who had known the woman, reached out to grab her and help her to the bed. She died that night, and the Ministry of Health sent workers clad in personal protective equipment (PPE) to draw her blood, which subsequently confirmed Ebola.

Phil is convinced that this was when Vincent became infected. Several days later the fever hit, and Vincent called Phil to tell him that he couldn't come to work. When Brisbane heard the news, he told Phil to make sure he came to JFK. He would need to be isolated, he said. The intervening weeks, which had seen JFK overrun with critically ill patients far out of proportion to the usual routine, had convinced Brisbane that what was happening was real. But by then it was too late. In mid-July, Dr. Brisbane started to appear fatigued. He walked slowly, weaving down the hallway, leaning up against the wall for support. Nurses avoided him. Soon he, too, would be unable to come to work.

I knew none of this at the time; there was hardly any news being reported, and I hadn't heard anything on e-mail from my contacts. On July 1, an especially ominous headline appeared from Reuters: "Ebola Outbreak Is the Largest Ever." There were at that point 759 official cases. That was more than double the size of all the Ebola outbreaks in history, with only one exception: the Gulu outbreak in Uganda in 2000 and 2001. The Gulu outbreak tallied 425 total cases, and it was clear from reading the Reuters piece that, whatever the final number, the West African outbreak would soon be more than twice the number of Ebola cases from the Gulu episode as well.

And then . . . almost nothing about Monrovia for three weeks, during which time I thought that perhaps my colleagues were going to be spared the worst. The disease seemed to be spreading in the countryside, but if Monrovia was being overrun, it wasn't making the reports. I started to contemplate an upcoming vacation to Canada with less foreboding than I had been feeling in June.

On July 27, however, the Associated Press reported my worst fears. "Ebola Kills Liberian Doctor, 2 Americans Infected," read the headline. Dr. Brisbane was dead. The two Americans were Kent Brantly and Nancy Writebol, a doctor and nurse working for the Protestant missionary group Samaritan's Purse, which, along with a second missionary group, staffed a hospital on the outskirts of the city. The hospital was called ELWA, the acronym standing for Eternal Love Winning Africa. Like the staff at JFK, Brantly and Writebol and the other ELWA staff kept providing care throughout June and July while the epidemic raged on the streets of the capital. Brantly and Writebol were airlifted to Emory University Hospital's Biosafety Level 4 unit, since Emory was equipped for such care owing to its proximity to the CDC headquarters and its laboratories in the Special Pathogens Branch. The news in the States was virtually nonstop from there on out.

In terms of my acquaintances, the situation was worse than I knew. Borbor had tested positive, and Phil Ireland had become symptomatic as well. Phil believes he became infected by caring for Vincent, who by then had been taken to an ETU that had been set up on the margins of ELWA's large campus. He was critically ill, though how ill no one could say, as the ELWA ETU was deluged with cases by that point. There was no easy way to get an update from the inside.

Four days before the AP story broke on July 27, Phil knew it was his turn. "I was having headaches that I had never experienced before, so bad that it felt like flashes of lightning," Phil said. He was in the outpatient clinic at JFK, where he used an oximeter to check his pulse.

"I was running 118. I've had malaria a thousand times and it had never done this. I checked my temperature and it was 38.1, and I thought, *This is Ebola*. So I went to the pharmacy, bought paracetamol, antimalarials, and ciprofloxacin. I went home and told everyone, 'I'm isolating myself in this room. Nobody come to me. Just stay away.' The next morning, I felt a little better. I drove myself to work, but I was feeling weak, so I went to the hospital kitchen to get a bun and some tea."

Despite the hope that some nutrition would revive him, the sight of food and drink proved too much for Phil. His abhorrence of food and especially drink reminded him of the characteristic presentation of a different disease that he had seen at JFK, rabies, but he knew he wasn't suffering from rabies. He got into his truck and drove straight to ELWA. Amazingly, they turned him away, saying that they knew he had been careful and tried to reassure him that he was just anxious. Shocked, he returned home.

Phil was too weak to return to work and would need to remain in his house, so he sent his wife and children out to stay with other family members. The thinning ranks of his colleagues from JFK, as well as physicians from the Ministry of Health, continued to check in on him. Several days later, when his symptoms had worsened, the ministry sent an ambulance to his house to take him back, dazed and confused by then, to the ELWA ETU for testing. At the entrance to the ETU, an argument ensued between the drivers and the staff as to who would assist him out of the ambulance. The unprotected drivers wanted no part of this, but the ETU staff insisted that until he got *out* of the ambulance, he was their responsibility. "I came to a little bit, and heard the argument going on, and whatever strength I had, I went to the ambulance door, kicked it open, and two guys in PPE came over and took me straight into the ETU," he said. After the test would return positive, he was given a cot. He would turn out to be only a few feet away from Vincent, who did not have much longer to live.

Until I learned that Borbor was infected, the Ebola outbreak had remained mostly an abstraction. Although I had been on Monrovia's streets and knew something of the place, the news of the ever-increasing bedlam still seemed far off. But when a phone call came from Trish

McQuilkin and the news about Borbor was conveyed to me, a switch flipped, and I realized it was time to find my way over there. I knew this man, and although I can't claim to have known him well, I understood enough to know how much a country like Liberia needed a man of Abraham Borbor's stature. He wasn't just another doctor who happened to be working in Liberia; he practically *was* internal medicine in Liberia. Because the Civil War hit the pause button on an entire generation of physicians (or health-care workers of any kind, for that matter), those few who were still standing by the tail end of their careers were the only ones left to train a new generation of physicians. Dr. Borbor was very nearly the sole Liberian internist who hadn't fled but had seen it through and was now around to help Liberian medicine get back on its feet.

Think about it this way: If I got run over by a car in the United States, it would be a sad moment for my family and my friends, but in terms of my impact on the medical community in central Massachusetts where I work, life would go on in much the same way as it did the day before. There are something like twenty-five infectious disease doctors in Worcester alone, to say nothing of hundreds of other internists. In terms of the impact on patient care, my passing would hardly register. But if Borbor were to die from Ebola, Liberian medicine would suffer an impact that couldn't be measured. He was irreplaceable in a country that was ill suited to lose any help, but especially the type that mentored a fledgling class of young doctors learning to find their way in a country in full reboot.

I had more on my mind than Borbor, however. I had barely gotten to know Liberia—the sum total of my knowledge was based on my brief visit, reading a few books about the country and its history upon my return, and some solitary time spent ruminating on what I had seen. To go charging into what increasingly looked to be a highly unstable situation with one of the deadliest viruses on the loose, completely overwhelming the government's capacity to respond, may seem like an exercise in folly. To do it to help people I hardly knew may seem like a death wish, but I could not shake a sense that I had a responsibility to be there. If you travel to a place like Monrovia, with its desperate poverty, and you are treated with such remarkable kindness and deference as I had been, it is hard not to feel a sense of obligation to these people, even those I hadn't met and about whose lives I could only guess.

Indeed, I had made it to Liberia because the institution where I worked, the University of Massachusetts, had fostered a relationship with the country since the end of the Civil War. In 2012, UMass had invited Liberia's president, Ellen Johnson Sirleaf, to receive an honorary degree at our medical school commencement, an act that couldn't have been a more public affirmation of our commitment to this country. The Web page of our Office of Global Health prominently featured a picture of our faculty standing in front of the main building of the University of Liberia. As an institution, we had proclaimed to the world our assurances that we were there to help them.

Now, *I* had become part of that relationship and was bound by that commitment. My feeling was that, even if you have a brief experience like mine in Liberia, and those people suddenly find themselves in a major crisis, and you *can* help them, you *must* help them. It wasn't *noblesse oblige*; it was keeping your word. If I failed to help when I could, in their hour of need, then what was my moral worth? Our good name as an institution and my good name as a doctor—my good name as a *person*—would mean nothing at all if I sat on the sidelines.

And this was no crisis of political instability typical for the region— it was a *health-care* crisis, and I was a doctor who could make a tangible contribution at the ground level. Trish and some other members of the Liberia group at UMass were making their difference by getting much-needed supplies to JFK and organizing the providers in the United States; I needed to make my difference by getting myself to an ETU and doing what I do for a living, which is take care of patients with infections. Once I saw that my new friends were being overrun by this pestilence, I had decided on doing everything I could to return to Liberia, come what may.

About the time I was flipping my mental switch into "go" mode, a family physician named Rick Sacra, who by chance also was on the faculty at UMass, had already gotten on a plane to work as a doctor at ELWA—not in an ETU, mind you, but mainly to deliver babies, given how starved the entire medical system was for competent medical help as Liberia's already tenuous health-care structure imploded. Rick would pay for that decision by becoming infected in short order. But Rick was deeply invested in Liberia, having worked at ELWA off and on for more than two decades. He had friends, colleagues, and patients whom he knew at an intimate level. However dicey a proposition it was to head into Liberia in the summer of 2014 to perform medical work without proper Ebola training and protective gear, for a man like Rick Sacra, there were clearly other matters that factored into the equation based on his long-standing relationship with the place, to say nothing of his permanent relationship with Jesus Christ. By contrast, I had merely been a guest on a quick flyby to a country I was only beginning to understand. I wasn't about to take that kind of risk, but I was determined to assist in what would surely be a massive international aid effort.

Of course, being resolved to help out is nice, but I didn't have the first clue about *how* to get over there with the right kind of organization. During the last few days of July I looked around on the websites of MSF, which had been holding increasingly strident press conferences saying the international response was far too inadequate and which led me to assume there would be some place where one could easily find out how to volunteer. But no such luck. Being an academic physician, I didn't know much about any other aid organizations, so I turned to the CDC website and decided to see whether someone at the Special Pathogens Branch might know something. The Special Pathogens Branch handles dangerous viruses that cause lethal outbreaks such as Ebola, so I thought that maybe someone there might be able to point me in a direction.

The Special Pathogens Web page listed the name of the director, Dr. Craig Manning, and a phone number. To my surprise, I reached him directly on the morning of August 1, and we began to talk. "Steve, it's interesting. You're the third call I've gotten this week, and I'm not sure what to say right now. Obviously the CDC is working on this but I don't know what to say for someone like you," he said. "I do have this friend from Ireland who works for WHO, why don't you send him an e-mail and tell him I sent you, and see what happens."

Off went an e-mail to Ireland. A few days later, I got a reply, the gist of which was: *Can't help you myself, Steven, but why don't you try my friend at MSF Belgium, and if that doesn't work try this person who works in a different division of WHO.* So I wrote the woman at MSF Belgium. "Thanks for your interest," she wrote, "but right now we're only looking for people who have experience working in Bio-safety Level 4 conditions. . . . If you're interested in placement in a different location, we'll be happy to send you an application."

That caught me quite by surprise, for it seemed as if MSF was ha-ranguing the world health community on a daily basis to step up its response. Now they were turning away people offering to help? More-over, surely given the size of the outbreak, weren't most of the people with experience in Hot Zone work already spoken for?*

Thus, a few days later, it was on to someone else at the WHO, this time in Germany. The next day or so came a reply. "You know, I have a colleague named Hilarie Cranmer, an emergency physician from Massachusetts General Hospital who is coordinating with Interna-tional Medical Corps, and I've cc'ed her on this message," said the note. "Hope that is a help."

Over the span of about a week, I had pinged e-mail contacts almost completely around the globe, and at the end I found myself connected to someone who lived only a few miles from my doorstep. Hilarie and I spoke that week for maybe ten minutes in what I later realized was something of an informal interview, and I recounted in a very cursory way why I not only wanted to go over but was "qualified" to do so: I was an infectious disease doc who had more than a nodding acquain-tance with hemorrhagic fevers, even if it was only the far less lethal dengue virus, and had been to Liberia, even for only a mere few weeks. "Got it, that makes sense," she said in the highly succinct summary

---

* Based on my brief experience with them, MSF appears to be less a single unified organization than it is a conglomeration of several semiautonomous groups: MSF Belgium, MSF Spain, MSF New York. Over the course of August I spoke with not only MSF Belgium as related above but also MSF New York, who gave me the same basic response after having me fill out an interminably long application. When I arrived in Bong County, I discovered that IMC had "picked up" several MSF alumni who had gotten a similar runaround. I wasn't completely surprised that MSF wasn't going to take me sight unseen for work in an Ebola unit, but I was nearly stunned that their organization's HR wing couldn't streamline their procedures for *their own physicians*, some of whom had worked for them for longer than a year.

for which ER doctors are known. "Let's stay in touch, and I'll let the IMC human resource people know to look for your CV."

By now it was approaching mid-August, and with each passing day the outbreak was on its way to becoming the lead news story in the world. Monrovia had been in chaos for well over a month, but now it was no longer a regional secret known only to those in the Liberian diaspora with direct contact with the city residents. *The New York Times* ran a long story about the turmoil, carefully parsing the various challenges that the central government faced in its beleaguered efforts to preserve order and stop the epidemic.

By that time, I was sitting in on weekly conference calls of a small group of physicians in the States keen to help in whatever way they could. For instance, Trish McQuilkin, working with contacts such as the head of the Liberian College of Physicians, Dr. Roseda Marshall, had managed to procure nearly $10 million in personal protective equipment for JFK—no mean feat that, given huge logistical challenges of obtaining that much material and sending it to a place that fewer and fewer shipping companies wanted to have anything to do with. All this from professionals whose expertise was in treating patients, not running international supply chains.

During one of these calls I learned that Borbor had been among the first people in the world to be given the experimental drug ZMapp, although my clinical opinion was that even if ZMapp were truly an effective drug—still an open question as I write this—it was probably too late to have an effect. ZMapp works by binding the virus with premade antibodies. It works a bit like a molecular vacuum cleaner: The body's natural vacuum cleaner (that is, the naturally produced antibodies specific for the Ebola virus) takes a few weeks to activate, by which point most of the damage of Ebola is already done, and the patient—if he or she has survived—doesn't require such antibodies anymore.

ZMapp provides a ready-to-go anti-Ebola cocktail in a bag, best used at the *beginning* of an infection. Borbor was probably already making his own antibodies by the time the ZMapp was being infused into him, so whether he lived or died had little to do with how much virus was in his body, but rather the extent to which his body's own immune system had gone completely haywire. All that, however, was but a guess. The fact that he was still alive several weeks into infection was encouraging to me, although I wasn't precisely sanguine about this.

I started alerting my superiors at UMass that I was looking for ways to get over there and work in an Ebola Treatment Unit. My division chief thought this was laughable almost before I could finish my first sentence. "You're fucking out of your mind," was his immediate observation.

Arguably true, but not fully relevant, I thought.

A few days later, after I took another pass at him: "Steve, I'm not letting you go over there."

Um, Doug? You're, um, not my dad.

That's how a few of the conversations proceeded in August.

As we neared the end of August, Monrovia nearly came apart at the seams. One of the densest parts of the city is a neighborhood known as West Point. Monrovia's center is a spit of high land at the mouth of the Mesurado River where it meets the Atlantic Ocean. From this outcropping one can travel either north onto Bushrod Island or east into Sinkor (the site of JFK) and farther on into Congo Town and the outskirts at Paynesville. Basically the main human settlements of Monrovia are shaped like a V flipped on its side, thus: ∟, with the city center at the pivot point. West Point is a small but densely populated peninsula, a dead-end nub of land just west of that northern corridor leading out of the city center. It had become one of the hottest areas of the outbreak, and with its concentration of human beings— somewhere between fifty and a hundred thousand people lived there, though nobody knew the population with any precision—the spreading virus had become the biological equivalent of a hydrogen bomb. President Sirleaf had made a fateful decision to institute a *cordon sanitaire*. That is, she placed the entire section of West Point under a quarantine. In effect, she was trying to dig a fire line with the hope of stopping the viral flames from spreading.

But quarantines are risky maneuvers even under the most optimal of circumstances, and these were not the most optimal of circumstances. Quarantines can be effective in *small* areas, say, a village of a few hundred people, but this was an attempted quarantine of tens of thousands, nearly all of whom were frightened, ill informed, and suspicious of the government—hardly a surprise given decades of civil strife during which time caution with respect to government pronouncements could be lifesaving. In doubting the reality of Ebola, they shared Dr. Brisbane's cynicism but lacked his education and perspective, and so couldn't easily shift their thinking in spite of the evidence accumulating all around them.

To cordon off that many people meant that at least some major and basic contingencies needed to be considered. These people needed food, they needed water, and a good many needed money, for a weeks-long quarantine meant lost income in one of the most impoverished sections of an already extremely poor country. Yet from what I could tell reading the news, there was no clear plan beyond putting up a rope, having the army stationed at the borders, and saying, "Don't cross this line."

Mayhem, predictably, ensued. Residents attacked an ETU that had been set up in the neighborhood, regarding as lies the government pronouncements that the virus should be isolated to minimize the spread. They carried away sick patients in their arms, took the sheets and mattresses, and forced the health-care workers to run for their lives. Days later, the West Point mob directly confronted the Armed Forces of Liberia, who at one point opened fire on the crowd, killing a sixteen-year-old boy in the process, another casualty of Ebola without ever becoming infected. He wouldn't be its last.

The West Point quarantine was not just a mess. It wasn't even a disaster. It was a calamity. And Monrovia itself hung in the balance.

Then, more news: Borbor was dead.

Somewhere between the final few days in August and the first few days of September, the Human Resource staff at International Medical Corps called me to discuss work in their new ETU that was currently under construction in Bong County. Mainly it was a more formal repeat of the conversation that I had with Hilarie Cranmer a few weeks before. I was eager to talk about dates and whether they were going to commit, in part because it was now obvious that help was needed immediately, but also because I had to start making arrangements to have my outpatient clinic and inpatient service time covered. I told them I could be available starting the third week of September and I could go until mid-December. They said, "Well, we're not deploying people more than six consecutive weeks given the stress of the environment, but mid-September seems good. We'll keep you posted."

But I did need answers from them, rather more quickly than they seemed prepared to provide them. Aid organizations, I didn't fully understand at the time, are considerably nimbler with their staff deployments, and nurses and doctors are frequently notified of their assignments a few days before their departure. Academic medical centers, however, make their schedules a *year* in advance, moving at a glacial pace compared to aid organizations like IMC. The kind of doctors who were starting to emerge as volunteers for this effort—people like me—were going to need some lead time to put things in order. But a group like IMC can't plan that far in advance; it's just not what they're built for. This interinstitutional tension was the first of many such instances in which doctors and nurses, myself included, found themselves trying to negotiate as best they could in order to serve in West Africa.

At any rate, about two weeks passed and I heard nothing from IMC. At one of the weekly conference calls of U.S. physicians focused on the Liberian crisis, someone mentioned that the Centers for Disease Control was in the midst of arranging a course for preparing health-care workers bound for West Africa. Until that point, the only way one could learn the proper procedures for working in the high-risk environment of an ETU was to be trained by MSF, which had developed the protocols years earlier based on its ongoing involvement in Ebola care. MSF had a three-day training session for expat workers in Belgium and was ramping up training in the affected countries, but more hands were needed on deck. The CDC had taken the MSF protocols and had created its own curriculum to increase the pipeline of properly trained workers. I knew I needed that training, for there was no way I was headed to a country filled with Ebola without it.

Having not heard from IMC, I contacted the CDC directly and was told that the course was already booked solid until mid-November. Did I want to put my name on the list? I had been lining up all of my colleagues to cover for me starting in late September and extend *into* mid-November. Was I now going to have to completely rearrange a schedule that I had painstakingly constructed and abuse the goodwill of my clinical chief, who was already gritting her teeth at the coverage chaos that my hasty departure would produce? I decided that I'd get over there when I could, and my division would have to deal with it. November it is for the CDC course.

A day or two later, IMC called again. "Are you available to attend the CDC course on September 21?" someone asked me. "We could then deploy you within a few days of the training." Oh, they *are* serious about me going, I suddenly realized.

"Well, yeah, but they told me they're booked solid until mid-November," I said. "I can't go over there without being trained." I was told to sit tight, they'd be in touch. Three hours later I received an e-mail from a woman named Martha Mock at the CDC telling me that I had a spot reserved for the pilot training course, could I please confirm that I will be coming?

Whoa.

A few days later I was sitting in on an IMC conference call with a small group of nurses and one other doctor to discuss the situation on the ground in Liberia. IMC still at that point hadn't formally offered me a contract, nor had they provided precise deployment dates, but by this point I was taking things on faith. They had gotten me to the head of the line for the CDC course, which I assumed they wouldn't have done unless they were very serious about getting me to Bong County.

Leading the conference was a man named Sean Casey, the head of operations for IMC's response in Liberia. Sean was calling from Monrovia, and he was the first person with whom I had spoken who was actually on the ground. I don't remember much of the call; mostly I sat and listened. The other doctor was talking a lot about convalescent plasma transfusions—that is, giving the serum from survivors, in theory rich with anti-Ebola antibodies, to infected patients in ETUs, a kind of poor man's version of ZMapp. I didn't know whether this would be within the capabilities of IMC's Bong County ETU, but based on what I had seen at JFK ten months before, my sense was that this doctor was running before walking.

My biggest concern was less about whether it was a reasonable suggestion (it seemed so) but the kind of urgency with which he spoke. I knew enough from working at JFK, as well as working in other countries with major resource limitations, that sometimes you have to just make do with what you've got. If you go into this environment with strong feelings—indeed, almost a sense of moral righteousness—about what should constitute standard of care and then the conditions fall short of it, you can become very dispirited. I was a little concerned that this person didn't realize what we might face.

I can recall one exchange from this conversation with crystal clarity, however. Sean had summarized the situation according to the latest tallies supplied by the World Health Organization. I don't remember those numbers, but I'll forever remember what he said next. "The current estimate is that Liberia requires twenty-seven ETUs to care for patients and prevent the outbreak from spreading further," Sean said, and paused for a split second before adding, "as of this moment, there are six."

On that same day in Guinea, the tremors that the world was sensing about the difficulties of containing a region-wide outbreak turned into an outright earthquake. A delegation of officials, doctors, and journalists, as well as a pastor for good measure, went to a place called Womey, a quiet village a few hours east of Meliandou, to aid in community educational efforts about Ebola. The idea was simple: Provide presentations about the virus and explain how it is spread so as to encourage optimal behaviors designed to stop it in its tracks. By now, the Nzérékoré Region in eastern Guinea had been inundated with Ebola cases, and hundreds were dead. Villages were being decimated and paranoia was running high.

The presentation began, but almost immediately the visitors sensed something was terribly amiss. At the sight of these outsiders, village women began to chant, "They are coming to kill you." Soon, several men from the village emerged with masked faces, armed with machetes.

It was clear that many villagers thought they had come to Womey to *spread* Ebola instead of help prevent it. The educational session quickly turned into a massacre. Eight members of the visiting party were hacked to death and their bodies were thrown into a community latrine; the remaining few ran for their lives into the jungle.

The story of the Womey massacre reached the outside world two days later, on September 18. It was a worst-case scenario. The very people who could provide the best hope of stamping out this pestilence were being rejected, and in as dramatic and violent a manner as could possibly be imagined, by those most at risk of being mowed down by the virus. Womey was a warning that those who wanted to turn the tide had to be prepared to make two potentially lethal gambles: The first was of becoming infected; the second was of being chopped, quite literally, to pieces. Or perhaps in the opposite order.

With the sobering reality of Womey on my mind, a few days later I found myself on a plane to Atlanta to attend the pilot CDC Ebola course. I had spoken with Pranav Shetty, the lead physician in charge of the Bong ETU, which had just opened for business about the time of the conference call. All was proceeding briskly, although I still had no contract and no assignment. I assumed that this was going to be rectified shortly, and I formally halted all of my clinics and told my division chief not to expect me back for six to eight weeks. I was told again that I was fucking out of my mind, and again I thought he may have had a point, though not for the reason he said.

Throughout September, I had spent so much of my waking energy thinking about *how* to get myself to Liberia that I hadn't taken so much as a second to reflect on *what* was driving me there. The explanation you read above is mostly a post hoc justification. At the time I had operated on pure instinct. Now I was reasonably sure it was going to happen. During the three-hour flight from Boston to Atlanta, I opened my laptop and with very little forethought just started writing. As if to compose an explanation to myself, and maybe the broader world, for what was about to happen, I typed the words "Why I Go" at the start and wrote for the next three hours, 2,800 words without ever raising my head. It was the shortest flight I ever took.

The plane arrived in Atlanta, and a small group of the early attendees waited at an assigned location to be picked up and taken to Fort McClellan in Anniston, Alabama, for the four-day course. A half dozen of us were there milling about, and we would form the first cohort to make the ninety-mile drive west from Atlanta to wait for the people coming in on later flights. As we stood around, I recognized the voice of a woman talking on her cell phone but didn't know why I would know someone here. I then realized that I had listened to this woman, whose name was Emily Veltus, in an interview on NPR only a few days before about her work with MSF in Sierra Leone. She must have practically gotten off the plane from Africa and come straight here. Some of the course leaders, I would later learn, did exactly that.

Eventually I started a conversation with a woman in uniform. Initially I took her for being in the military, as uniforms equal military to my civilian eyes, but she was a lieutenant commander in the U.S. Public Health Service whose name was Elizabeth Lybarger.* The USPHS was a group that President Obama was preparing to deploy to Liberia in an effort to build a state-of-the-art ETU to care for the healthcare workers at such high risk, not only those working in existing ETUs but those like Zoeban Parteh, who were continuing to see patients at hospitals like JFK without any serious protective gear. Elizabeth was in charge of making sure her USPHS troops were trained, and as such she was attending this CDC pilot course as something of a reconnaissance mission. As we started out making small talk, I observed two salient features about her: First, she felt a deep responsibility for those working for her, and second, she swore like a sailor. Which is to say I liked her tremendously right from the start.

We rapped the entire way from the airport to Alabama swapping our life stories. In the mid-1990s we had both read *The Hot Zone*, and we both had developed a passion for the virus as a consequence. Unlike me, however, whose career ambitions to do work in Ebola or Marburg got sidetracked by family priorities, Elizabeth really did go into this line of work. Her life had *become*, in some sense, exactly like the kind of people that Preston wrote about. She had worked at

---

* Now LCDR Elizabeth DeGrange.

USAMRIID—the United States Army Medical Research Institute of Infectious Diseases, a place that filovirus aficionados regard as a sort of mecca. She had worked at CDC as well, in both places working on Biosafety Level 4 agents. And now she was working for the U.S. Public Health Service facing potential deployment to a Hot Zone of unprecedented proportions, a fact that was creating some unpleasant scheduling conflicts with her upcoming wedding.

For the course, the CDC had commandeered a small corner of the vast army base at the southern tip of the Blue Ridge Mountains in eastern Alabama, sharing that part of the campus with a bunch of firefighters undergoing hazmat training, which was part of the base's permanent educational activities. We were assigned dorm rooms that were Spartan but clean, and given time to relax while we waited for the rest of the participants to arrive. Elizabeth and I made our way to the mess hall and ran into some other uniformed personnel, this time actual military in the form of Lieutenant Colonel Tom Wilson and Major William Thoms of the U.S. Air Force, who were there to think through the logistics of flying infected soldiers back to the States if worst-case scenarios took place. "The grub here is pretty good," one of them said, and after the initial sampling of down-home Alabama fare, with menu items like glazed ham and scalloped potatoes or country fried steak with gravy and green beans, I thought, *Yes, but it's missing eighty milligrams of Lipitor for dessert.*

The next morning the class of "Camp Ebola," about fifty people in all, was in one of the classrooms in a huge concrete office building about a mile and a half from the dorms. It must have been sixty degrees in the nondescript classroom. I ended up sitting in the back with the military people, who by that point had expanded to include Major Matthew Chambers of USAMRIID and Commander James Lawler of the Naval Medical Research Center in addition to Elizabeth and the USAF guys. *One of these things is not like the others*, my mind would sing to itself from time to time during the course, as my uniformed colleagues may not have been fully aware that they had something approaching a more well-behaved version of Abbie Hoffman sitting beside them.

The course was a Who's Who of the international health scene. In addition to all the military folks, several of whom had been doing Biosafety Level 4 work for decades, were the aid organizations: MSF sent a nurse and a social worker, each with Hot Zone experience, to help guide the proceedings; about five members of Paul Farmer's group Partners In Health were present; a person from Save the Children had come; there were people from various institutions such as Johns Hopkins and Emory; and of course there was a big CDC presence. The lectures were devoted to all topics Ebola: the history of the outbreaks; the dynamics of the current outbreak, which was literally changing by the day; the clinical presentation and course of the disease; the infection-control procedures necessary to contain the virus; and so on. Lectures were held in the icebox in the morning, with the practical exercises of learning to wear (don) and take off (doff) personal protective equipment in the afternoon. I thought that wearing PPE in Alabama in late September was going to be good training for the physical stress of working in Liberia, but it turned out we came during an unseasonably cool stretch, and during our three-day PPE practicum, the temperature hovered in the low seventies without a hint of humidity. I hardly broke a sweat during the exercises. That was about to change.

One evening a group gathered at the campus bar, where we shared the space with the firefighters turning in from their hazmat work, and sat on a porch listening to the workers who had just returned from the outbreak to hear their informal impressions of what would await us. Nahid Bhadelia, an infectious disease doctor from Boston University who had been working at an ETU in Kenema only weeks before and who had seen some of the worst of what this epidemic had to offer, made a comment that seemed both completely unsurprising and simultaneously shocking. "Guys, it's not like you haven't seen this stuff before. It's just sepsis. They've got sepsis," she said, referring to the physiologic process of the body's severe reaction to bad infections. In saying that, she was trying to communicate that we had *all* seen sick patients; there wasn't anything bone-jarringly weird about a health-care worker tending to the ill, so it was best to mentally recalibrate.

But then came the counterpunch. "It's not the sepsis," she added. "It's the *volume* of patients with sepsis that is the challenge. You're going to see a lot of people die."

And I thought back to that day at JFK when I witnessed seven young patients expire in one day.

The third day of the course, *The New York Times* ran a story that got everyone's full attention during one of the morning breaks. "Ebola Cases Could Reach 1.4 Million Within Four Months, CDC Estimates" was the headline, and although the text of the article indicated a more nuanced reality—mainly, that the 1.4 million figure was a worst-case scenario—it was hard not to escape the notion that Liberia, along with its two neighbors, were on the fast track to total collapse.

I thought again about Womey, where Ebola had managed to kill even without direct infection; the terror that the virus had unleashed upon the countryside was causing the social fabric to rip, turning mild-mannered rice farmers and palm oil harvesters into cold-blooded machete-wielding murderers. Womey suggested that as the virus became harder to contain, the violence would expand, hampering the efforts that might stanch the bleeding, and in doing so make the virus harder to contain, in an escalating feedback loop. It could make other humanitarian aid organizations hesitate to join forces with MSF, IMC, IRC (the International Rescue Committee), and the few other groups that had established beachheads to help fight the outbreak. It looked grim.

During that break, everyone was discussing the *Times* piece. Nobody was really surprised, for we had all thought previous media reports about *thousands* of victims to be a gross underestimate. But it was a different matter entirely to see one's worst fears posted on the front page of the Paper of Record. When we started the training, in more poetic moments I conceived of what was taking place in that cold little conference room in Alabama as something like being at the first wave of D-Day: a perilous action but also something at which the survivors would someday look back with a certain level of pride in their accomplishment. After I read the *Times* piece, I thought the more apt allusion could have been the Charge of the Light Brigade.

At dinner that evening, I had pulled aside Mary Jo Frawley, a nurse who had done stints with MSF in prior Ebola and Marburg outbreaks. I started to talk about the staff with whom I would be working: By mid-September many articles had highlighted just how risky treating Ebola patients had become for the nursing staff. I knew that IMC's ETU would be much safer than the local clinics where many of these nurses had become infected, but I also knew that even if the national staff worked at an ETU with the proper equipment and procedures to ensure maximal protection, these people still had to return to cities and villages where the virus was running rampant and could just as easily be infected there. And although I would like to think of myself as being a progressive and egalitarian doctor when it comes to the subject of teamwork, I am still a touch old-fashioned when it comes to the notion that, as the physician, I was responsible for *everyone's* life in that ETU. I thought of those nurses dying on my watch, and after three days of preparing for the end of the world, I sat there and held Mary's hand and wept like a child, the tears flowing down my face and off my cheeks onto a plate of roast beef with gravy and mashed potatoes, which until about a month ago was, at least in the aggregate, much more likely to be deadly to me than Ebola.

The public display of raw and uncensored emotion no doubt must have caused some alarm to my colleagues walking by, who may have concluded that I was emotionally unfit for what was to come, but my frontal lobes have always functioned with just enough oomph to make me aware that my displays of emotional intensity can be jarring to people but not so much that I modulate my behavior unless it's absolutely called for. And at that moment, I didn't give a damn.

Later that night we went to the campus bar for pitchers and karaoke. After the third beer, I unwound by singing Gordon Lightfoot's "Sundown" to mild amusement and playing a game in which Emily Veltus and one of the docs working for the CDC named Rupa Narra would toss popcorn into my mouth from ever greater lengths, and I would bark and clap my hands like a seal if I caught them. Later still, a group of about ten of us caught a taxi into town, or whatever constituted "town" in rural Alabama—which by my definition meant a cluster of buildings, of which one had a perfectly functional bar—and

I added a few glasses of bourbon to the beer that had become part of my bloodstream. The next day I left Camp Ebola with enough of a headache to last the bus ride back to Atlanta but not so much that it was still there by the time I arrived in Columbus for a previously scheduled visit to my mother, as the training session had overlapped the first day of the Jewish New Year.

IMC had finally sent me a contract, making everything official. I was to be deployed soon. I began the laborious task of formalizing my temporary leave with UMass, asking colleagues to cover my panel of patients during my absence and letting go of my teaching responsibilities for at least the next few months. I was supposed to be in Columbus for about three days and then make my way from Columbus to Chicago to Brussels and then Monrovia, but a freak incident occurred at O'Hare airport the day of my departure, where a disturbed man tried to set fire to the air traffic control tower, shutting down O'Hare and therefore a huge number of the flights going through the Midwest.

It was a weekend day, so I made frantic calls to the on-call travel agent to try to find an alternate way out of the country, and came within minutes of a flight going to Philly and then Brussels, but too much time was required for someone at IMC to sign off on the plan. So I remained stranded in Columbus for an additional two days, since there were no longer daily flights going to Liberia, as most of the carriers had suspended their service to all three of the affected countries. I decided to stay at the airport hotel rather than return to my mother's apartment in case I got a call for some crazy new plan that required my returning to the airport immediately, but nothing transpired, and two days later I found myself sitting in the terminal somewhere in the vicinity of 5:00 p.m. glancing at the television, flicking through e-mails on my phone.

Then I saw it.

The TV was tuned to CNN, and the headline ran across the bottom of the screen: "FIRST DIAGNOSED CASE OF EBOLA IN THE U.S." I blinked a few times, and then picked up my phone and called my best friend. "Mark, you're not gonna believe this," I said to him, then relayed the news. "I'll tell you this. America's about to lose its mind." I read the updates as they flashed, which was that a Liberian expat had become symptomatic at a hospital in Dallas and not much else was known. We chatted for a few minutes, but I had to board my plane to make my connection. As I got onto the plane, I thought that Liberia might be a better place in which to find oneself over the next few days. Then I thought about what was actually happening in Liberia, and I realized that was wishful thinking.

I got to Newark airport with about two hours to spare before catching the red-eye to London. The O'Hare connection to Brussels was full, so I was now going on an even more adventurous pathway through Newark to Heathrow to Casablanca and then finally to Monrovia. About an hour before boarding, they announced that first-class upgrades were available if anyone wanted to inquire at the desk. I am normally not given to even considering flying first class—as pleasant an experience as it is to fly in such manner, it has always seemed an extravagance that can't be justified, and it rubs hard against that part of my personality that is adamantly socialist. But an upgrade on a red-eye heading into what was going to be a long few days meant that I might get some much-needed rest, which I definitely wasn't going to do in the upright seating of coach. So I went to the desk to inquire and was cheerily told that upgrades were definitely available and would cost $575.

This seemed a ridiculous amount of money for a six-hour flight.

Ah, to hell with it, I thought. I probably wasn't coming back anyway, so I might as well enjoy it. And I handed over my credit card.

3

THE BLUE WORLD

The current scientific understanding of Ebolaviruses constitutes pinpricks of light against a dark background.
—David Quammen, *Ebola*

The Royal Air Maroc Flight 559 from Casablanca landed in Monrovia at two-thirty in the morning. The Roberts airport is more than an hour outside the capital, its lone airstrip not far from the Atlantic Ocean, so that a passenger's slightly unnerving point of view makes it seem as if a water landing is being attempted. For Americans, air-*strip* is probably a more helpful description. What one normally envisions when the term *airport* is used—long concourses, electronic signs indicating flights arriving and departing, so much artificial lighting that it seems perpetual daytime—is nowhere in evidence here. Roberts airport in its entirety consists of one low-slung concrete building about the size of a car dealer's showroom, a small outpost of partial light gamely fighting back the dark African night. The signs are all either painted or are printed on poster board; there's nothing electronic here.

Even in the middle of the night, emerging from the air-conditioned plane into the air of Liberia is like entering a sauna. The few of us who were on the plane, mainly a collection of health-care workers, news reporters, and a few Liberians, disembarked by descending a rickety aluminum portable staircase and walked about one hundred feet to the entrance of the building. I had been here before, but this time as we trudged along, there was definitely a sense of transition, of leaving one kind of world and emerging into an entirely new and different one. We were first guided to a series of plastic buckets containing a light bleach solution with a tap at the bottom and were told to wash our hands. Then we stood in line, for the building couldn't be entered until one passed through a group of workers who stood by to check everyone's temperatures, holding onto infrared thermometers shaped like guns that were aimed at one's temple. As we waited, contemplating our thermal regulation while we perspired in the heat and humidity, we were provided with fliers about Ebola, explaining the signs and symptoms and what to do should we become sick in Liberia. It was no longer a training exercise.

Despite the fact that the plane was mostly empty, it still took more than an hour to get through Immigration and Customs. Afterward, the ride from Roberts airport to the IMC guesthouse in Monrovia took another hour. I shared the ride, which ambled down a one-lane road in utter darkness, with Steve Whiteley, an emergency doctor from California. Steve had extensive experience in disaster situations and had done prior stints with MSF. He had been all over the world and done medicine in some very trying situations. As an infectious disease doctor with no specialty in disaster response, I could not help but find this intimidating. I began to worry about whether I would be seen as a legit player here, and I hadn't even been on the ground long enough to see daylight.

We were greeted at the guesthouse by a Scotsman named Jimmy Steel, who told us that we would be meeting at just past seven for debriefing. I got to bed a little after five and awoke less than two hours later, bleary-eyed, and headed to the living room to meet.

The debriefing, as best I can recall, was a short meeting in which I was told, "Welcome to Liberia. Ready to go to work?" Shortly thereafter we drove to Monrovia's heliport, where a chopper waited to take a group of us to Bong County, where we were going to perform various jobs at the Ebola Treatment Unit. Normally transport to Bong County is done by car: a five-hour, 120-mile ride over a tattered highway that was in the process of being reconstructed. But we were needed there with all haste, as we were scheduled to replace some of the staff who had been working weeks without a day off, and were set to depart on their R & R over the next day or two.* Thus, we were booked for the helicopter ride to maximize overlap between the incoming and outgoing workers.

What you see of this country when you take that one-hour, bird's-eye-view trip is a *lot* of jungle. Small villages dot the landscape, but there is hardly any large urban development once you get past the outskirts of Monrovia. Every few minutes, a part of the jungle would suddenly assemble itself into improbable order. At first I thought it was a trick of the eye due to my exhaustion, but I kept seeing this repeated pattern in the canopy where the trees aligned perfectly into a grid. It reminded me of cornfields, but why would Liberians want to harvest *trees* in the same manner? The answer is that they were rubber trees: The tire corporation Firestone, which has been in Liberia for nearly a century, owns a significant amount of land in the country.

We landed on the soccer field of Cuttington University and, under the watchful gaze of curious onlookers, loaded our bags onto a waiting bus. Cuttington had been founded by the U.S. Episcopal Church in the late nineteenth century and over the past century had been the training ground for much of the Liberian elite until the Civil War tore the country apart in the 1990s. The school reopened at the end of the Civil War in 2004 and now found itself closed again a decade later, this time because of Ebola. IMC had commandeered some of the student and faculty dorms to house the staff.

Not having ever been involved in a disaster situation and not having ever worked with IMC, I hadn't really thought through the point of flying by helicopter. That flight wasn't cheap—money was time—and the money was being spent so that we could go to work immediately.

---

* R & R was mandatory for the full-time workers for International Medical Corps in disaster situations. It typically consisted of a ten-day spin pretty much wherever the staff person wished to go; many of the staff traveled to sunny, beachy places across the globe. The purpose of R & R was, as the letters imply, to get some rest and relaxation so they are fit to return to the hard work in the stressful environment in which they work. Ironically, however, it was not unusual for staff to return from R & R *more* spent as a consequence of partying a bit heavily, at least in part as a coping mechanism to deal with the psychological trauma of the work.

Yet all I was thinking about was to catch a nap and put my luggage away somewhere, so I was taken by surprise when the bus drove straight through the campus and headed out to the main road. We were bound for the Hot Zone right away.

The International Medical Corps Bong County Ebola Treatment Unit sits atop a hill in the middle of the jungle, off the main road that links Bong's capital, Gbarnga, to Monrovia. It's pronounced BAHN-gah. Liberian English seems to have an often apathetic relationship with its consonants, frequently dropping its *g*'s and *k*'s so that, for instance, the tribal language of the largest ethnic group in Liberia, *Kpelleh*, is pronounced something between "peh-leh" and "pay-lay." The one-lane muddy road knifes through the jungle for a little over a mile and emerges into an open area where the forest has been torn apart, leaving a bald gash about two hundred meters across. From the bottom of the hill, you would be struck by the wound inflicted on this patch of earth by humans, and your eyes would scan from a dense green to a gap marked by dozens of people scurrying about a bare landscape, and back to the green as if the jungle were heroically trying to ignore its unwelcome neighbors, hoping that they might yet go back to wherever they came from.

The barren nature of the ETU becomes even more pronounced as you move closer to the gate. The ground is entirely gravel; an incredible amount of it must have been trucked up to this site, for its length is nearly a quarter mile. Many separate, small buildings dot the landscape—so many that it wouldn't be immediately apparent which buildings constituted the patient care area. But what would grab your attention even more than the hive of human activity, the staff darting to and fro among these buildings, is the unnatural amount of *blue* pouring in through your eyes. The buildings are, in fact, little more than hastily hewn two-by-fours hammered together, placed on concrete floors, all wrapped in ocean-blue tarps. Once you are inside the compound, you cannot escape the color.

Despite the number of structures, the layout of the ETU is very simple:

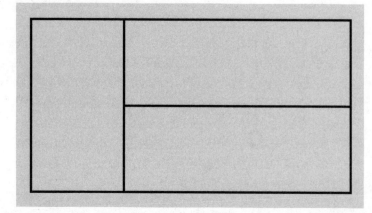

The vertical rectangle on the left represents the staff area. One building housed the changing rooms, a pharmacy, and a storeroom; a second, the medical staff workspace; a third, the administrative offices; and so on. This was formally known as the low-risk area, although I sometimes called it the "Warm Zone" to distinguish it from the other two rectangles, which were the high-risk areas of the Hot Zone. The only problem with my "Warm Zone" term was that it implied that beyond the gates of the ETU was a Cool Zone, and in the Liberia of October 2014, there was no such thing as a Cool Zone. The virus could be anywhere, and the fear was that it was nearly everywhere.

The bottom-right rectangle represented the area where the suspect ward building and its patients were housed. This was the way station for patients who came to the ETU with various symptoms or contacts that were suspicious for Ebola but whose blood tests had not yet returned. If the test returned negative, patients were discharged back to the community. But if their tests did show infection with Ebola, they were transferred into that final rectangle, the confirmed ward.

These were not hermetically sealed places, of course: Doctors, nurses, and patients all flowed through these areas. Structures dotted the boundaries. Patients entered the suspect ward through a triage building (the box at the bottom) that was attached to a driveway where the ambulance dropped the patients off. The staff met them by entering through the "donning," or gowning, station, thus:

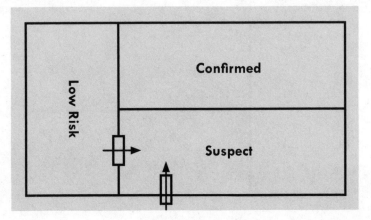

Once inside the Hot Zone, the staff moved in a counterclockwise direction into the confirmed ward, and then reemerged into the low-risk area by means of the decontamination chamber:

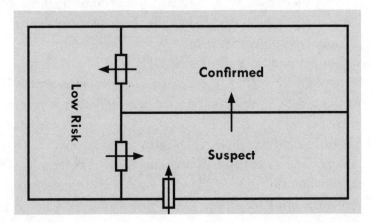

The laws governing the motion of this humanity and matériel were rigidly enforced, and the structures that formed the boundaries between these spaces were always the points of maximum attention, concern, sometimes stress, and occasionally anxiety. Within a few short minutes of arriving at the ETU, I would be directly introduced to that domain and those laws.

As I walked into this blue world, I had two competing sensations. One was of wonder that I really had arrived in this place, had come to the end of the world, and was about to engage in the battle of a lifetime. The more pedestrian feeling was one of such utter exhaustion that all I really cared about, Ebola or no, was to curl up as soon as possible at the most convenient location and take a nap. Since nobody was explaining to me the schedule, I thought that perhaps this was a quick tour of the facility, after which we would be taken back to the Cuttington campus, put up in housing, and be allowed to take the day to acclimate ourselves and get some sleep. I was rudely disabused of this notion when Pranav Shetty, the chief medical officer with whom I had spoken two weeks before, had just completed introductions and then asked Steve Whiteley and me if we were ready to round on the patients.

I had gotten about five hours of sleep over the past forty-eight, having hopped through four countries and a quarter of the earth's circumference. I felt dirty, I was exhausted, and I hadn't had a chance to settle myself. Now I was being asked to do some extremely dangerous work for the very first time. I shot a quick glance at Steve, whose travels began in California and were even longer, but he was expressionless. I felt the urge to voice some concern about this plan. I had to make a quick decision.

"So, what are we waiting for?" I asked, with a let's-rock-and-roll tone in my voice.

It was the right move for more than one reason. First, I was about to get one hell of a jolt of wake-up that would sustain me well into the evening. More important, I would come to learn the critical importance of having a positive attitude. That little piece of Dale Carnegie may sound painfully banal, but in a disaster environment, where there is so much chaos and suffering, being chipper and staying upbeat with a *Here we go!* attitude is that much more important. When everyone is stressed and stretched to their physical and emotional limits, a sour attitude doesn't poison the well—it poisons the *fishbowl*, as the boundaries are that much more constrained. Everyone's working on top of everyone else, and nobody's going be getting away to a nice restaurant, movie, or bookstore for a little mind clearing anytime soon. Not that I understood this at the time; I was just following my intuition.

I went to change into scrubs and boots in the dressing room, and then we entered the donning station. I had performed the gowning process three times at the CDC training course in Alabama. Now, however, it was for real. It isn't exceptionally difficult to put on PPE, but it does involve several small steps, all of which must be perfect, lest one create a situation where exposure to the virus can occur inside the Hot Zone. Three times is plenty to learn to wear PPE; one of the main points of the training is just to become sufficiently familiar with the procedure that you aren't paralyzed by fear when you enter for the first time.

First come the gloves: a pair of regular exam gloves overlaid on surgical gloves, with the inner pair protecting the skin to the mid-arm and the outer pair providing stability, as exam gloves can more easily tear. Next comes the suit itself: a sun-yellow outfit made by DuPont Corporation known as Tychem that zips up from the crotch all the way to the top of the neck. As I put this on, by the time the zipper was midway up my chest, I could already feel the sweat beads form on my head, neck, arms, and back. I never failed to marvel at how quickly I would break into a sweat after I put on the suit.

After zipping up, we put on small face masks to protect our mouths and, after that, a white hood that covered everything except the eyes. The hood was, for me, the moment of real transition, as I couldn't get past the idea that it represented some kind of a shroud: I could only see that white go over my eyes momentarily, but I could *feel* my head and neck become encased in it, like some pharaoh of ancient times getting wrapped in linen to help the journey into the next life. After that hood went on, I was in the land of death, and later, when it came off, that marked the moment when I returned to the land of the living.

Then came a large plastic apron to provide an extra shield against body fluids laden with Ebola; an outer pair of surgical gloves, which we wrapped up with duct tape; and finally, we put on the goggles, marking the moment where we completely sealed every surface of our bodies from the outside world. It wasn't designed to be airtight, but you could get pretty far into a pool before you ever got as wet with anything other than your own sweat, although you would produce a shocking amount of that.

The total time to put on such gear, if only one person were being tended to by the gowning team, was about ten minutes. However, nobody ever goes in alone, and typically there are upwards of six people donning gear in the cramped station, which is not much larger than a decent-sized walk-in closet, so the entire process usually took more than twice that. When it is your *first* time going in, the anticipation is a bit breathtaking. This wasn't a typical inaugural session for a new job.

In we went.

The one-foot journey from low risk to the Hot Zone was like stepping onto the moon. Suddenly all my senses were operating at full throttle—the sensation made stranger still because all my sensory organs were trapped behind various layers of petrochemical polymers. The hum that I felt was not just a first-time experience. Although I would gradually normalize many of the tasks I performed in the high-risk area, I never quite lost that sense that I was moving around in a place not of this earth, one with rules so different it was almost like gravity didn't exist. Those differences required a recalibration of how I moved about and my general level of attention to my surroundings. Every sense was heightened in high risk, even during my most pedestrian moments and even when the work, at first so electrifying, turned into routine, as it inevitably does in any job. Ultimately, I came to see that as protective, and I didn't try to suppress it. Vigilance was required in this place. There wasn't anything casual about what I was doing.

That lesson became clear immediately when Pranav, Steve, and I entered the hallway of the suspect ward. There, lying in front of us, sprawled lengthwise, was a patient, delirious and shaking. When we approached him, it was clear that his pants were soiled with diarrhea and his shirt stained with vomit. He was covered in his own body fluids. The moment that I saw him, my mind simply went blank except for the word *Ebola*. It was not totally dissimilar to the sensation that Phil Ireland had when he realized that he wasn't infected with malaria, although because he was infected, that word must have seemed like a roar. I thought, *You asked for this assignment, Steven, and now you have your wish.* We had been in the high-risk area for maybe five seconds.

But it's actually what happened the *following* second that marked the moment when theory turned into practice and I started to learn the art of Ebola care. Pranav surveyed the situation, walked directly to the patient, whose name was Aaron Singbeh, and tried to get his attention. Aaron wasn't responsive, however. Steve and I walked over, and Pranav said that we should get him back to his bed, change his clothes, and wash him up, and without more than a moment's consideration, the three of us picked him up and carried him back to bed. My mind was still very much in *Ebola* mode—here was a guy who was covered in billions if not trillions of copies of the virus, now only a few millimeters from my skin—but I was also aware that suddenly Aaron had magically transformed into something with which I was much more accustomed, namely, a *patient* for whom I could give something known as *care*.

But how to care for a patient with Ebola beyond just standing there in PPE and cleaning him up? As if to answer this question that I hadn't actually asked aloud, Pranav walked to the next room, which had served as the ward's medical supply closet, and started looking around for something. I asked him what he was looking for, and he said, "Valium." That simple, matter-of-fact reply almost made the ground shake under me, for the drug Valium is commonly still used in the United States and Europe for delirious patients. We didn't have much to offer, but we did have something *specific* for a *specific* problem. In short, we had medicine.

I was even more flummoxed when Pranav thought of a solution to the problem posed by the Valium itself, which was how to get it *into* Aaron. Because he was delirious, we couldn't give him the pill to swallow, since he'd most likely either let it just sit in his mouth or possibly choke on it. We couldn't give intravenous Valium because Aaron had no IV catheter. So he took the Valium pill, crushed it, poured the contents into a water bottle, and then took one of the IV bags and cut the tubing used to infuse the fluid into the veins, fashioning a crude straw out of it. Aaron would be offered a little Valium juice. I was simply amazed at Pranav's ingenuity. And because of it, the shock was starting to wear off, and I was beginning to think like a doctor again.

Not that it made much of a difference to Aaron, who was unable to sit up and sip from Pranav's ad hoc straw. As I looked at him, I thought that he would not survive the night.

An ETU is, at its barest, nothing more than a hospital: If you looked past the hasty construction, it would fit the image that most people around the world conjure up when they hear that word. There are patients who lie in beds, and there are doctors and nurses who come to round on them. There are medicines dispensed from a pharmacy, which are given for various conditions. There's a laboratory for testing, although in our case the laboratory was off site (at first, *very* far off site, then blessedly closer). There is charting and paperwork—the bane of any medical staff, and no different here. And finally there is a morgue. The structure of the facility is similar in all the essentials. As I took my first walk rounds that day, I had the dawning realization that, despite the fact that this was where Ebola was being treated, it was an environment with which I was intimately familiar, and its structure and rhythms would provide a great deal of comfort in the weeks to come.

Although an ETU is a hospital, it is unlike any other *kind* of hospital. Normally, people conceive of hospitals as places where they go for care. This is no less true in an ETU, but Ebola changes the playing field between patient and provider, so that the rules governing the relationship between the two become inverted. For instance, the first rule of an ETU is, quite simply, protect the staff. Although patients are there to be treated, they themselves constitute a threat to others because of their contagiousness, so every detail of the ETU is designed to minimize their ability to infect anyone who has come to care for them. In every Ebola outbreak since its initial discovery in 1976, one of the most important features has been the infection rate among health-care workers: Sick patients, naturally, come to clinics or hospitals, and without adequate protections from the virus, the staff become infected and are often among the hardest-hit groups. This was no less true in the West African outbreak, as hundreds of doctors, nurses, and other health-care staff became infected and died.

Thus, staff safety reigned supreme in an ETU. While patient care was obviously central to this hospital, it was not the highest priority, so that if the two were in conflict, safety would trump it. What does that actually mean? Picture the following: An Ebola patient has a seizure. A seizure is typically a grade A emergency in health care: Every available member of a medical team would come running as fast as possible to administer whatever care was needed. But if a patient with Ebola seized, you would *not* come running. Instead, you would get into PPE as slowly and methodically as you did any other time. That could mean that the patient would have an uninterrupted seizure lasting as long as ten to twenty minutes, which given the other ravages of Ebola could easily lead to death. But no staff member ever enters the high-risk area without adequate protection; there are simply no medical emergencies in an ETU.

Moreover, an ETU is designed as much to treat the surrounding community as it is to treat the patients. That is, patients are just that—people harboring an infection—but due to the nature of the disease, infected people pose considerable risk to everyone around them. They are, from the standpoint of outbreak epidemiology, storehouses of virus that can keep the epidemic spreading. Thus, the ETU is designed to get as many copies of virus out of circulation as possible. It exists as much for the people who will never see the inside of its walls as it does for those who become its temporary residents.

Then, and only then, do patient concerns come to the fore.

There was an extensive network of pipes beneath the gravel surface, all of them leading to clusters of three sets of spigots throughout the compound. These provided direct protection against Ebola and were constantly in use. The first spigot was white, which indicated well water; the second, colored green, was a bleach solution of 0.05 percent chlorine. The green tap was meant for contact with humans: The 0.05 percent solution could deactivate the virus on contact, but the solution was light enough that it wasn't especially harmful to the skin, eyes, or mouth.

Finally, there was a red spigot, containing a 0.5 percent bleach solution. The red tap was the industrial-strength deactivator of the virus. Anytime workers were hauling commode buckets filled with fluids containing jillions of Ebola particles or carrying corpses, they would rinse their gloves and some parts of their PPE like their aprons with the 0.5 percent solution. Indeed, once inside the high-risk area, *any* activity in PPE, even as simple as seeing a patient, was followed by washing with the red tap. The decontamination procedure was done by spraying the 0.5 solution onto providers as they took off their PPE. But this solution was far too corrosive to be used directly on skin; once, one of the members of the national staff had washed part of his face with the red tap, not understanding its strength, and shortly thereafter his left eye had swollen shut.

Hand washing became an obsession in the ETU. Ebola's main point of entry to the body is through mucous membranes, mainly the eyes and mouth. Because people incessantly and instinctively touch their faces throughout the day, keeping one's hands as sterile as possible represented one of the best chances to prevent an infection among the staff. If you had some body fluid containing Ebola splashed onto the skin of your arm, you wouldn't necessarily become infected—not, mind you, that I would recommend testing this—but if you *touched* that fluid with your hands and then moved your hands to your face as humans habitually do, this is the most likely way you would allow the virus to enter your body. So the green 0.05 percent tap, in particular, found itself in frequent use at its various locations. It almost didn't make sense *not* to splash your hands if you were walking past it.

I came in the next morning to learn that Aaron Singbeh had died. He wandered the halls of the suspect ward that night in a delirium. On evening rounds, he was found in the bed of another patient, Josephine, the two spooning peacefully. She, however, was already dead, though Aaron was blissfully unaware of this as he cuddled with her. He was escorted back to his room by one of the staff. It was as if he wished to accompany her to the other side in a gesture that was simultaneously touching and horrifying. Soon, he would get his wish, as he passed on in the middle of the night.

Both Aaron and Josephine, and many others besides, had actually been in the suspect ward for several days. When I arrived, the Bong County ETU had been open for about two weeks, and during that time, only one laboratory in the entire country was devoted to Ebola testing. Located in Monrovia, the lab was operating well beyond its capacity in late September, with hundreds of samples per week pouring in from all parts of the country. It took nearly a day to send the vials of blood from Bong to Monrovia, and because of the backlog it could take three to four more days to receive the test results. That meant that the turnaround time on a suspect case—that is, to actually *know* whether a person did or did not have Ebola—was roughly five days. And that was under optimal circumstances. As a result of being inundated, tubes could occasionally be misplaced by the lab, or the lab could not properly identify the sample because the chlorine spray used to sterilize the outside of the tube also happened to be effective at washing away the ink used for its identification. During those first few weeks of operation, when the Bong County ETU relied on the Monrovia lab, it was not unusual for patients to linger in the suspect ward for a week or more.

This delay proved itself to be particularly alarming once it became clear how many patients in the suspect ward did *not* have Ebola. It would take a few weeks before the pattern became discernible, but about half of the patients were uninfected. No Ebola. This would be borne out by the data from other ETUs run by different organizations. For every patient who came in with the disease, there was another who had some other problem.

There were at least two major implications of this large number of uninfected patients being brought in for suspected Ebola infection. The first was that there were many *other* medical problems that might appear at first blush to be Ebola but in fact were different medical conditions. The ETU had one and only one test: an Ebola "PCR," a test that relies on late-twentieth-century science but has found everyday widespread use since. PCR relies on amplifying specific sequences of nucleic acid, the molecular "letters" that form the design instructions of all living organisms. Ebola PCR merely amplifies nucleic acid sequences specific for the virus. If you weren't infected, the molecular "primer" (or search string) would not bind to anything, and no signal could be amplified; if you *were* infected, the primer would bind to the Ebola's nucleic acid, a signal would be amplified and detected, and the number of virus particles in the blood could even be quantified.

Beyond knowing whether someone did or didn't have Ebola replicating in their blood, nothing could be known with anything resembling certainty, and so other diagnoses were mostly based on educated
guesswork. In terms of diagnostics, the ETU practiced twenty-first-
century medicine for Ebola and nineteenth-century medicine for
everything else. At the time I arrived in Liberia, there was no functioning health-care system besides ETUs. Essentially all the hospitals and
clinics were closed. So these people in some sense represented all of
the *other* conditions that were being ignored in the midst of the Ebola
crisis. It wasn't merely killing the people it infected; it was killing
people who were dying of everything else that could be treated, since
there was nowhere to turn.

The second, more unsettling implication in terms of our job, was
that the uninfected half in the suspect ward was in perilously close
proximity to those who *did* have Ebola, possibly placing them at
greater risk of catching the virus than they were in their own communities. The lag time in the test results only added to the risk; the longer the delay, the longer the Ebola-negative patients in the suspect
ward had opportunities to become infected. That also meant that, if
such delays were to continue, ETUs across the country had the potential to *spread* the infection rather than halt it.

The screening strategy represented the double-edged sword of
Ebola epidemic management. If half the patients who came through
the suspect ward were uninfected, it meant that the net was being
cast wide in an attempt to catch every case and take as many Ebola
patients as possible out of circulation. In other words, there was a
low threshold to be considered at risk for Ebola. That was good for
the community, for the risk of having an infected patient outside the
ETU was deemed greater than the risk of having an uninfected person
sleep a night or more in a Hot Zone.

But would *you* want to sleep in there for a night without any protections if you *didn't* have Ebola?

And how many nights must uninfected patients remain in such a
place before it becomes difficult to justify? This was the unpleasant
question facing the staff of the Bong County ETU in late September
and early October. For it became fairly clear to us after a patient had

been admitted to the suspect ward for three or four days whether they had Ebola. A patient whose illness did not progress or, indeed, improve over that time might assume they were uninfected and could minimize their interactions with other patients. But what to do when one encounters Aaron, sprawled across the corridor, his fluids flowing across the floor, teeming with virus? What to do when Aaron, in his delirium, waltzes directly into one's room?

Fortunately, we did not have to dwell on such troubling matters for long, for a solution was coming, one that would take that five-day turnaround and turn it into a five-*hour* turnaround.

The solution came in the form of about four or five guys who set up some supplies in an unused part of Cuttington University. They all worked for a gentleman named Barack Obama. They were with the U.S. Navy.

During my first few days working in high risk, I gradually made the transition from thinking my patients had Ebola to realizing that I was a doctor treating patients who happened to have a viral illness. It was certainly a deadly viral illness, and one that required me to care for them while looking like a space alien, but I understood that what I was doing was more or less what I do back in the States. These were people, like the rest of us, with family and hopes and dreams and all the rest, who through some bad luck were infected with an exotic virus never before seen in this part of the world. Treating them as such, I would realize, became an important part of Ebola care: You ignore the Ebola aspect as much as possible, although not to the point where you risk your own infection.

Learning to care for these people was like going back to medical school again. The first patients I encountered were quite ill, whether in the suspect or the confirmed ward, and beyond checking their temperatures and looking at their medication records, I wasn't sure what to do—precisely the feeling that marked some of the more humiliating moments of my early training. I did have a checklist of symptoms to review with them, but it was written in a small font, and my glasses were fogged with sweat, and the goggles over the glasses were misty, so that reading became an exercise in squinting out what material I could.

Only gradually did I realize that I didn't need the checklist because I could *talk* to the patients. It sounds so silly now to write this. But it wasn't immediately obvious to me in those first few days: I could listen to them explain the recent history of how they became ill and ask questions of them to get a detailed story. It is what all doctors everywhere are trained to do. Just because they did (or might) have Ebola didn't mean that I had to change the rules about how I interacted with the patients. So as that first week wore on, I settled into a routine that I understood.

I also needed to learn to do physical exams again. Examining patients in full PPE is an exercise in realizing one's limitations and trying to glean as much information as possible from what little data can penetrate the goggles, hood, mask, and gloves. First, that ubiquitous tool of modern medicine, the stethoscope, can't be used, for there was no placing anything from the high-risk world into ear canals where a hood might tear. Any details about the physical exam that a stethoscope helps elucidate could not be easily known to us, which meant that all our clinical work could not be communicated to our colleagues, at least some of whom would be picking up our work in the months to come, and yet others still who would treat patients in the future outbreaks that were sure to arise.* So our ability to take our wisdom as clinicians—and our training was the product of *hundreds* of years of accumulated experience of the physicians that came before us— and add to it on this disease was limited in the extreme. It was like being an anthropologist at the astonishing discovery of a first-contact society, only to discover that you have no recording technology, and that you have suddenly gone deaf.

Mostly, what I would do was *look* at patients—although I could often see as well as a driver trying to negotiate a country road in the middle of a thunderstorm without windshield wipers—and *feel* them, or what is known in the business as "palpation." It was not much.

---

* Trish Henwood, whose specialty within ER involves expertise in using ultrasounds, effectively performed an end run around the stethoscope problem by bringing portable ultrasound technology to the confirmed ward. Ultrasounds are basically higher-tech versions of stethoscopes that provide even greater detail than Laennec's invention and avoid the infection-control problems associated with the stethoscope. But the ultrasounds arrived at the Bong ETU after I left.

Why was it important in the first place to perform any physical exam? Wasn't this just Ebola anyway, and who cares about doing an exam? The answer relates in part to Ebola's history. All previous outbreaks were relatively short affairs, and so what was known about the disease was still largely hastily gathered impressions, since the principal goal of the prior outbreaks was simply to stop them. But the West African outbreak was different; as much as containing and eliminating the epidemic was still of paramount importance, the sheer number of cases, and the size of the medical staff tasked with caring for patients, allowed for a more thorough study of the disease.

To a layperson's ears, that may sound heartless, with clinicians coldly appraising the precise manner of a victim's physical decay. But having the ability to recognize a possible Ebola patient *before* a test, to seek telltale signs that would prompt suspicion by a doctor or nurse in some rural clinic five years from now, when the West African outbreak is only a memory, could be the difference between a mini-outbreak and another epidemic that slays tens of thousands of people. Or, given the speed by which humans can travel around the globe, worse.

Moreover, doing a reasonably decent physical exam was critically important for those 50 percent of patients in the suspect ward who would turn out *not* to have Ebola, because it raised the question of what they *did* have. Any information, even a crude physical exam, when coupled with some clinical reasoning, could lead to a potentially lifesaving diagnosis.

At the very least, having a working idea of what was wrong with these patients gave us some peace of mind. On my second day, Pranav introduced me to a man in his mid-forties named Ballah who had come in coughing up blood. He was emaciated, probably not much more than a hundred pounds, and hadn't had a fever—which suggested he didn't have Ebola—and Pranav figured it was tuberculosis. But when you cough up blood in the middle of an Ebola outbreak, nobody's taking any chances, so when his family carried him to the local hospital, they referred him to the ETU, and he lingered in the suspect ward waiting for a test.

Pranav was sure that this was tuberculosis for more than one reason. First, if we *weren't* in the middle of an Ebola outbreak, TB was far and away the most likely diagnosis, as the disease is still widespread in this part of the world. Second, he had been having symptoms for a week or two; if it was Ebola, he would in all likelihood have died days ago. But how to clinch the diagnosis? We had only our Ebola PCR test to perform, which told us that he either had it or he didn't. And since he probably didn't have it, while we waited, any other diagnosis would have to be made by looking, touching, and making a best guess.

I thought about this for a moment. Not only is TB widespread in the region, but so is HIV, and TB and advanced HIV could easily go together. As an infectious disease doctor, I saw patients with stories like this even in the States. If he had HIV, the diagnosis of TB in this man was quite probably correct (though not necessarily the other way around). But without an HIV test, how to diagnose HIV?

"Sir?" I said to Ballah, who looked up at me with tired eyes. He could barely lift his head. "Would you mind opening your mouth?" The question was at first unintelligible to him, partly because of how the thick mask of PPE muffles the voice, partly because Liberian English and American English aren't exactly the best of friends. But after a few seconds of charade-like gestures that had the appearance of clowns at a circus, followed by a slow repetition of the question, Ballah got the idea, and opened his mouth.

The inside was coated with a white plaque instead of the normal dark pink that one would expect to see. This was a fungus called *Candida* that forms part of the normal microbiological ecology of our mouth but runs rampant when the immune system fails and can no longer limit its growth, resulting in the condition known as thrush. That was as good a diagnosis of HIV as one could get in this environment. That also meant that Pranav's diagnosis of tuberculosis was highly likely to be correct. *Chalk one up for the ID doc in his first week*, I thought as I made my way among these battle-tested emergency physicians.

I didn't just have to relearn how to practice medicine during that first week; I had to learn how to move around in PPE. The limitations imposed by the suit and the apron and the rest of the outfit were considerable. Much of what constituted my vision was limited by mist and the sweat that dripped onto my glasses and goggles. Reading a chart, even if it involved only recording and surveying a patient's temperatures, became an exercise in interpreting hieroglyphics. Because the blue tarp that formed the walls of the ward kept out light very well, the interiors of the wards were dark places, which made reading the charts that much more difficult. To make sure that I knew what I was seeing, I often had to move my head to adjust it to the light to get the correct angle on the paper. To an observer, it must have looked like I was a museum curator holding up some ancient artifact, considering it from all angles. I often felt like I was in one of those diving suits from the early twentieth century, completely sealed except for that one shield of glass in front, surrounded on all sides by water. Except in my case, the water wasn't part of the external environment, it was, until quite recently, a part of *me*.

Moreover, the peripheral vision in PPE was nonexistent. Anytime I heard a noise or wanted to grab some item sitting next to me like a medication or a chart, I had to turn to look at it directly. Negotiating narrow spaces had to be carefully thought out lest I scrape up against the wooden frame that had a nail or piece of wood sticking out that could tear my suit. That wasn't a theoretical concern: Steve Whiteley discovered one such nail sticking out of the construction in the suspect ward during the first week.

Plus, my hands were sealed in three layers of gloves, and although the layers were thin, it caused enough loss of dexterity that I had to move slowly through any tasks requiring fine motor skills. Among the most important of those, I would soon learn, was hooking up IV lines. I ran more IVs in my time in Bong County than in my entire career combined, and during the first few days it was a matter of getting the muscle memory for the motions. But I also had to keep at bay the extra folds of latex from the outer layer of gloves, as they seemed to be insistent upon trying to tear themselves up when, for example, I would seal an IV cap, only to find a small piece of that third pair of gloves stuck up inside the cap. It was like getting a run in your stockings, but with slightly higher stakes, especially since the IV lines always involved getting blood on your gloves. When that would happen, no matter how much I got used to working in the Hot Zone, bright red blood on my hands always guaranteed a fresh flash of *Ebola* through my head, producing a small jolt of adrenaline, as if my pituitary gland was sending a chemical memo to remind me where I was.

But if I had to describe the experience of PPE in one word, it would simply be *sweat*. The sweat began to flow—and I do mean *flow*, as opposed to *bead*—even before I had finished donning every item, and it didn't stop until I emerged from the decontamination chamber. I sweat so much that I could see it drip above the edge of the gloves and pool in between each layer.

It wasn't just that I was soaked in sweat, as if I had gone for a run on a hot and humid day. I pooled in sweat. The sweat from my head and face would come into the mask, which became so saturated that I would suck in a fair amount of sweat with each breath. My socks didn't just become wet; I could feel the sweat accumulate over the course of my rounds so that the liquid sloshed back and forth in my boots, usually about three-quarters to the top. When I emerged from decontamination, I would sit down, remove the boots, and just pour them out as if they were pitchers.

With all of that sweat went a lot of electrolytes, and the first few days I didn't properly appreciate the need to hydrate before a spin through the high-risk area. The staff, like the patients, tried to stay hydrated by means of drinking oral rehydration solution. It was only a small improvement over seawater. On my second day, I spent just under two hours in PPE and I hadn't had any oral rehydration solution before going in. I emerged dazed, and it took me nearly as long as the time that I spent inside until my body began to feel normal again.

A major priority for me was to make as many inroads as possible with the national staff. I used whatever gimmicks I could to get to know the Liberians on a personal level. It was not always easy. At first, I relied on some of the goofier tricks in my arsenal, like showing a tendency to pantomime my basketball jump shot as I walked between buildings. That proved a big hit in the opening days, and some of the Liberians would want to engage in a momentary one-on-one in the midst of the various tasks that needed to be done. It lightened the mood but didn't prove especially useful to meeting people. I was going to need to overcome a fair amount of my own social anxiety and start talking to people if I was going to integrate even remotely with the locals.

Many of the national staff lived in nearby Gbarnga, a city of thirty thousand, and a bus ferried the IMC workers living in and around the city. It was a risky decision in September 2014 to apply for a job at the ETU. I became friendly with one of the members of the psychosocial support staff, a woman named Garmai Cyrus. She was tall and had her hair braided close to her head, with tiny shells laced in between the various braids, which made her hard to miss in a crowd. Garmai said that many of her neighbors had stopped talking to her once she got the position, and she was avoided on the street. She said this was not exceptional treatment. Everyone from the national staff working at the ETU had to make a calculation about their financial needs from a job that paid very well versus whether they would be considered a member in good standing in their communities ever again.

I also started to talk to Sam Siakor, one of the senior people working in the water, sanitation, and hygiene, or WASH, group. Take away the scrubs that Sam changed into when he came to work each day, and you could envision him as a rural African prince, for he stood taller than me, easily six three and perhaps taller, with a bald and noble crown, dark brown skin, dark eyes to match, and a magnificent smile. Sam was about thirty years old, which meant that he must have had to endure some dicey situations while growing up during the Civil War. I quickly came to discover how much I admired and liked him. He had grown up in Bong County and attended college, no small accomplishment in this environment. Just before the outbreak started he was working as a teacher in a local high school. His was truly a Liberian success story—which, for someone his age, was a rarity given Liberia's recent history.

I eagerly soaked up what I could about his life and his culture. Sam was a devoted member of his local church, and eventually our talk turned to matters of faith. For me, faith is a tricky subject when I speak to those who possess it, since I have none myself. I do not, however, take any pleasure in debating the matter, finding the argumentative tenor in the atheism of a Hitchens or a Dawkins to be off-putting. Instead of a bunch of theological discussions, we settled on a common language that gave both of us pleasure, for we both reveled in song. Sam had surreptitiously photocopied one of the pieces from his hymnal that he carried with him to work each day. The photocopy machine, a piece of equipment that didn't find the damp of the jungle air to its liking, barely functioned. Despite this, he managed to eke out two perfect images from his book one afternoon: A great miracle happened there. I went home at night with my assignment to learn it within two days.

When I first set about to learn the song in my flat that night, I had been so wrapped up in the idea of using the music as an opportunity to make a connection that I hadn't really considered its meaning. Sam, however, was wryly trying to teach me a particular lesson about his faith and perhaps how he thought the divine presence manifested itself in the Blue World.

> *You are the Lord, that healéd me,*
> *You are the Lord, my healer,*
> *You send your word, and you heal my disease,*
> *You are the Lord, my healer.*
> *I am the Lord, that healéd thee,*
> *I am the Lord, your healer,*
> *I send my word, and I heal your disease*
> *I am the Lord, your healer.*

During those first few days, I got to know many of the patients who had been admitted prior to my arrival, but there were of course still patients coming in, and these I met from the beginning of their time at the ETU. One of the first of these new-admit patients was Pastor John from Margibi County. Margibi County lies to the east of Monrovia and is south of Bong, a drive of several hours to the ETU. Our ambulance service had been dispatched to retrieve him. One of his congregants had been very sick and died, and he had ministered to the person, gathering the family in prayer. I don't think that we knew for certain whether that person had ever been tested for Ebola, since many patients who became ill and died at that time couldn't or didn't want to get to an ETU. Regardless, now, several days later, it was his turn. He was lying in bed in his suspect-ward room, awaiting the results of his blood test, sweating from fever nearly as much as I was from PPE.

"Pastor John," I said to him as I walked in, "I'm Doctor Steven. I'm going to be one of the doctors taking care of you while you're here, okay?" That was okay with Pastor John, who, after politely answering a battery of questions about when his illness started and what his specific symptoms were, took over the encounter and told me that it was time to pray. "You believe in Jesus, yes?" he asked me.

It seemed not the right time for me to get into an involved discussion about being both Jewish and mostly atheist, so I glossed over the question and suggested that we indeed pray. I was already on the pads of my feet in a catcher's stance, and I knelt.

"Good Lord, we ask that you protect us," he started. "We ask that you guide Doctor Steven and give him the knowledge and wisdom to help us fight this curse of Ebola. Protect him while he does your work here. We ask that you guide the nurses and the other workers that are here today." And on he went, with a great deal of energy, gaining strength as he warmed to his subject. I was moved, not only because of the gesture, but by the eloquence with which he prayed. It was clear that he excelled at his calling. I also couldn't believe that this man, who was almost certainly infected with Ebola, was praying for *me* and *my* soul.

I contemplated all of this for some time, as the prayer continued beyond five minutes while I sat there dripping sweat all over his bed. Realizing I had more than a dozen other patients to see and that every second in PPE was a race against the clock, I tried as gently as possible to encourage him to reach a conclusion (*Um, Pastor John? Just so that you're aware, I should be moving along . . .*), taking a moment of high drama and watching it quickly morph into screwball comedy.

Late in the afternoon the day after Pastor John had prayed at length for me, the Ebola test returned as positive. I accompanied him from the suspect ward to the confirmed ward, finding him a room toward the back. He walked slowly and gingerly. I showed him his bed, and he said he wanted to pray for me again. Very pleased with this, I knelt. This prayer lasted no more than a minute, and he was noticeably weaker, although beyond his weakness and fever, there was nothing about his condition that would have made you realize he was infected with Ebola. I finished up my rounds and wished him a good night. When I returned the next day, his weakness had accelerated. He barely noticed me when I came to see him, and I had to ask *him* to pray for me. The prayer lasted only a few moments. The following day, there was no prayer.

He was among the first patients I watched this virus claim for its own. That was only the beginning, however.

4

INFERNO

Traditionally, the spirit world is made manifest in Liberia by
various means including the use of carved wooden masks,
a notable feature of cultural life in many Liberian rural
communities. The use for religious purposes of masks, behind
which a person becomes unrecognizable and in which a spirit
is deemed to take visible form, says much about traditional
Liberian attitudes concerning both the spirit world and the
hidden nature of reality.

—Stephen Ellis, *The Mask of Anarchy*

Back in the United States, the Ebola scare moved to an entirely new
level. The man I had seen on the news as I was leaving the States was
identified as Thomas Eric Duncan. He was a Liberian national who
had returned to Dallas from Liberia on September 20, at that time
feeling healthy. On September 24, however, he became ill with symptoms consistent with Ebola and decided to go to the ED of Dallas
Presbyterian Hospital the following day.

There, a series of questions should have identified him as a person
at risk for Ebola so that appropriate isolation precautions should take
place. There is a sizable African expat population in Dallas, so the
presence of a man with a Liberian accent and a fever should have been
a major trigger to more than just the triage nurse, but for whatever
reasons, the alarm was not raised. This means that Duncan had sat in
the waiting room for about ninety minutes before being ushered into
the treatment area. According to an article appearing in the October 25 edition of the *Dallas Morning News*, Duncan presented to the
ED at 10:37 p.m. on September 25, was seen by the triage nurse at

11:36 p.m., and brought into a treatment room at 12:05 a.m. That's actually pretty fast for that time of night.

For those who have never been to an ED in an urban area on a Friday night, there are usually a *lot* of people sitting around or milling about waiting to be seen, so surely Duncan must have exposed a large number of people by doing nothing other than sitting there. He *then* went for evaluation and was seen by the ER doctor, the nurse, and other staff. He was referred for a CT, which meant that he exposed the people who transferred him onto a stretcher and the radiology techs working the shift that night. He got discharged almost exactly five hours after he had arrived with a working diagnosis of sinusitis and was given a prescription for antibiotics.

I don't like second-guessing physicians or nurses through the retrospectoscope unless I know all the details of a case and there is a clear and unambiguous error that can be identified. I've seen too many cases where something appears obviously wrong in the rearview mirror until you speak with the provider at the time, and when you hear their logic, you discover how reasonable their actions really were. We know *now* that Duncan had Ebola, but how many cases of vague abdominal pain does an ER doc typically see over the course of the week? Or sinusitis? The answer is a whole lot more than cases of Ebola.

That said, the only issue to which I confess some puzzlement is how Duncan evaded proper identification as someone at risk that first visit. Liberians have an obvious accent, and Presby has a patient base that includes a fair number of West Africans. Surely not only the doctors but a number of the staff must have been on the alert for West Africans presenting with fever—the whole country was increasingly anxious about this—and yet his presentation didn't trigger any follow-up questions by anyone caring for him. I worked in a hospital in the Chinatown neighborhood in Boston during my residency in April 2003 when SARS, a virus even more scary than Ebola, was being reported not just in the Far East but among Chinese nationals in Toronto. You can be assured that everyone working in the ED at New England Medical Center at that time was on the lookout for any person recently returned from China with acute respiratory symptoms, which then was a not insignificant number of people.

At any rate, Duncan returned to his home, a small apartment with one bathroom that he shared with his partner and their five children. There he continued to deteriorate for another two days until he called 911 and the EMTs arrived, transporting him back to Presby and exposing themselves in the process. Finally, in the ED he was identified as being at risk for Ebola and was properly isolated.

One would have hoped that after his appropriate identification and isolation as a possible Ebola patient, Duncan posed a much smaller threat to everyone and our list of exposures would stop there. Unfortunately, almost every aspect of his care over the next week was botched. The initial protective gear worn by the health-care workers was inadequate, leaving critical parts of their bodies exposed. Moreover, the decontamination process, which in many ways is even more important than the protective gear itself, was neither well understood nor standardized.

As his symptoms worsened and he became progressively more infectious, he was moved deeper inside the hospital to a different unit. The transfer itself increased the chance of depositing virus in fluids on floors, walls, and anything else that came within contact of him. Instead of assigning a small number of health-care personnel to his care and thus minimizing the number of further exposures, the administration tried to distribute the risk among a bigger pool, and he was seen by a rotating cast of doctors and nurses as he became more ill. It was about as close to maximizing the chances that the contagion would spread to as many people as one could envision. The entire Dallas metropolitan area would be on edge for weeks.

Nobody knew it at the time, but it would later be revealed that Duncan had escorted his neighbor's daughter into a taxi for transfer to an ETU in Monrovia and accompanied her during the taxi ride, obviously at close quarters for a prolonged trip, on September 15. She would die in the ETU.

Duncan died on October 8, at the beginning of my second week of work in Bong County.

In Monrovia, Phil Ireland began the slow process of convalescing as he tried to resume his life. Though he was not yet ready to return to work, his strength began to increase. It was not, however, the end of his troubles. "After I got sick and I went back home, I saw some of the guys where I used to live," he said. "They said to me, 'We know you work for the government, we know what you guys planned, you weren't sick.' Some of my *relatives* said this." Even by that point in Liberia, some people were still inclined to view Ebola as an outright hoax.

To counter this, the Liberian government began a campaign, elegant in its simplicity. "Ebola Is Real" was the slogan. A huge mural painted onto a wall on Tubman Boulevard proclaimed this. It was situated only a few blocks from President Sirleaf's residence. Adjacent to the slogan were rudimentary life-size paintings of people exhibiting the most common manifestations of the disease: a child squatting with diarrhea exiting his body, a person vomiting, a face showing the sclera—the whites of one's eyes—a pinkish red. And so on.

Yet the fact that the Ministry of Health needed to launch an "Ebola Is Real" campaign served only to underscore many people's skepticism that a biological disaster was actually in motion. The level of trust in official government pronouncements was dismal, created in part by a system in which the powerful and wealthy lived in gated compounds and drove around in SUVs expensive even by American standards, while the vast majority of Liberians toiled for appallingly low wages, which forced them to live in domiciles that only rarely possessed plumbing or electricity. The lack of plumbing, in particular, was critically important, for the inability to wash one's hands meant that Ebola could spread more easily, as the uninfected would touch the infected yet have no easy manner by which they could literally wash the virus away.

The lives of so many Monrovians were, from a structural standpoint, almost indistinguishable from that of a Londoner in 1750, except for the cell phones. And they didn't have to travel to Europe or North America to see the developed world and understand that they were not a part of it, for the developed world drove by them on Tubman Boulevard as they made their way on foot or on the back of a motorcycle from home to work or the market. At a population level, the kind of middle-class life that someone like Phil was living was almost nonexistent, providing no societal ballast in a crisis like this.

That chasm between wealthy few and impoverished many fed true cynicism, so even perfectly sensible advice given out by the Ministry of Health could produce the entirely unintended opposite effect. And there were other, older frames of reference to make sense of the events taking place in Monrovia. Tribal animistic beliefs were still alive and well in West Africa. They did not vie with Christianity and Islam for primacy as a coherent view of the world, but rather complemented those religions. It wasn't at all a contradiction for a Liberian to go to church and praise Jesus Christ on Wednesday and on the following day proclaim that evil ancestral spirits had infested their house because a jealous person had cast a spell on them. This way of understanding natural phenomena was seen by many as perfectly legitimate. When ETUs started to spring up around the city with their rigid boundaries, strange rules of engagement, and faceless PPE, tens of thousands of frightened Monrovians reacted in bewilderment, without any frame of reference to make sense of these events.

Rumors started to circulate that ETUs were a government plot to *spread* Ebola in order to secure further international aid as the flood of dollars unleashed by the end of the Civil War was beginning to abate. The proof could be found in the workers who walked all around the ETUs, and throughout the city, spewing fine liquid droplets onto patients and the surfaces they contacted with a two-foot-long nozzled stick, the tank of liquid strapped to the back of the sprayer clad in PPE. *This strange mist* contained *Ebola*, they said. The government and the aid agencies weren't putting up the ETUs to treat it, they were doing so to bring people in and incubate them with the virus.

Never mind that this was totally preposterous even after a few moments of concentrated thought, because nobody in their right minds would waltz into an ETU without symptoms in order to be sprayed by someone who would give them the virus. If that really was the case, how was it that that people were becoming deathly ill *before* they were ever hit by the spray? But reason wasn't winning the day on the streets of Monrovia. Terror was.

Compared to that, life in Bong County by contrast seemed to be perfectly ordered. Not only was I meeting patients, I was becoming acquainted with the national and international staff. Simultaneous with my arrival, another emergency medicine doctor from California named Colin Bucks had joined the group. With three fresh M.D.s now holding down the fort, Pranav took a much-deserved break, heading back to the States. Colin and I took to one another immediately, and I couldn't help but fancying our fast friendship as a kind of modern version of Hawkeye Pierce and B. J. Hunnicutt. My life's goal in some ways was to be Hawkeye, so having a wisecracking doctor from California in my midst provided the perfect Hunnicutt equivalent.

But there were many others as well, among them Godfrey Oryem, a Ugandan in charge of the WASH team who had been working with IMC for years; Rosa Nin-Gonzales, a Spanish nurse doing her first stint in Liberia; A. Weheley Duo, one of the Liberian physician assistants who would often round with me; and many others. I reveled in the companionship. The stimulation from finding myself in such company was balanced by the steady flow of death that took place on the other side of the plastic orange fence that separated the high-risk area from everything else.

Sean Casey, who presided over all the activity, was fascinating to me. About ten years younger than me, he had grown up in the suburbs of Philadelphia, but after high school had made one in a series of unorthodox but intriguing decisions by attending the American University of Paris. Since then, his life had been equal parts business administration and international aid work. He was as comfortable, and authoritative, talking about stock portfolios as he was about the latest educational reform measures in Zimbabwe. With the epidemic banging and shimmying its way through West Africa, each day brought a new crisis, but Sean approached the running of the ETU with a coolness that was enviable, as I only rarely exhibit such poise, and even then usually with the help of medications. Nevertheless, he pulled off this Spock-like calm while being entirely approachable, as quick to laugh about the little absurdities of our work situation as anyone else in the room, which was of immense help when a laugh was needed. You *wanted* this guy to be your leader. I have known many accomplished managers, but I had never met anyone who had quite the combination of skills that Sean seemed to possess, and who could utilize such skills so effortlessly. I didn't know if we would ever work together again (assuming that we both got through the next month alive) but I did know that if it ever came to it, I'd walk on hot coals if he asked me to. He was a singular leader.

At the end of my first week, early one morning not long after the morning staff meeting, a small commotion was taking place at the main entrance. Sitting in the administrative hut, we poked our heads outside to see what was going on. A beat-up old Nissan hatchback sat next to the guard post, and nearly a half-dozen people stood around an older couple, though all kept their distance. Sean was already on his way over; I looked around for a pair of gloves and goggles, but nothing more, and joined them afterward.

The Nissan was actually a taxi, which is to say it was a car owned by a man who made a living out of driving people around. Cars, and the petrol used to power them, are incredibly expensive assets for the average Liberian. I surmised that the man sitting in the driver's seat was of pretty high stature in the community simply because he owned this vehicle. But as I looked at him, with his hands gripped tightly onto the wheel at ten and two, I saw the slightly wide-eyed look with which I was becoming increasingly acquainted in the high-risk ward. He was scared, very scared.

I then darted my eyes over to the couple, a man and woman probably in their sixties, who were already talking to Sean. They held a bundle that I couldn't initially make out, but they were gesturing to the backseat of the car. Sean looked over to me and told me there was still a passenger in that seat, but the car windows had a dark tint and I couldn't see anything. Then Sean came over to explain.

"They have a baby," he started, and I quickly processed the mental image of the bundle I had observed, realizing almost with a smack to my forehead that *of course* that's what they were holding. "The mother is their daughter, and she bled during the delivery. They said her boyfriend had recently been treated for Ebola and was discharged from an ETU in Monrovia." We quickly decided that I would talk to the mother and we would make a decision from there about what to do.

This was not how the triage process was drawn up in the playbook. Until that moment, when I encountered patients suspected of being infected, I saw them at a safe distance in a special "triage hut" in the high-risk area where patients and the staff were separated by a metal mesh divider. But now I was only feet from a potentially infected woman in the backseat of a car, who had delivered a baby who was quite alive, being held by two individuals who were clearly exposing themselves if she was infected, and had now possibly exposed an unassuming third party in the taxi driver.

I put on two pairs of gloves, a light disposable molded face mask to keep out fluid particles, and the green, polyvinyl chloride splash-safety goggles used in high school chemistry classes. This was the triage hut safety kit, and in that setting, where we stood usually between one and two meters from patients, that was a perfectly safe combination. But I didn't put on the ski-mask goggles and N95 face mask, each with their tight seals, that we used for the Hot Zone work. Nor did I get into the suit. The splash goggles and gloves served as protection, but at close quarters, it was definitely not ideal protection.

I walked over to the car, and when I got to within three feet, I asked the driver to lower the back window so that I could look in and ask her questions. The electric window slowly slid down about three inches, and then went no farther. The driver gave me a look as if to say, *That's what you get, buddy,* like he knew something of the international code of taxi driving despite working in rural Liberia. I got up on my tiptoes and peered in but couldn't see a thing.

What happened next is one of those *Rashomon*-like moments where different people who were present will describe the events differently. I no longer trust my own memory of what took place, but the next action I took was almost certainly the most lethally stupid mistake of my time in the ETU—actually, you can drop the "almost" from that—and indeed in my career in medicine.

To get a better sense of what was happening, I opened the car door.

Nothing in the dark interior was moving. As my eyes adjusted to the contours of the form a little more than an arm's length away from me, I could see a woman spread across the seat and rolled into position with her head facing the back. There was no way for me to make eye contact with her, assess her breathing, ask her questions, nothing.

I thought I saw movement but could not be sure. I inched closer to try to glean any information I could.

We'll never know just how many inches separated my suboptimally protected face from this woman, who I realized later was, as a statistical matter, almost certainly infected with Ebola no matter what her clinical state. But I do know that I should never have been that close. My recollection is that I got to within about two feet of her. Some say they saw my head go completely inside the car. Whether that's true or not, there is, thank goodness, no photographic evidence to confirm. But even if I did not put my head inside the car, I definitely put my head inside the mouth of a lion with very sharp teeth, and this wasn't a circus act. As I realized what had just transpired over the past thirty seconds, I backed away, and felt the ticking of a twenty-one-day clock start inside my head, waiting for the onset of fever and muscle pains. Audrey Rangel, one of the core expat nurses from the States, looked at me as if I had just emerged from one of those science-fiction movies, playing the character who has been jabbed with a substance that will melt them away in a matter of minutes. Sean, whatever thoughts were flying through his head, displayed no reaction.

Fortunately, I didn't have more than a moment or two to ponder any of this. We told the driver to take the path used by the ambulance service and head to the formal triage area, where I could properly suit up to examine the patient, much to the relief of everyone who had just witnessed my ill-considered, unprotected spur-of-the-moment evaluation. In the meantime, we still had to deliberate on what to do with the baby—a girl. If the mother was infected, which was something we suspected but could not yet prove, then this baby was coated in virus, and at very high risk to become infected herself. But should we take her into the suspect ward? How would we test her blood, which would be a challenge for even one of the best nurses to draw from such a small child? Who would be able to care for her in high risk? The tenants weren't exactly predisposed to care for newborn infants requiring twenty-four-hour attention. We would probably be sentencing the child to death if we brought her in.

But what to do if we sent the baby home? Here the dilemmas multiplied and were even more worrisome. I strongly doubted that she could survive Ebola. If the grandparents were to care for her, they put themselves at risk of infection. Would the couple try to find a wet nurse? I didn't know enough about the cultural practices of rural Liberians to know whether they even utilized wet nurses, but if they did, then that meant other people besides direct family, not unlike the taxi driver, might die in the wake of this micro-outbreak. The longer that baby lived, the more people she potentially threatened, and I rapidly oscillated between my misgivings about the lives that might end the longer she hung on and the horror that I was secretly hoping for this beautiful wonder of creation to die, and die soon, so that the web of death might stop there. Barring a miracle, which was a scarce commodity in Liberia at that moment, there was simply no good way out of this, no happy conclusion to the usual story of hope and promise that accompanies the birth of a healthy child.

Sean called a contact, an MSF Ebola expert named Anja Wolz, to see what protocols they had in place for such a situation. After several minutes of talking with her, he returned to the group. "She's never heard of anything like this before," he said. She didn't think it wise to bring the baby into the suspect ward, and what ensued was a long discussion with Sean and Audrey about how to give formula and what supplies we should equip the grandparents with in order to nurse the baby while allowing them to remain relatively protected. Since formula and the health needs of a newborn infant were far beyond my clinical expertise, I merely noted my concerns about having a wet nurse involved, then headed to the gowning area to suit up and go see the mother.

Ensconced in the theoretical safety of the space suit, I opened the car door again and this time put my hands directly on the woman and shook her. She didn't move. She was hot to the touch. I had placed a thermometer under her arm and it got to 104. An "axillary" temperature like this meant that her core temperature was hotter still. I felt for a pulse on her neck, and felt again and again, and nothing. She had died, though whether it was from a postpartum hemorrhage or from Ebola, I couldn't say. But that fever—though *fever* is really too meek a word in this instance—didn't bode well.

The story of the boyfriend seemed highly suggestive, but it also didn't make complete sense if we were to believe that he had infected her. We didn't know the details about when he entered or left the ETU, but assuming that he had been seen in one of the Monrovia ETUs, he probably had been there for at least two weeks and wouldn't have been discharged unless the viral load in his blood was undetectable. So he shouldn't have been able to infect her *after* his discharge. However, if he infected her *before* he was admitted, then why had she taken so long to incubate the virus? Until the West African outbreak, the maximum incubation time ever witnessed was twenty-one days. We know this because a few people in previous outbreaks had brought the virus to their previously uninfected villages, serving as the "index cases," and their travel histories were traced to attending funerals where Ebola was in circulation exactly three weeks before their illness began.

At the time, I hadn't carefully considered this. It wasn't until many months later, when some new information had filtered in, that I could conceive of a different scenario by which she was infected. At any rate, as I informed the burial team that they would be required to suit up to retrieve the woman and prepare her for interment, I had to explain to the driver what was happening and offer him what preventive measures we could. At the very least we were going to recommend that the inside of the car be completely sprayed with the high-grade chlorine solution. As for him, we urged him to step out of the car and take a bucket with the low-grade chlorine solution meant for human skin and wash himself off. This, of course, meant he was walking into the Hot Zone totally unprotected, and even if he knew at some level his car was quite likely contaminated, his driver's seat must have seemed like a life preserver in the midst of a heaving ocean in which he suddenly found himself. He did it though, and jumped back into the car, turned it around, still wide-eyed, and headed back down the jungle road.

That covered about an hour's worth of work that day.

As the first week progressed into the second, we fell into routine.

Wakeup for me was just after six. I can't function in the world without a morning shower, even when working in an Ebola Treatment Unit where nobody cares how my hair looks, so I was an early riser.

My flat at Cuttington had a bathroom that was not much different from any standard bathroom in the West, although it was more weathered, with fixtures that hadn't been replaced in more than thirty years and tiles missing here and there. The plunger to the toilet didn't work, so flushing it consisted of pouring a pitcher of water into the bowl, the water retrieved from a large blue fifty-five-gallon polyethylene drum that took up about half the maneuvering space in the small area. The shower head came directly from the faucet in the tub, with a long metallic snake to reach upward. There was no place to attach the shower head, so bathing consisted of holding it above my head to let the cold water run down, then placing the apparatus on my shoulder while I shampooed, and finishing with a rinse. It was a cumbersome production but worked, all things considered. One morning I entered only to find a spider—a *huge* spider, whose body was a little larger than a quarter but whose legs stretched out beyond the size of my hand—on the wall by the bathtub. He moved quickly at the sight of me and was halfway across the wall before I could even catch my breath. *Give me Ebola* any *day over that spider,* I thought. That day I went to work grubby, and I tiptoed around my bathroom for days, performing an elaborate series of checks before I felt comfortable enough to tempt fate by bathing or utilizing the toilet.

Ebola seeped into every corner of our lives, even in the humdrum routine of daily grooming. During my training at Camp Ebola with the CDC, I had a long conversation one afternoon with Navy commander James Lawler about the philosophy of shaving. You read that correctly. His thoughts were carefully considered and the result of years of work with Biosafety Level 4 agents. He pointed out that male facial hair presents a dilemma with respect to Ebola. The virus enters the body most efficiently through the mucous membranes. Touch an infected person and wash your hands, you stand a good chance of never getting sick. But touch that person and then rub your eyes or touch your lips, and the virus has its opening. (As I mentioned earlier, this was the reason the lack of running water was so important to Ebola's spread in West Africa. Give people plumbing, and it's far less likely that thousands would be suffering from the disease.)

Therefore, to stop the virus from finding its entry into the body during work in the Hot Zone, the two most important pieces of protective gear for someone working with Ebola patients were the goggles and the N95 face mask. If the seal on your wrists wasn't perfectly airtight, it didn't guarantee Ebola an entry since you washed your hands in some form of bleach solution more than two dozen times before you emerged from the Hot Zone. But if your goggles missed the seal against the rest of the mask by even one millimeter, it could be a lethal error. So too the mask. You needed to breathe, but you wanted as little as possible beyond air to enter that mask.

Back to the shaving issue. The problem for men and masks is that, as their beards grow, they push out against the mask and ruin the seal. Given just how much sweat your body could produce during rounds, it was not too hard to think that the virus could enter from the outside, hitch a ride on a bead of sweat, and get sucked up into the mouth during the labored breathing that was certain to ensue.

It would seem the obvious solution was to shave, but shaving introduces its own problems in the form of microscopic cuts. Even when men have a "perfect" shave and there are no appreciable nicks in the skin, they are nonetheless there, and from the standpoint of an Ebola particle, such a tiny cut must look like the Grand Canyon. Colin, Steve, and Pranav remained clean shaven during their time in Bong County; the African staff, whether the Liberian national staff or expats like Elvis Ogweno (who is Kenyan) or Godfrey Oryem (Ugandan), generally didn't grow big, bushy beards for this to be a problem. I opted for a different approach and settled on keeping my Vandyke trimmed so that the mask seal remained as tight as possible and shaved the rest every three or four days.

I would go through this morning routine and then putter for a few minutes, checking my e-mail if I had a Wi-Fi signal. The SUV would pick us up just before seven; during the ten-minute ride to the ETU, we filled the time either with small talk about spiders or Wi-Fi or some such, or with big talk about what was happening in the unit and how this or that patient had fared overnight. We arrived and wandered about for a few minutes, looking at the board to see whether any developments had taken place.

The morning staff meeting took place in the medical tent just before eight. Upwards of twenty people working in all aspects of the ETU operations were crammed in for the proceedings: the medical staff, the operations team, the financial people, communications, information technology, and so on. We sat around the room on cheap white plastic lawn chairs with matching round white plastic tables meant for a summer patio but were cumbersome in the small space, leading to people sitting at odd angles. I would fill a mug with boiling water, spoon two heaps of instant Nescafé and grab a sugar cube. The sugar was frequently covered by small brown ants who found our little coffee bar an unexpected but delightful source of sustenance, so I'd have to brush them aside and plop two cubes into my coffee. I'd wash it down with dry biscuits, and that became my morning eye-opener. It seemed the height of decadence, and I looked forward to it every day.

The meeting covered an impressive range of items and made me realize how little I understood about the behind-the-scenes details that made hospitals run. There was an imposing amount of operational aspects to consider, even though this was about as rudimentary a hospital as one could imagine. The medical summary during the morning meeting sometimes seemed the most trivial: We would announce the total number of patients in each ward, how many had been admitted over the past twenty-four hours, how many tests were positive and negative, whether there had been any deaths, and who was awaiting discharge if their blood test was negative. Invariably I forgot to log this information when it was my turn to present, and I never failed to be surprised when I was supposed to be announcing the tallies. Someone would need to feed the data to me, to the slight irritation of my medical colleagues. To summarize the clinical situation took all of about thirty seconds, even though the meeting usually lasted a half hour.

During the meetings we would deliberate over the other questions that were central to the ETU getting through a day: Did we have enough petrol to run the generators to keep the place lit at night? Was there enough housing at Cuttington University for the various expats who were now coming and going with greater frequency? How should we coordinate with the driving staff, who had to operate on a fairly tight schedule, when we needed to courier the blood to the Navy lab for Ebola testing, which could be anywhere from ten in the morning until noon? How should we handle the all-important goggles, whose tight seal against our skin protected us from the virus but whose structure became less pliant by the repeated washings in high-concentration chlorine bleach? We reviewed supply problems, prepared for any visitors, and considered all the other aspects of the running of the facility. While this meeting was taking place, the national staff had their morning devotional, and a loud, beautiful song would waft through the compound. Those tasked with presenting during the meetings had to review their business items while talking over the singing.

Following the meeting, we headed to the changing rooms to prepare for rounds. Inside the locker room sat two large, industrial garbage cans filled with the laundered, folded scrubs that we wore underneath our PPE. I was taller and larger than almost all of the Liberians and most of the expats, so there was a premium on extra-large scrubs. Each morning I had to dig through the garbage cans to find a shirt and pants that fit, ultimately turning the nice stack of folded apparel into a heaping mess. Eventually I got so frustrated by this cockamamie process that I snuck the properly sized scrubs into a tucked-away corner in the medical staff office, hoarding them for later use.

Once the scrubs were on I had to search for the appropriately sized boots, which after soaking in chlorine were left to dry on sticks impaled in the ground in well-organized rows adjacent to the structure. They were arrayed in a completely random manner, so you had to walk through the lattice of boots to find a matching pair. Again, since I was tall, only one available size would suffice—forty-four. Finding these rare items became a scavenger hunt that in retrospect seems comical but at the time was sheer crazy-making. *Aha!* I would think as I walked down the rows of drying boots, spotting that second boot bearing the magic number 44, only to discover on closer inspection that it was a forty-four *left*, a version of which I already held in my hand, and still had to continue the hunt.

Gowning and gloving could take upwards of an hour. We tried to phase the staff into the Hot Zone in some kind of order. The WASH staff started the process as they moved through to spray down surfaces that may have become covered with virus, as well as collect the trash, sending it to the incinerator at the far boundary of the ETU.

Next, the nursing assistants, so they could distribute food and drink to the patients. This was followed by the nursing staff, who would collect vitals, start IV fluids, and distribute medications. Eventually the M.D. and physician assistant came in. The final group to enter was the psychosocial support team. Since our gowning and gloving station was so cramped, the process of moving those headed in to round on the patients, perhaps ten or more in all, moved at a snail's pace. The food was prepared in the kitchens of Cuttington, and sometimes it would arrive late, which would disrupt the order and lead to prolonged discussions about how best to phase each group in.

Once in, rounds lasted a little more than two hours. The nurses, who started earlier, were frequently inside for up to three hours. We had heard rumors that other ETUs were running in one-hour shifts for staff safety, given the heat and possibility that someone might faint. Colin, who had taken over as medical director while Pranav was taking R & R, had once proposed that we limit shifts to this length. That experiment lasted exactly half of one day, since it was impossible to make it through even the suspect ward in that amount of time and moreover didn't make much sense since everyone could easily tolerate the first sixty minutes in PPE. But you started to notice your body after the first hour, and you could feel the strain around ninety minutes, and things got progressively more taxing from there.

The distribution of medications was a key feature of morning rounds. We were giving patients an enormous number of drugs: We gave antibiotics for, well . . . *something* is the best thing that can be said, and we gave antimalarials since large numbers of patients were simultaneously infected with the parasite, and Ebola might in theory increase their susceptibility to malaria's more deadly effects. We also gave antinausea medications, antianxiety medications, and acetaminophen to try to halt the roaring fever of Ebola and also take the edge off the muscle pains that were common.

But it was one pill that encapsulated, as it were, the problems with providing this miniature formulary: vitamin C. Somehow vitamin C ended up on the WHO's list of standard treatments for Ebola, so the aid organizations were essentially obligated to put this on the list of required drugs for patients. It made the alternative medicine types back in the States crow with joy, for they believed it underscored that natural remedies, and not all those sludgy, toxic medical-industrial-complex products designed to enrich the salaries of pharmaceutical company executives, could solve the Ebola crisis.

I had virtually no doubt that vitamin C made no appreciable difference to the patients' overall prognosis, and while I don't object to giving harmless pills in most cases, vitamin C in this case *wasn't* a completely harmless pill, for it was *huge*—a horse pill if ever there was one. Providing them that vitamin C pill put patients at risk of throwing up the other pills, a few of which, like antibiotics, might actually make a difference.

During the rounds, the job of "doctor" would often morph depending on the circumstances. It became clear to Colin and me after about a week that an ETU was for the most part a nursing production. The care of patients was driven largely by protocols drawn up by MSF and WHO, and consequently there wasn't much "big" decision making for the patients—that is, do we give *this* drug to this patient or *that* drug to that one. Those kinds of decisions, however, are often where physicians provide their value-add to patient care, and in the daily routine of the ETU, it was the nurses who brought much more immediate value with their technical skills: the ability to obtain blood samples and throw IV lines, among other procedures. It wasn't that I couldn't do either of those things, but I hadn't done them regularly since my residency, which I had completed more than a decade earlier. To relearn the art of IV line throwing would likely involve missing a vein here or there and could conceivably lead to a needle stick exposure, but working with Ebola patients left zero room for error, and so I left that work to the nurses who had the hands for it. I did draw blood on a few occasions, a skill I felt more comfortable with.

Ideally, the M.D.s could have become data-collection and data-processing machines, which was desperately needed given the potential spread of the epidemic over the next several months. Previously, Ebola had always been managed in emergency situations, usually by MSF, whose priority has never been clinical data collection but instead has been, appropriately, crisis management. Now, though, with the epidemic already much larger than all of the previous outbreaks combined and with no sign of stopping, one small upside was that the virus could be studied. I know that seems coldhearted, but to study patients with Ebola carefully *now* meant that we might know more about how to approach *future* patients in outbreaks that have not yet happened. It is how medicine progresses. If the international health community executed its response to the West African outbreak as it would in a small village in the Congo, a great opportunity would be lost to help anyone unlucky enough to be infected by Ebola five or ten years from now. The best we could do for those people was to be scientists and be meticulous about what information we could glean. That mainly consisted of recording temperatures and checking boxes that aligned with specific symptoms that were already printed out on the paper, like filling out a questionnaire that neatly systematizes and documents horror.

The act of recording such information may sound simple, but in the physical environs of the Bong ETU, the systematic gathering of data was a good deal messier. Every patient had a chart, which was basically a series of photocopied pages stapled together. (That doesn't sound like much, but under normal circumstances you can do a lot with a couple of pages of paper per patient, provided the recorded information is carefully organized.) Each chart page itemized various parameters that could be measured on a daily basis: what meds had been administered, their temperatures, their symptoms, and so on. In theory, we could record and tabulate that information and would be sitting on a treasure trove of material that might provide clues to help unlock the mystery of why Ebola killed with such ruthlessness, and might even suggest which treatments were helping (like, perhaps, antibiotics) and which were not (like, perhaps, vitamin C).

Unfortunately, the heat and humidity of Bong County proved a worthy adversary to this project. The damp would cause the paper to soften and curl, making the process of recording information cumbersome. Then our sweat would drip onto the already moist paper, sometimes making the ink from previous entries run or causing the pen to rip the paper like a knife through butter when recording a measurement.

The page devoted to recording symptoms was so carefully thought out that if we had a well-gathered set of this data from the patients we had seen in the first three weeks, we could easily have submitted a paper to *The New England Journal of Medicine* that would have been taken very seriously. It listed more than twenty signs and symptoms, each known to be associated with the disease, and placed all of these items in a grid so that they could be marked as to whether they were present or absent each day they were there. You could then see when the muscle aches tended to abate and when the severe nausea began, or learn when the more unusual symptoms, like hiccups or confusion, were associated with better or worse prognoses.

To look at this page while sitting in an office in the States, you would think it was a model of scientific and clinical precision, and if the data was logged with accuracy, it would make a lasting contribution to the field of Ebola literature. But out in the field, the eleven-point type was nearly impossible to read in the dark interiors of the patient rooms, especially with misty goggles, and the grid separating one day from the next was sufficiently small that one could easily mark a symptom as happening the day before or the day after it actually occurred. It seemed like the classic problem of myopic bureaucrats who had no understanding of the situation on the ground. But it wasn't, for unless someone had done Ebola work in a space suit in a dark tent before, there was no conceivable way in the crazed run-up to the preparations for running an ETU that such difficulties in data collection could have been anticipated. And the charting was just one in a thousand details the staff threw together as fast as it could to get the ETU up and running.

Even if the data could have been recorded in a more optimal manner, there was the additional problem of getting the information *out* of the high-risk area. It seems laughably simple: *Just record the data, and then enter it into a computer!* But you can't take a computer inside the high-risk area because it can't come out—and even if IMC had decided to purchase a laptop in Monrovia for the purpose, the high-risk areas, while having electricity for lighting, weren't constructed with outlets, so it couldn't be recharged.

Nor could the paper charts be physically exported for the same reason that almost no other inanimate physical object could ever emerge. Informationally, the Hot Zone was quite close to being a black hole; even if the charting data wouldn't be known to posterity as being the highest quality, it was still important and worth sharing with the broader medical community. But the only way we could extract the data was to have someone suit up, retrieve the charts, move to the boundary of the Hot Zone, and sit and *read* the information to someone on the outside who would then manually record the data *again* before heading back to the tent where it could finally be digitized by reentering the data on a laptop. Eventually, Colin and I did just this, which led to a string of odd moments where I would find myself sitting on a lawn chair in the high-risk area with my legs crossed, comfortably chirping away patient temperatures as if I was sitting on a porch in the Midwest, idly conversing with a friend on a summer afternoon.*

The goal of exporting the temperature data was to see whether there was any correlation between the Ebola viral load and how long the fever persisted. It was relatively easy to move those numbers from the inside to the outside, for it didn't take much time to plow through one patient's chart to read those numbers. But the even more valuable information, the clinical symptoms, would require hours and hours of transcription, and there were far too many other tasks that commanded our attention for this kind of work to proceed in any systematic manner. I belatedly understood why the clinical data from previous outbreaks was fairly spotty. We came better prepared than those medical teams, but we still encountered tremendous obstacles that were difficult at best to anticipate. Most of that information never did escape the gravitational field of the high-risk area, and my inability to find a way for it to cross the four feet that separated the Hot Zone from the world in which information can be recorded and shared is among the regrets that I will carry to my grave.

So with that important doctor-based function being limited at best, we took to helping out in what other ways we could. Sometimes that

---

* Trish Henwood, seemingly the whiz kid of the physicians, later found a better way around the data-extraction problem by taking pictures of each chart page with an iPad as I held the page up at the boundary, then the data was manually reentered on the other side. Again, it's one of those logistical matters that seems the obvious solution in retrospect, but we were thinking about a good many other challenges at the time, which is why she got a publication to her name in *The New England Journal of Medicine* and I did not.

led to more problems than it solved, as the expat nursing staff, which in October consisted of a formidable collection of some of the most talented medical professionals with whom I have ever worked, were trying to coordinate the efforts of the national staff, so the offers of help that Colin and I made were sometimes perceived in ways that we hadn't intended. After a few weeks, we had worked out enough of a system so that I would like to think we brought some additional expertise to the various chores that were the daily bread of the ETU. But the immediate tasks of patient care were overwhelmingly performed by the nursing staff. The doctors weren't entirely superfluous to the running of the ETU, but the nurses were, without any question, completely indispensable to it.

That was rounds. We made rounds about four times each day, after which we would "run the boards." Running the boards was a process of reviewing the names of the patients on a laminate board, and the clinical team who had just seen the patients would summarize their status. Because the patient charts could not leave the high-risk area, we were forced to remember what we had encountered because that information had to be passed along orally during these rounds. It was the only way we could effectively communicate what was happening with the patients to the rest of the medical staff. We ran the boards at the shift change at 7:00 a.m., then later in the morning, again in the midafternoon, and finally at the handoff back to the night shift around 7:00 p.m.

When I got out of PPE, soaking wet from my sweat and the chlorine spray, I wanted to go straight to run the board so that I could expunge the tenuously held data in my head lest I forget details or confuse patients. Thus: "Joseph Dwolo is a twenty-nine-year-old man here in the suspect ward, who came from Ganta with fever and chills last night, and his test is still pending. He looks pretty good right now. Hasn't gotten nausea, but he does have conjunctivitis." We used every trick we could to remember who was in what room. Mostly it worked, with each staff member serving as a kind of cross-check of information. Every once in a while, two people would have conflicting impressions of how a patient was faring, which led to interesting conversations— or, on occasion, depending upon how stressed out we all were, wrestling matches. Verbally, anyway.

Death disrupted our neatly organized plan of assigning patients to rooms. If a patient died, the roommates immediately fled to other rooms and would not return even after the body had been removed. The spirit world made itself known at these moments, and no amount of coaxing could bring any of the patients back. It added layers of complication to our memorization schemes, since we would go in expecting to find George in room C5 but instead see him on a bed in C8 where you *thought* you'd find Fatu. As long as there were enough beds to go around, the staff dealt with the problem as best we could. But what would happen if we hit full capacity?

Depending on how physically brutal rounds had been, after we ran the boards we'd spend usually a half hour or more recovering, just sitting in the medical staff quarters rehydrating and reenergizing. We had a small refrigerator that housed dozens of cans of a popular Liberian soda called Rox, which I thought of as the West African taste equivalent of Diet Mandarin Orange Slice, and as such I avoided it unless I thought that my blood sugar was running at dangerously low levels. I had gotten used to the taste of oral rehydration solution—or at least I was so desperately thirsty after emerging from a spin in the high-risk area that drinking saltwater didn't seem so bad. But no wonder it wasn't popular among the patients. When a shipment of Coca-Cola arrived, it seemed like manna had fallen from heaven. And because my weight was starting to plummet from all the sweating, it marked the only time in my life when I could drink as much Coke as I wanted without any guilt whatsoever.

I liked to round in the morning and let Colin take the afternoon shift. That allowed my afternoon to be set aside for paperwork: filling out death certificates, cross-checking the demographic data in our logbooks, moving the charts from suspect to confirmed folders and so on; or checking the inventories of our supplies and tending to other administrative tasks. There tended to be downtime during the afternoon activities, a chance to catch up and talk about how the patients were doing, think aloud about the physiological changes wrought by Ebola infection, and, when we took a deep breath, socialize.

By four we usually heard from the Navy lab as to which samples were positive and which negative. They tended to run half and half, which meant that we would bring news to those in the suspect ward that would seem either like a liberation of ecstatic proportions or a death sentence. Someone from either the psychosocial team or the medical staff or both would return to the suspect ward and escort the infected to the confirmed ward, and guide the others through a symbolic River Jordan of bleach solution poured on their heads and bodies, thence to freedom. Not surprisingly, emotions ran high in the wards during this time in both directions.

Then, we waited for the ambulances to arrive.

It usually happened around six, just before sunset, and the short equatorial sunset made the gathering of histories of the patients a hectic and somewhat chaotic exercise, as darkness soon engulfed the proceedings and writing in the weak light of a single incandescent bulb became a formidable task. The ambulances were nothing more than pickup trucks with a metal frame attached to the back part and an orange tarp laid over the flatbed to provide the patients with privacy as they were shepherded to the ETU. On the flatbed were foam mattresses for the patients to lie on if they could not sit and pickle barrels to serve as commodes on their journey. These were the very same commodes that they would find in their rooms.

The conversion of a 4×4 into an "ambulance" may sound like the ultimate in résumé padding, but they were in fact a good deal safer than the few true ambulances zipping around the Liberian countryside at that moment, such as the one that bore Phil Ireland to the ELWA ETU. The complete separation of the driver's cab from the patients meant that the drivers could not be exposed, and thus they required no special training provided they kept the doors closed on their runs. Actual ambulances, with their open communication between the driver's seat and the back portion, were real hazards to drivers. Sometimes we would see these ambulances operated by groups other than our own, with drivers wearing full PPE, in theory totally contaminating the interiors, the drivers not knowing anything about proper doffing and spraying of bleach to inactivate the virus. I felt sorry and mildly embarrassed for them for their misunderstanding that the wearing of the suit was the key, as if the polymers that formed the barrier left them totally safe when in the presence of patients and could just be casually peeled off afterward. We had no time to convey to them that the tricky part was getting *out* of the suit and was the time when they were at greatest risk of becoming infected. I have no idea if any of them actually did become infected, but I wouldn't be surprised if a percentage of them did.

The ambulances would proceed along a path that abutted the wards, and the patients disembarked from the flatbeds and entered the triage hut. There we would talk to the patients, obtaining their histories—that is, the stories of what symptoms they had, the timing of those symptoms, whether they had been in contact with anyone ill, and so on—while documenting these details onto forms sent by the Ministry of Health. Processing the Blue World's new arrivals took at least an hour, after which a member of the medical staff escorted them to their assigned rooms for the night, almost certainly among the longest nights of their lives. And with those tasks behind us, and the night-shift workers now in motion, we would head home to our flats in Cuttington.

The more days passed, the more acquainted we all became with the virus, and although it did not ravage the body in quite the way most of us would have guessed, its ability to destroy human flesh was still impressive. Each day brought at least one death. We would round and find ourselves having to recalibrate our census as the WASH team would send a group in to move a patient to the morgue.

The first lesson hit me completely by surprise: The hemorrhagic fever of Ebola wasn't so hemorrhagic. I already had a notion that this might be true. When I was applying for training programs in infectious diseases, still fueled by the adrenaline rush that reading *The Hot Zone* had provided a decade before, I told my mentor that I was interested in working with hemorrhagic fever viruses. At that time, the only research being done in Massachusetts on hemorrhagic fever was by a group at UMass working on a mosquito-borne tropical virus called dengue. The classic presentation of dengue was something known as "breakbone fever," which is about as painful as it sounds and is caused by the severe muscle aches the infection produces. But the less common, lethal form is called Dengue Hemorrhagic Fever, or

DHF. That was what interested me when I started out in infectious disease. After all, *The Hot Zone* said people bled. The question that had gripped me in this phase of my career was simply, *Why?*

But after I came to UMass and worked with the dengue group and I learned more about DHF, I realized how rare it was for patients to have frank bleeding. *Hemorrhage* was a misnomer, reserved for only the worst of the worst cases. As the years passed and I read more and accompanied my mentor to hemorrhagic fever conferences, I would come to discover this to be equally true of other viruses that fell under this category, such as Lassa Fever, Hantaviruses, Rift Valley Fever, Yellow Fever, and several others. Still, I assumed that the filoviruses of Ebola and Marburg would live up to their reputations.

And when I arrived in Bong County to work, almost immediately they did. The first few days that I had rounded, I met a woman named Fatu. She was in her mid-thirties, perhaps five foot five, and had a stocky frame, her hair a tangled mess from having been lying prostrate in her bed in the ETU for several days. When we first met on my very first day, I had come to her room at the end of the hallway of the suspect ward to find her vomiting into the commode bucket. When I retrieved the bucket, the liquid was unmistakably tinged with red. I assumed that she had almost no chance of surviving, but I came back the next day to find her doing the same—still with blood—and was surprised to find her still sitting up in bed the *next* day. I got down on my knees that day and looked into her eyes, which were not scared so much as weary, and I asked her to tell me she was going to survive. She just looked at me, blinking. Then I asked again, and she looked at me again. And I asked a third time, and she slurred out the words that she was going to survive. I made her repeat it. I left to round on the other patients, assuming it would be the last time I would see her alive. She looked terrible.

The following day came, and with it, the official confirmation from the Liberian Ministry of Health that she was infected. (This was before the Navy had shown up and provided that same-day turnaround time on tests.) If she was still alive, I would finally tell her that her test had come back positive and that she would need to be escorted to the confirmed ward. She was sitting upright, looking more animated than I had ever seen her. She looked at me with a certain level of rage and summoned the energy to say, "I'm gonna *beat* this virus!" And sure enough, she did, and was among the first survivors that I had cared for from the beginning of their hospitalizations.

Yet Fatu proved to be the exception, and in the days that followed I saw essentially no other cases of bright red blood. I sheepishly confess to a degree of disappointment—I had come all the way to an Ebola outbreak, and yet I certainly didn't feel like I was walking around in Richard Preston's account. In more flippant moments, I thought about writing his publisher and asking for my money back. One day in the first two weeks I saw a young man in the confirmed ward who appeared to be more stable than the others, a good harbinger in this part of the ETU. As I came in to talk to him, however, a small trickle of red blood ran out of his left nostril. My pulse quickened. *Here it was,* I thought, *the Ebola epidemic*! "Your nose is bleeding," I said to him gingerly, worried that the observation alone might cause him to shrivel up.

"Oh, yeah, I've had problems with bloody noses since I was a child," he said, casually waving his hand as if this were a tedious subject. I couldn't stop from feeling deflated, and that left me deeply irritated with myself, for I certainly was not there as part of a grand hemorrhagic fever tour, starring Bright Red Blood. At any rate, that was about as close as I ever got to seeing the precise kind of horror that I had come to expect. But I still encountered horror in abundance.

What I *did* see was a lot of gastrointestinal fluids. The amount of diarrhea and vomit that went into the commode buckets of the patients was remarkable. As we continued to care for patients, we used our laptops to read up on the scientific and clinical literature of filoviruses as much as we could, and it became clear that, while bleeding was very much a known quantity, it was the vomiting and diarrhea that dominated the pathology of Ebola. They usually started about a week into infection and were such a cardinal feature of the disease that they received their own special designation in the clinical literature of the "wet symptoms." The phrase doesn't sound nearly as terrifying as the word *hemorrhage*, but it was easily as efficient as blood loss in terms of how it could snuff out a life. Phil Ireland's early illness, when he still was lying in his bed in his house, weren't marked by wet symptoms, but within about twenty-four hours of coming to the ELWA ETU, they hit him with such force that he could still wince when describing the sensation to me nearly one year later.

The wet symptoms were much more important to Ebola's deadliness than hemorrhage, and they were also much more prevalent. That managed to explain why it had been confused with cholera in the early phases of the epidemic. I have never seen a case of cholera. The one major epidemic in my time was a tragic episode in Haiti that started in 2010, a few years after its calamitous earthquake; thousands of people died, although that outbreak didn't receive anywhere near the same amount of notoriety as Ebola. Despite never having encountered a patient with this infection, I used it as a template for my revised clinical impression of Ebola.

There was, of course, a range of pathology in Ebola, with some patients having some symptoms and other patients having different presentations. But if one were to boil it down into a bite-sized morsel for a medical student or a resident, a simple way to remember the typical course, it was this: You started out with a week of influenza, and then you graduated to a week of cholera. By the end of the second week, you were either dead or on the very slow road to recovery. I would also tell those students and residents to get *bleeding* out of their mind-set and perhaps in suggesting that, take away a little of the primal fear that the word *Ebola* can induce.

During these first weeks several of us had noted that we had gone from *watching* the world's leading story to *being* the world's leading story. Along with MSF and the other aid groups, IMC was engaged in a worldwide media blitz to raise consciousness, awareness, and impel governments, foundations, and anyone else who could make a tangible contribution to contain the outbreak to do so. Every few days we'd have some reporters, mainly based in Monrovia, come up for a day to tour the facility and interview people. We hosted some French writers from *Le Figaro* (who managed somehow in the midst of the damp African heat to nevertheless look chic, one casually taking notes and ambling about the compound wearing blue jeans, a dark gray T-shirt, and a fedora). There were two amiable TV crews, one from Germany and the other I think from Sweden, each spending a day or two shooting and interviewing. An American photojournalist named Morgana Wingard, who was working for USAID, the U.S. government agency whose money had in part funded the construction of the Blue World, came around a few times.

Sean mostly escorted those brief flybys around. I wasn't paying a huge amount of attention to their comings and goings, but it seemed that the print journalists were there to *understand* people by asking questions and listening carefully to the answers, while the TV types already seemed to know what they had in mind and barreled in with an I-came-I-saw-I-shot-pictures approach that, at least speaking for myself, underlined why I have such contempt for TV journalism in the first place. A big CNN crew had come to do some shooting, and I don't think they were there for more than an hour or two, perhaps because they were so skittish about being out and about in such a dangerous place and were eager to return to the relative safety of Monrovia, probably at the posh Mamba Point Hotel, hoping they could get back on a plane to get the hell out of this country. Two hours is enough time to, well, pretty much do nothing at all except take some moving images of people milling about in PPE, allowing CNN to drive home what was almost certainly a message of absolute fear that was working its way up to full steam in the wake of Thomas Eric Duncan's infection in Dallas.

Among the print journalists, three reporters working for *The New York Times* had become part of our hastily arranged family. The Australian photographer Daniel Berehulak had been shooting in Liberia since at least September, and his photographs had penetrated my consciousness well before I met him. One picture stood out in my memory. The article, which appeared in the *Times* in mid-September, detailed Obama's plan to step up the U.S. military presence to three thousand troops and equip the region with a variety of supplies for the outbreak.

Yet for all the article's verbiage, it was Daniel's photograph that seared into the memory banks: a picture of a man, obviously dead, lying on a street in the city center, a rug under his body and covered by a sheet, with a crowd surrounding him. A stream of fluid that appeared to issue from his own body flowed to the right, directly into the midst of the crowd. Standing to the left of the body was a man wearing latex gloves, gesturing at the corpse with both palms open as if to say, *This is what we are left to cope with on our own!* Possibly his intent is to warn the crowd away from coming any closer. Regardless, this gesticulating man was just feet away from a biological bomb with no real protection to speak of. Standing near the body's head was another young man wearing latex gloves but clad in nothing but shorts, a T-shirt, and flip-flops.

Daniel's work was remarkable not only for its ability to capture the terrible essence of Monrovia at that moment but because of the risks required of him to obtain such shots. It was phenomenally dangerous work, making our efforts in the ETU look like a walk through a rose garden. Six months later, I would end up speaking with a reporter for NPR named Nurith Aizenman who had been present at the West Point riots. When I learned of this, my reaction was similar to how I responded to Daniel's work: *Are you* totally *insane?* It was bravery of the highest order. Now Daniel had come to Bong County to document the workings of the ETU and the patients and families who found themselves caught up in this death trap.

In addition to Daniel, there was Ben Solomon, an American in his mid-twenties doing video journalism. He interviewed people about their jobs with a video camera and as such was doing much the same thing as any television reporter. But unlike the TV reporters, whose work usually finished in a matter of hours, Ben stayed with us for at least a week, making long, detailed videos that I couldn't watch until I returned to the States because of the limited bandwidth in Liberia. Like Daniel, Ben had an easygoing manner, and his levity provided a much-needed distraction amid a busy and sometimes tense working atmosphere.

Finally, Sheri Fink was fully embedded with the team for several weeks. Sheri and I had met at Camp Ebola, and we had talked a few times in the interim while I sat around my hotel room waiting for a flight and Sheri sat around waiting for the *Times* and IMC to pound out the details of her embed. Sheri was a doctor by training but had become involved in journalism devoted to humanitarian crises. Her first book dealt with the war in Bosnia; her second, *Five Days at Memorial*, based on a Pulitzer Prize–winning article, was a bestseller about the terrible decisions that medical staff faced while tending to patients who could not be evacuated from the Hurricane Katrina disaster in New Orleans. Because of our brief acquaintance, her arrival in the first few days provided an emotional anchor in the tumult of meeting dozens of new people, acclimating to a new work environment, and settling in to new living quarters. Her presence was a great comfort to me not only because I enjoyed her company but also because at that point I had known her longer than anyone else.

On rounds one day I had made my way over to the confirmed ward. I always made mental tallies as I moved about the wards, dividing the patients into three broad categories: the recovered, the tenuous, and those on the precipice of the abyss. I was nearly finished, with only two patients left to see. One of these patients was a woman named Yatta, and her status was somewhere between tenuous and the precipice. On this particular morning, she had not looked well at all, and I thought that she might not live to see the next day. She leaned over the side of her bed while I was talking to her and vomited into her plastic bucket, and the casual, automated quality of the maneuver suggested to me that she had been doing this so much over the past day or two that it had become part of her routine, as if everyone should just stop themselves in the middle of a conversation in order to heave up gastric contents.

I suddenly heard an electronic chime in the room. After a few moments I realized it was coming from under Yatta's pillow. She turned from her bucket, nonchalantly reached under the pillow, and an insistent cell phone emerged in her right hand. We halted our already halting conversation while she answered the call. It was her brother, and she proceeded to say something that I've heard so many times in my day job that I wondered whether I really was on a remote jungle hilltop in rural Africa or whether I was on the seventh floor of a hospital in central Massachusetts: "The doctor is here. I'll call you back in a few minutes."

The cell phones made clear that this was a twenty-first-century outbreak, for at least half of the patients had come with them and regularly kept in touch with their families, and in this respect they were no different from typical patients in the West. The absence of other accoutrements of comfort—toilets, televisions, actual *walls*—only underscored the weirdness of the advanced technology. Some aspects of the operation would have seemed unremarkable to the forebears of these patients, like the rough-hewn timbers that formed the skeletons of the structures. But the cell phones allowing for distant communication *out* and the radios providing distant communication *in* would have blown their minds.

Needless to say, the patients weren't the only ones plugged into this ethereal hive of communication. The expat staff all brought their laptops, which allowed us to pretend that we were just in another office space down the corridor from our colleagues, each screen a two-way window on the world. Given our interests, we spent a large portion of time following the Ebola coverage, comparing and contrasting the perspectives of print media versus television coverage, the Europeans versus the Americans, and so on.

One of the strangest (though simultaneously, most banal) ways in which we remained connected to the rest of the world was through a website that allowed us to post little updates on our lives and share them with various "friends" of our choosing. It may be true that the revolution will not be televised, but I am certain that the end of the world will be Facebooked until there is no one left standing. We had all become objects of intense curiosity to our friends, and our posts were followed and shared and liked. Some of us in the ETU had "friended" one another during the proceedings, and we could follow each other in virtual reality even as we lived the real reality separated from one another by a few feet.

The Internet access relied upon mobile Wi-Fi hot spots purchased by IMC. They were moderately temperamental devices about the size of a cigarette pack. We could count on perhaps an hour or two of access, although the connectivity was intermittent. Our e-mail messages could get cut off, leading to the occasional profane remark from someone who just lost fifteen minutes of carefully worded work. We eventually got good at saving our e-mails before sending them, something I almost never do in the States. Elvis Ogweno, one of the Kenyan expat nurses, used an old agricultural metaphor in wondering whether the hot spots were working. "Do the cows have milk?" was his oft-repeated question. Within a few weeks, the logistics team set up a satellite, and the hot spots became less important, for we had a creamery.

The laptops themselves were powered by an ersatz electrical system nearly as mercurial as the wireless access. Plugging into the outlets directly seemed a highly risky proposition, in part because the wiring wasn't perfectly grounded, in part because the workspace where we accessed the plugs was better described as a sturdy tent than a true building, and we were still in the rainy season, where rainwater easily penetrated the periphery of the structure. Any metal piece on the laptop served as a conductor and therefore one's own personal miniature electrocution system. MacBooks, we soon discovered from the various cries of "Youch!" and "Fuck!" emanating from the Apple-owning expat staff, had a lot more metal than PC laptops.

Touching the outlets could prove to be even more dangerous than working in the high-risk area. To avoid directly plugging in (and to accommodate the multiple users) we used power strips purchased at an electronics supplier in Monrovia. The strips, however, were of inferior quality made by a Chinese manufacturer. They were designed to accommodate various types of electrical outlets used in that part of the world, for Liberia, which uses 120-volt electricity, is different from its neighbors, all of which utilize 230-volt systems with a different style of outlet. These power strips as a consequence didn't accept the American plugs very well, leaving them as loose as a five-year-old's primary tooth ready to depart from the jaw, and the plug would receive the power only if it stayed in the outlet just so. Even the slightest movement could cause the plug to lose the connection, and the laptop's battery would start to drain again. By the end of the second week, I found this process to be excruciating, and I decided to risk either me or my computer's motherboard being fried and just went ahead and plugged it in directly to the outlet. As I am typing these words on the very same laptop, I seem to have made a good gamble.

The communications system wasn't the only aspect of the operation where the mix of nineteenth-, twentieth-, and twenty-first-century technologies all had to comfortably coexist. As doctors and nurses, we ran what seemed like a hospital: There were rounds, there were tests, there were medications. Yet because we worked with this particular virus, whose clinical behavior was only dimly understood and whose lethality imposed severe restrictions on just how we could behave as clinicians, we were sometimes—well, often—left to incomplete trails of evidence by which we based our treatment decisions.

Our possession of the space-age technology of the Ebola PCR test was hampered by the circumstances the virus imposed, which frequently turned the care of patients into a maddening exercise in medieval medicine. *Why*, in fact, were people dying at such appalling rates? It is the kind of question that drives every physician who thinks about disease, and unlike what most of us did in our regular jobs— which was simply treat disease that we more or less understood—we were asking this question aloud on a daily basis like physicians living in the pre-microscope era had asked about cholera. And we felt a sense of urgency in trying to arrive at some kind of an answer, even if only a crude one, so that we could put a dent in the mortality and save a few lives in the process. But how to glean information and make reasonable scientific observations in a clinical environment devoid of even stethoscopes? Everything was a guess.

One of the topics that came to dominate the discussion for weeks was the problem of potassium. We had all been surprised to see just how much fluid the patients were losing, and we all understood that electrolyte levels must be going haywire. The fluctuations in these electrolyte levels might hold the key to at least part of the high-grade mortality of the disease. Manage the electrolytes well, and maybe you can help people to ride out the storm.

Managing potassium is one of the most critical activities of doctors and nurses the world round. Sodium, calcium, magnesium, and chloride all can tolerate wider swings before causing real trouble, but potassium levels must remain within a narrower window, mainly because of its effect on the electrical conduction of the heart muscle. Go too low, or especially too high, and the heart can experience a total electrical shutdown.

Potassium can be depleted by diarrhea, and it didn't take a superior clinician to see just how much diarrhea the patients had. Patients would lose liters of fluid each day. We would come in on rounds, find someone lying still in bed, and see a bucket at their bedside with several inches of murky liquid within. So we had good reason to believe that patients' potassium levels were becoming dangerously low. Perhaps they would benefit from potassium supplementation. We had been giving potassium in the form of oral rehydration solution, but the overly salty taste made it understandably unpopular among patients. As an alternate, we had potassium pills, but they were large; just the sight of them was enough to cause nausea, or worse, in some patients. Bananas were cheap and abundant in that part of Liberia, and while they often contained only a small dose of potassium, at least their easy-on-the-stomach quality provided hope that we could replete them a little, and that *might* constitute the difference between life and death for a few patients while they went through the crisis period.

The tricky part about profound diarrhea is that such fluid losses *also* lead to kidney failure, and the kidneys regulate potassium levels. So one other interpretation of why patients were dying was not because their potassium was falling too *low* but instead because it was going too *high* when the kidneys shut down. In that case, trying to provide patients with more potassium, whatever the route, might be doing exactly the wrong thing.

The simple way to resolve this dispute, in a manner that could have been performed in even a backwater regional hospital in the United States of the 1950s, is to check a patient's serum potassium level along with their kidney function. There are machines now that can perform these laboratory tests without the need for specialized technicians or even a central power source. But we had no such capabilities. Running such tests introduced complexities into lab protocols that would require careful consideration far too slow for the pace of the outbreak, for working with the blood of such patients constituted genuine risk for whoever was handling the samples, and such advanced technology might not work in the African humidity, or might require special outlets not available in rural Liberia, and on and on the logistics problems went.

So instead, the doctors and nurses kicked the problem around in the manner of a Talmudic discussion. *Well*, the reasoning went, *it's probably hypokalemia* (low potassium), *so we should provide potassium supplementation. . . . But since they might be dying of hyperkalemia, we'll just be giving them bananas, which aren't really going to bump their potassium much anyway.* When we finally did come to something approaching a consensus on the bananas, I realized I had succumbed to the kind of medicine I swore I would never perform. I was practicing homeopathy.

The high-risk area, especially the confirmed ward with its mounting dead, was capable of being a depressing place. But mainly the staff focused on the positives. Once patients survived the worst of the virus, they still had to remain in the isolation of the Hot Zone while their viral loads drifted back down to undetectable and therefore would no longer pose a risk of transmission. This could last for weeks. Surviving a near-death experience, followed by lounging around with very little to do, is probably the all-time award winner for anticlimax, but most bore the tedium well. Genesis, one of the first survivors I knew, had a viral load that kept tailing off, and our predictions that he would be able to leave after the next blood test was taken proved to be wrong a few times. When the test would come back, still positive, I'd look for some glum humor in the situation. "Genesis is still waiting for his Exodus," I said the first time we were caught by surprise, which helped lighten the mood a little. When the next test came back positive a few days later, I noted, "Well, Genesis has decided to take a pass on Exodus and has just gone straight to Leviticus." This time the remark was met with wan smiles.

Yet when his moment finally did arrive, there was jubilation. Every discharge was a celebration, with dancing and singing and smiles in abundance. A picture of Genesis hearing the news of his negative test was featured in *The New York Times*. His arms are raised into the sky, both his fists clutched together, a triumphant smile across his face. Every patient who received such news reacted similarly. It was not a happy moment only for them or even for the staff; the other patients, some of whom were still about to face the worst of what Ebola had to offer, could at least see this and take heart. Whatever the rumors were circulating out in the community that the ETU was just a place to die, here there was evidence to the contrary that couldn't be missed.

I found other ways to experience and transmit joy in the midst of the death. Like most people, I take pleasure in physical contact, but IMC's rules in the middle of the outbreak were, understandably, that nobody touch one another during the crisis. I literally never shook hands, patted anyone on the back, or gave a hug to any of my colleagues. We were even discouraged from touching our *own* faces for fear of possibly bringing a stray virion that we might have picked up. But with the safety of PPE, touching was perfectly safe—or at least not forbidden, since Hot Zone work couldn't exactly be described as "safe." So rounds provided a ritual for contact. Those who were healthy, I high-fived; those who weren't, I stroked their arms and foreheads. Kids, in particular, provided all sorts of opportunities. If any of the children needed to be taken from the suspect to the confirmed ward, I'd volunteer to be the one to do it. I made a point of picking up and spinning around the kids who had survived on the confirmed side each time I came through. Their laughter was the antidote to Ebola's ominous silence.

The opportunities to use touch as a way to improve the morale of the adults was no less profound. I had watched a woman named Alice get worse and worse, and then one day I came in to find her sitting in a chair in her room instead of lying on the bed. "Alice, how are you feeling today?" I asked. "You look better!"

Until that point, Alice's face had always been an expressionless mask of illness, but suddenly she looked up with a pouty tilt of her head to the left, and her eyes bored straight into mine. "My *neck* hurts," she said, and pointed to the offending area.

If you have been suffering from an Ebola infection, and you now complain, sitting upright, that your neck is hurting, you are *not* going to die from Ebola.

"Well, Alice, we should do something about that," I said, and then I proceeded to come over and rub the back of her neck for about five minutes. The sweat I was dripping all over her didn't seem to bother her in the least. This became a daily ritual during Alice's two-week convalescence, and I thought at times of adding a line in my future CV: "Steven Hatch, staff physician, and Alice's personal masseuse, Bong County ETU."

At the end of the second week, Sam Siakor came up to me, asking me to step aside into a private area, which was difficult in the fish-bowl environment of the small compound. The outbreak had touched a family to whom he had been close, and now he was hearing that another member, a woman named Siatta, had fallen ill as well. Because Sam's duties were with the WASH team, he wasn't sure how to arrange for an evaluation. Because I worked inside the unit and wasn't part of the ambulance team, I didn't know either, but I quickly called Elvis, who was out on one of his runs. We arranged for Siatta to be picked up, and later that day, she was sitting in the suspect ward with a fever. The following day, when the test returned, we moved her over to the confirmed ward.

Clinically, she looked no different than anyone else with Ebola. To me, however, she was entirely different from all the other patients. I knew Sam and called him a friend by that point, and Siatta was a direct extension of that friendship. Everyone else in the ETU were people that I thought of in precisely the same terms that I think of the patients I care for back in Massachusetts, but I was bound to Siatta through personal connections. Intellectually, I understood that her chances of surviving the next seven days were just south of 50 percent. Emotionally, I was never going to forgive myself if she died.

5

THE UNBEARABLE CRY

Human suffering anywhere concerns men and women everywhere.

—Elie Wiesel, *Night*

In Monrovia, the ETUs still operated at full tilt. A story had reached us via the journalists that a patient there had accidentally been declared dead. She had been lying in a body bag awaiting transfer to the ETU's makeshift morgue. The protocol for removing corpses from the wards involved repeated dousings of bleach; before the body bag was zipped up, a worker would spray the solution directly on the body to decontaminate to the fullest extent possible. When the woman was sprayed with the bleach solution, she sprang to consciousness. Our staff reacted to this news with complete horror. There were enough contingencies to contemplate, but burying someone alive was a scenario too terrifying to consider.

In our corner of Bong County, the work continued apace.

The evening was one of the periods of maximum frenetic activity. Depending on when the ambulances arrived and how many patients needed to be processed, those of us working the day shift would head back home to Cuttington somewhere between 8:00 and 9:00 p.m. Two or three SUVs would ferry the expats back to campus, while a larger bus would transport the majority of the national staff to Gbarnga. If it was raining, as it often was as the rainy season neared its end, I would wrap my computer bag in one of the sample PPE suits tucked away in various nooks of the medical staff office, as their composition proved not only able to hold deadly viruses at bay but did an excellent job of keeping a computer warm and dry in a moist and rainy jungle.

On the way out we would grab dinner in a Styrofoam container, typically some theme-and-variation on grilled chicken in a spicy West African sauce with a side of noodles with chopped ham and a biscuit. Everything was prepared with palm oil, which is to margarine what cane sugar is to saccharin, and so everything tasted very rich. Since the ETU work had put me into a major calorie deficit, I didn't mind all that palm oil so much. Sometimes there would be a slice of watermelon, which looked delectable, although I never consumed anything that wasn't cooked for fear of catching some gastrointestinal pathogen. When I first came to Monrovia the year before, I had managed to allow this to happen, and it wasn't fun. But in this instance, two days with fever and diarrhea would not only prevent me from caring for my patients, it would also lead to my own workup for suspected Ebola, something I was determined to avoid at almost any cost.

The drop-offs at Cuttington took about ten minutes, and we headed to our individual flats sprinkled along a half-mile circular road around the periphery of the campus, each a few hundred yards away from the other. The housing was available because the faculty, in whose living quarters we stayed, had fled. I always wondered where they went. After the drivers dropped us off, we tended to go our separate ways. For the first three weeks, I lived alone, but I shared a building with Colin and Steve Whiteley. Steve worked the night shift, so he was always going when we were coming and vice versa, and we tended to see him only at the change of shift, with few opportunities for us to socialize. But after I dropped my stuff off I would often walk to Colin's place and rap with him about the day's events.

My mainstay in the evening, however, was to sit at my dining room table and spend an hour or so on the Internet. As remote and isolated as I was in the Liberian countryside, in some ways, it was as if I hadn't left. I never lacked for correspondents; even the tedious official e-mails from the medical center back in Massachusetts announcing some new high-level hire or that the main visitor parking on Level 6 would be temporarily closed for repairs, became a source of small comfort. I got an e-mail from a colleague at UMass, who asked me whether I thought it okay for a patient to receive a particular drug used in parasitic infections, and when I replied that it sounded reasonable, she asked me if I would mind seeing her in the next week or two. "I'm a little busy as I'm out of the country, but I can forward this along to someone else in the division if you want," I replied.

I'd spend some solitary time with contacts back home, idly munching on some Pringles, touching base with friends and colleagues, reviewing the happenings in Massachusetts and beyond, trying to keep my finger on the pulse of regular life that seemed increasingly distant while I was engaged in what I couldn't stop myself from feeling was a one-way ticket.

The single best e-mail I received was from a senior medicine resident named Sunkaru Touray. It came several weeks into my tour, when the excitement of the initial experience had faded and the exhaustion of the work had started to set in—just the time when a pick-me-up would hit the mark. Like my boss Doug, Sunkaru thought I was in the midst of a psychotic break when I told him I was going to go to Liberia. Doug, however, didn't really take me seriously until I was already on a plane, so our conversations tended to have a dismissive tone to them. By contrast, Sunkaru knew me well enough to know I wasn't kidding when I told him of my plans, and before I left he spoke with me at one point and I could see genuine fear on his face. But I had left, and now there I was, checking my e-mail weeks later. He apparently still felt the need to express some form of concern to me, even if affectionately, even though the die had been cast.

"Doctor Hatch," he wrote. "How's the suicide mission going?"

For the most part, I slept like a baby during my time in the ETU. I needed stamina and focus to work inside the high-risk area, so I made a point of going to bed no later than eleven in anticipation of a six o'clock wake-up. There was no air-conditioning, but because we weren't fully into the searing temperatures of the dry season, the room was comfortable, and a decrepit but functional fan did the rest. During the first two weeks I had a recurring dream of waking up in the confirmed ward wearing a pair of jeans and a shirt, but without any PPE, standing there in my bare feet. It wasn't a long dream, and it wasn't a nightmare. I would wake up from it, jolted, but not in a soaking sweat feeling my heart pounding. It felt more like an electrifying curiosity than anything else, a little like how the astronaut Dave appeared at the end of his journey in *2001: A Space Odyssey*. With his space suit, however, Dave would have been adequately prepared if he found himself on the hall of the confirmed ward, so the simile ends there.

I could afford to be amused about the time that I received that e-mail, because we were seeing survival. Our ETU's mortality rate, which started out at about 70 percent, looked like it was slowly trending down to about 50 percent. Sean mentioned in one of the meetings that this wasn't isolated to just Bong County, since other ETUs across Liberia as well as Sierra Leone and Guinea were reporting similar numbers. Nobody had any clear explanations for why this was happening. One of the survivors was Siatta.

But even as those numbers seemed genuinely encouraging, the more we worked in Liberia, the more it became clear that Ebola's toll could not simply be measured by the numbers it killed directly. The tree in Meliandou had died from Ebola though trees aren't infected by it; the boy shot by Liberian soldiers as part of the West Point riots in September had died from Ebola without having it; the dignitaries who traveled to Womey had died from Ebola even though they were trying to help eradicate it. All these indirect casualties meant that Ebola's impact was much worse than what was even being reported, and those numbers were unprecedented.

One of the most important ways in which Ebola killed indiscriminately was by the simple fact that it had completely shut down the health-care system. ETUs were open for business, and that was about it. Local doctors and nurses did not want to risk their lives caring for patients, and so clinics and hospitals throughout the region shuttered their doors. Even those that stayed open were often avoided. JFK, for instance, never officially closed, but its census remained low. If medical professionals could not know who had Ebola, they would be risking their lives each time they evaluated someone, since adequate safety measures were only in place where people had been properly trained. So even matters like routine trauma could be deadly if they could not be evaluated or treated.

One of the groups most affected by this shutdown was young women, especially if they were pregnant. Vaginal bleeding during pregnancy is a very common problem, and sometimes it indicates a life-threatening condition that requires immediate medical assistance. But bleeding from anywhere at all in an Ebola outbreak all but guarantees that a patient will not be evaluated. So what happens to these patients? They get referred to the ETU, which can do nothing for them except prove that they don't have Ebola.

One such woman came to us around this time, in obvious pain, lying in the suspect ward. A doctor named Rene Vega came up to me while we were rounding to tell me something shocking: He thought the woman had an ectopic pregnancy—a condition in which the fetus develops not in the uterus but farther up in the fallopian tubes. Rene was part of an early class of physicians bound for other ETUs whom we had begun to train on-site to help bypass the bottleneck created by the fact that there were only two other places in the world where organized training was taking place: the MSF course in Belgium and the CDC's Camp Ebola in Alabama. Sean Casey had taken to calling our site in Bong County "Ebola University," which, given the comparison to Camp Ebola in Alabama, seemed reasonable, since although the course would be the same in the essentials, our location was in the middle of an *actual* outbreak. Rene worked for a group called Heart to Heart, and their ETU would be going up in neighboring Nimba County.

Ectopic pregnancies can rupture, and if emergency surgery is not performed, the patient usually dies. Rene's history and examination, despite the limitations of PPE, suggested that at the very least an ultrasound was in order. We had no ultrasound, and even if we did, what would we do with that information? We decided to give our colleagues at Phebe Hospital down the road a call. Phebe was a typical example of why any doctor or nurse not working in an ETU was wise to close up shop for the outbreak. Their first staff member, a nurse there, had fallen ill in June. By the end of September, six of seven full-time nurses were dead, and the sole survivor, a woman named Comfort Harris, was just coming out of IMC's ETU as the first person to be discharged from our facility. The staff at Phebe were terrified, and they declined to evaluate virtually everyone, with good reason.

But once this woman's test returned as negative, *our* reasons to have them evaluate her were actually better. It took some complex negotiations that would have made the U.S.-Iran nuclear deal look easy, but with repeated reassurance, along with a second negative test, we eventually managed to convince the docs at Phebe to take a look at her, providing many outfits of PPE to help them in their efforts. The night after that second test came back, the surgeon and anesthesiologist reluctantly agreed to take her to the OR to remove the ectopic pregnancy that Phebe's ultrasound machine proved was there. I am fairly proud of my work in the ETU, but Rene Vega managed to do something incredibly rare during the outbreak: He actually saved someone's life.

But she was the exception who happened to be lucky enough to have a savior like Rene Vega cross her path. Ectopic pregnancies aren't the only potentially deadly routine complication associated with obstetrics, and there must have been hundreds of women who had these kinds of problems in the middle of the outbreak, with nowhere to turn. Their lives, some unknown number of which almost certainly ended as a consequence of not having proper medical attention, will never be reported when the final numbers are chiseled.

Also around that time, we were training a new physician named Kwan Kew Lai, who had joined the IMC group as we prepared for our departures—the first of whom would be Colin, then Steve a week later, and me the week after that. Kwan Kew had done previous stints with MSF in Africa and expressed interest in working in one of their ETUs, but as with other qualified MSF alumni, she had no luck, and so IMC was only too happy to pick her up. She came to Cuttington and began her hot training just as I had done with Pranav.

During one of her first mornings, the suspect ward was busy, so we didn't head for the confirmed ward until two hours after we had entered. I could typically feel my body start to get stressed somewhere after one hour, and I got progressively more taxed every ten minutes or so. The longest amount of time I had stayed in during the daytime was three hours, and I was so dehydrated by the end of that spin that it took me more than an hour to recover. So I knew that we would need to move through the confirmed ward with efficiency, and efficiency has never been one of my strong suits.

Kwan Kew followed along as we entered the confirmed ward. In the first room on the left were three children: a brother-sister pair aged thirteen and eight, and their cousin Tolbert, who was nine. Tolbert's status had been tenuous since coming to this side a few days before. Neither the diarrhea nor the fever ever stopped, and in the past twenty-four hours he had to be placed in diapers and bathed twice each shift as he could no longer care for himself. The nursing crew had already rounded about a half hour earlier, but when I touched base with them they said nobody had died, although about three or four looked tenuous, and Tolbert was among them.

When I entered he wasn't moving. I started with a gentle nudge and said his name. Nothing. Then I moved to the head of his bed and placed my hand on his chest and slightly rocked it, this time cooing his name, "*Tolllbert . . .*" Again, nothing. For one instant, I thought of the cousins: Rebecca, who looked no bigger than a typical five-year-old in the States, had been lying on the floor sleeping when we entered, but she quickly moved onto the bed with her brother and clung to him.

It occurred to me that Tolbert was very likely dead and that the children might be better served by being escorted out while we made soothing noises about taking care of him or some such. I write that now in retrospect and it seems obvious. At the time, though, that thought was only one of many flashing through my mind, and my main focus was on the question of Tolbert's status. Had he died? The lightbulb had gone out, which was a not infrequent problem that plagued us, so in the darkness of the room small movement could be missed. If he had died, he had *just* died, since he had been responsive when the nursing staff saw him the hour before. I thought about the rumor we had heard about the woman who had nearly been buried alive; now only days later I faced a situation where I could commit the same error. So whatever thoughts I had about Tolbert's cousins were quickly chased from my mind as I focused on him.

First I looked into his eyes, but in the dim light and without a flashlight, there was no way to assess whether his pupils would contract when exposed to a beam of light, which is one of the principal ways medical personnel assess death. I then felt for his pulse on the carotid artery in his neck. A robust pulse hit my fingers, with a *bang!* on my skin that felt so strong I almost jumped. The rate was somewhere around one hundred. I took my hand off his neck and looked again at the child, who lay perfectly still. How could someone with such a strong pulse look like this? Then, standing there and touching nothing at all, I noticed something in my fingers of which I hadn't been aware until then: a rhythmic throbbing at the tips. That pulse I felt was almost certainly *mine* as my heart reacted to the stress of two hours in PPE. I repeated the carotid check a few more times, moving my fingers here and there, growing more frustrated by being unable to distinguish my pulse from what might be his. I felt nothing, but I thought of that woman in Monrovia. Maybe my fingers were incapable of detecting a pulse that distant. I needed to find another way to confirm his status.

I grabbed the bottle of the rehydration solution at his bedside and shook a little onto his face. Still no movement. It was just then that Kwan Kew, who had been silent throughout much of the rounds, chose to speak. "Don't you think we should escort these kids out of the room?" she asked reasonably. "I don't think they need to see this."

Reasonable though the question was, I was not in a state of perfect reason at that point, as my frustration at being unable to assess death—normally not a challenging task even for the stupidest clinician—had left me irritated and testy. "Look, these kids are already gonna have a lifetime of nightmares from their time here," I snapped in reply. "What the hell does one more moment like this really mean? I need to figure out what's going on here!"

I am far from the perfect clinician, although I generally believe that one of my stronger suits is a sensitivity to delicate situations and a knack for using words to heal rather than to hurt. So it shouldn't come as a total surprise when I say that, in a clinical career that has lasted just under two decades, this is about the most awful thing I've ever said to a patient or their family. Kwan Kew ignored my response and silently took Rebecca and her brother by the hand and led them to another room, which was all the more impressive given that she had never been in the confirmed ward before. Meanwhile, I stood there fuming at my ineptitude, though after a variety of maneuvers over the next several minutes I believed I did establish his passing. But it was not a great start with my new colleague, to say nothing of the fact that I probably added to the trauma of two children with my casual dismissal of their fear. The only upside was that they probably didn't understand my American accent and weren't fully aware of what was being said. That's what I tell myself now to find some sort of comfort, anyway.

Other failures of mine were equally painful. One of the most difficult moments of each day came in the late afternoon when the Navy lab called in the results. Almost invariably the list was a mix of positives and negatives, and the reactions of the patients in the suspect ward understandably ran the gamut. One day, however, nearly everyone was positive, eight patients in all. Organizing that large a group and moving them over to the confirmed ward was going to require some coordination.

With a smaller group, we would take the patients and their personal effects in one single move as they relocated across the compound. Because new arrivals to the suspect ward would arrive in a few hours and would come to occupy their rooms, we had to make sure no cross-contamination occurred. Everything the newly confirmed patients had touched on the suspect ward was either incinerated, doused in the high-grade bleach solution, or taken with them to the confirmed side. Obviously, we preferred to have as much material move with them, so all their belongings—cell phones, soap, thermometers, toothbrushes and toothpaste, their linens, the medical chart—got placed in their commode bucket after a rinsing and accompanied them across the divide.

But these people were of course often quite ill. Many were weak, and some suffered the wet symptoms whose severity would likely determine whether they lived or died, so asking them to carry a bucket weighing upwards of twenty pounds was asking a lot. Indeed, asking some of them simply to *walk* the twenty meters from one building to the other, carrying nothing at all, was risky. And nobody wanted to be picking up someone from the ground outside, where the rocks and the wooden posts created opportunities for tears in the PPE, to say nothing of hurting one's back seriously. So some patients had to be escorted by leaning on the staff. The lighter patients, typically the children, we could carry.

Yet the ETU rules of movement always dictated that once on the confirmed side, the staff could not return to the suspect ward to retrieve anything. You always moved toward a hotter zone, never backtracking. Most of the time, if we were moving three or four people, we could have one person assist a patient, while another would carry two or three buckets, and the remaining one or two patients could fend for themselves. But eight patients strained our capacities. As I organized the team that afternoon, we had to draw up the game plan on paper to figure out who was assigned to whom, like a football coach drawing up a Hail Mary, down by four with seconds to go in the game.

As technically challenging as the move could be, we also had to help our patients cope with the psychological distress of that brief walk. It seemed so odd to me: Physiologically, there was nothing different about the infected patients once we gave them the news that most of them already suspected was the case. Whether they were on the suspect side or the confirmed side, they still had virus inside their bodies, replicating at a furious pace and setting in motion changes in their immune systems that would determine their clinical course. There was nothing particularly magical about being on the confirmed side. The suspect patients could see those on the confirmed side during the day, lazing about at plastic round tables in their lawn chairs, listening to Radio Gbarnga, which was most often reporting on the events of the outbreak. Many of those on the confirmed side looked perfectly healthy, as indeed they were, having won their battles with Ebola as they waited for their viral loads to become undetectable. They could chat with these healing patients at the orange-plastic-fenced boundary between the two and take real courage in the evidence that people survived.

Yet some of the newly confirmed patients looked at that short distance, especially the one-meter zone that divided the two areas, as a chasm into which their bodies and souls would fall and never be seen or heard from again. It took some gentle encouragement to have these patients assent to the move.

And this day, with these eight patients, more than a little encouragement was needed. The patients spanned a wide age range. A woman in her sixties, wobbly on her feet, who needed special help walking over—that meant one person would be unable to assist further after accompanying her to the other side. A few of the patients were adults who were able to tend to themselves as we organized the caravan. One or two were in their late teens, and they were scared. We held their hands and stroked their foreheads and assured them that nothing was different on the confirmed side. With great reluctance, they gathered their belongings.

And then there was Josephine. She was six.

That was grim news, but what was worse was that her mother's test had returned as negative. There is a unique cruelty in separating a mother from her child, especially when the mother has been handed a new lease on life while being forced to watch her daughter be carried away to the confirmed ward, helpless to hold fast to her as the undertow of molecular biology pulled them further and further apart.

I knew we were going to need to be exquisitely sensitive to the fears of this child. After we had organized our game plan upon entering, I walked over to the boundary and got the attention of Siatta, who had by then recovered and had become something like a den mother of the confirmed ward. I asked her to gather the healthy women so that they could come out and receive Josephine with open arms.

My goal was not only to have Josephine feel assured that there would be people to look out for her but also to calm her mother, who would soon be discharged to her home and leave her child behind to heaven only knew what fate. As I explained my plan to Siatta, I could see the look of understanding come over her face. Josephine was sitting on her mother's lap only a few paces from me, and so I tried to convey this plan without explicitly stating my reasons for organizing a welcoming committee. After a few clarifications that were required to overcome the difficulties of understanding my American accent, and doing it through the muffling quality of the mask, Siatta stared at me for a moment. I couldn't believe my good fortune that without my having to explain my intentions, despite all the barriers to communication both physical and cultural, I was, if not perfectly understood, then at least understood well enough, on something this sensitive at a critically important moment.

By the time that I had spoken with Siatta, the staff had begun to escort the first wave of patients to the boundary. We made the decision to move in two successive groups, picking the most physically able for the first pass since they could walk themselves into the confirmed ward without further assistance, while three of us that remained would escort the weaker few, including Josephine, carrying their belongings. I turned and slowly came over to Josephine and her mother to break the news to them, as neither Josephine nor her mother understood what was to happen, and put in motion what was probably going to be the hardest thing I would ever do in the ETU.

As I walked over I reviewed all of the lessons I have ever taught my students about how to make a connection with patients. *Make your patients feel as comfortable as possible*, I tell them. *Think about every movement you make in terms of sending nonverbal signals. Speak to them at eye level, getting down on your knees if you have to. Hold their hands. Speak gently and slowly.* For Josephine, to say nothing of her mother, I was going to need to succeed at every single gesture.

I crouched down and held on to the arm of the chair for balance, and immediately I could see Josephine recoil into her mother's arms as she moved away from me. Her eyes stared right into mine and I could tell that she thought she was looking at a monster, a faceless creature in yellow whose eyes were the only part visible, and barely so, hidden behind the mist of the goggles. Then I shifted my gaze to her mother, where I was met with much the same look. "Josephine, I'm Doctor Steve," I said. I slowly explained to both of them what had taken place and that we would need to take Josephine over to the confirmed ward. It was then that I gestured to Siatta, who saw what was happening and, as if she had read my mind, was standing at the boundary with one arm outstretched, ready for Josephine's hand if she could just get up and walk the few meters to greet her.

Josephine, however, was having none of it. Her eyes conveyed undiluted terror. I tried to put my hand on her arm and she pulled away. I did the same for her mother, and although she did not react with the same level of fear, it was impossible to miss the dread on her face. By now the others had already been escorted to the confirmed ward, and I wanted to be over there to make sure that everyone had been situated and settled. Siatta stood there and spoke to both of them, telling them that there would be several women to take good care of her. A few of the other women had come out to join Siatta, and her lone voice grew to a small chorus. As I saw the scene unfold, I thought that we couldn't have orchestrated this move any better.

But Josephine and her mother had other notions. After perhaps ten minutes of encouragement, I finally managed to coax Josephine, and along with her the deadly virus to which her mother was being exposed by the second, to take my hand and make that short walk to the confirmed side. During this time, I mulled over the precise nature of her fear. It would be arrogance in the extreme to think I could articulate her viewpoint, but it did not stop me from wondering. Maybe she wasn't scared in some nonspecific and wordless way of going over to the "sicker" part of the hospital as other patients might have viewed such a sentence, but perhaps she feared the boundary as if it were the event horizon, a line that once crossed would never allow her to return and reunite with her mother. I sensed that her mother, who was nearly equally reluctant to let go of her child, harbored a similar notion, that this would be the last she would see of her baby girl.

And they were right. About four days later Josephine died, terrified and alone despite all of the care that Siatta, the other patients, and the rest of us offered. Her mother never did have the opportunity to say good-bye or even see her child at the interment. They had correctly surmised at the moment when I had separated them that separation would be irrevocable.

Josephine was correct: I *was* a monster—her own personal monster—at the moment I escorted her on what would be her final journey. And I had patted myself on the back at the time, thinking myself so swell for being such a sensitive and caring physician, even as I facilitated a horror from which Josephine's mother will never fully recover. My smugness gnawed at me for weeks after she died, then months. It gnaws at me still.

Other moments were painful not because of my own inadequacies but because of the sheer misery the place was capable of producing.

There was a two- or three-day span when a crew from *60 Minutes* came to do a story. Like the other television crews, they didn't have the opportunity to absorb the ETU at its deepest levels. It was get in, do some interviews, set up some facility shots showing people moving about doing their work, and get out. The reporter was a woman named Lara Logan. I knew nothing of her at the time, only to learn a few days after she left that she had done extensive reporting on the volatile Egyptian protests at Tahrir Square, which had gotten out of control, leading to her being brutally assaulted and raped. It would have been understandable if she took a desk job for the rest of her career, but she had come with her crew to Liberia to report on the outbreak, which when I heard about her past had dumbfounded me. And she had been incredibly kind, bringing some chocolates for the staff as a gesture of thanks. But television was television, and no matter what experiences she and her crew had lived through and reported on, I was skeptical they'd relate a story that went beyond the superficial.*

Just as the *60 Minutes* team had arrived and was setting up its cameras, we admitted a woman whose husband was already in the confirmed ward, having come the week before. By the time she spent her first night he was in the crisis phase. The following afternoon he died, and Fredericka Feuchte, the German expat in charge of the psychosocial team, had suited up to relay the news to the wife, who was still waiting to hear whether she was infected.

One of the qualities that had always surprised me about when we delivered these messages was the almost emotionally flat manner in which the news was accepted. There was very little gnashing of teeth

---

* On the whole, I was right about this. *60 Minutes* aired "The Ebola Hot Zone" a few weeks later. The good news about the report was that it did an outstanding job of providing a viewer with a sense of how an ETU works in about fifteen minutes and included two great interviews with Colin and Kelly Suter. Watching it back in the States, I thought it helped provide people with a real understanding about the form and the function of the ETU, and I was impressed. But the bad news was that Liberians, who comprised two-thirds of the staff, were almost completely ignored. Even the patients themselves mainly served as window dressing. Unfortunately, it was exactly what I expected from a TV crew working for a major U.S. network. By contrast, Ben Solomon's video dispatches of the outbreak for *The New York Times* included extensive interviews from many locations throughout West Africa.

and rending of garments. Whether this was the cultural norm or distrust of showing intense emotions to outsiders or the extraordinary circumstances of the outbreak, I still do not know. But on the occasions when we did have to relay news like this, the silence could be deafening.

This woman, however, did not take Fredericka's condolences quietly. While I was sitting in the staff quarters tending to some paperwork, a sharp scream pierced the ETU, and everyone instantly stopped and looked up from whatever they were doing. Then the scream continued. And continued. She wailed for nearly fifteen minutes, during which time the *60 Minutes* cameraman panned the compound while the noise halted virtually every activity.

That moment would feature prominently when the story aired weeks later. Yet during my time there, it was a singular moment. I thought that it would be good for viewers to be shown such footage back in the States, since listening to this woman's agony certainly humanized the Ebola story, forcing viewers to think about an actual individual's suffering instead of scary space suits and bleeding. But I also couldn't help but feel that these particular journalists were in part given a gift that they hadn't quite earned, especially when their brief tours of our facility were stacked against the work that Sheri, Daniel, and Ben had been doing over several weeks, gritting it out on a daily basis as they churned out lengthy and complex stories for *The New York Times*, spending hours on end talking to dozens of people on the staff, developing a deep sense of what was going on beyond the chlorine, the Tychem, and the morgue.

Death was part of the daily routine, but some deaths affected us more than others. Each of us grew attached to certain patients as we would have done in any hospital, but one loss hit us all with equal force. We had cared for George Beyan, a quiet man in his mid-thirties who had acquired the virus by tending to a sick friend. George had made the slow recovery after emerging from the abyss in mid-October and waited around for the virus to clear, hardly making a noise as he sat outside listening to Radio Gbarnga in the hot sun.

Daniel Berehulak had featured George in a photo essay in the *Times* that ran at the end of October. He had created an ersatz studio in the lone unused office of the compound taking portraits of the patients and the staff. He used sheets as a white background and the portraits shared a highly formal quality; they reminded me of the work of Robert Mapplethorpe. Say what you will about the potential for cross-cultural misunderstandings, as well as the risks of projecting oneself onto another's inner mental state by looking at their facial expressions, but there is simply no mistaking the absolute, unadulterated joyous state of George Beyan in Daniel's portrait. "I got up in the morning, I prayed. In the evening, I prayed. At dinner, I prayed. Prayed to get well," the caption quotes him as saying. "Yesterday, they said, 'You, you're free.' I danced, I jumped." The picture attests to the veracity of his statement.

George got the news of his impending freedom from the Navy lab one late afternoon. As much as patients understandably wanted to get the hell out of such confinement upon hearing the news, almost nobody left the day they received it. Coordinating the discharge paperwork and setting up a plan for them to return by alerting family of their departure all took time. Moreover, this was the same time that some of the staff were busying themselves with the patients in the suspect ward whose tests returned as negative, as they were prioritized to leave the high-risk area as soon as possible to avoid further risk of exposure. Others were working on taking the patients whose tests returned positive to the confirmed ward. Patients like George, who had lingered for weeks, were not going to suffer any ill effects from hanging out in the ETU another night. For all their understandable jubilation, in terms of the tasks to be performed at that hour, they were not the top priority.

George savored his triumph over death, dancing and jumping, but bad news was about to arrive in the form of his wife and two sons, one aged five, the other a toddler. They all had some form of symptoms. That night he stood at the boundary talking to his wife across the one-meter divide that separated the suspect from the confirmed ward, the boys in tow. The following day would be a waiting game for the blood tests.

That next morning we sent George through the decontamination

shower as he returned to freedom after nearly three weeks in isolation. I assumed he would have regarded this as a pyrrhic victory since
his entire family now awaited word as to whether they would have
to endure a similar experience, but I was surprised by the serenity of
his appearance as he sat outside the main staff quarters. There is always the chance that given the cultural barriers I was misinterpreting
his reaction, but I had seen anxiety, dread, and fear on enough Liberian faces to sense that this was different. Having lived through what
he had just lived through, however, it was certainly not for me to judge
him. Daniel took him into his studio, and his reaction was captured
for posterity.

The question arose as to whether he should return home in the
morning or spend the afternoon waiting for his family's test results.
George chose to wait. He was going home with his family, you could
almost hear him think. Only fate had a crueler plan in store for him.
We again got the call from the Navy guys in the late afternoon. His
wife and younger son tested negative, but his elder son, Williams, was
positive, and shortly we would need to escort him over to the confirmed side. He was obviously ill and was too young to fend for himself. He was going to need help or he would surely die. The women
on the confirmed side could not be expected to provide essentially
twenty-four-hour nursing support to this child, busy as they were
with other children, to say nothing of their own illnesses. And we
would not allow his mother to take him to the confirmed side, even
if she wanted to.

That left only one obvious choice: We would have to ask George to
return to the confirmed ward to nurse Williams. We knew that this was
asking an enormous amount of him. Yet we also knew that this would
not endanger him and that it was Williams's best chance for survival.
After a brief team conference where we all agreed this was the best
course to pursue, I walked over to hand George the news and our singular and extremely unpleasant request.

Although he did not explicitly say so when I first explained the situation, I had the distinct impression that he thought I was utterly out
of my mind. He gave a little shake of his head at first and said quietly
that he wasn't going back *in there*. I told him his wife couldn't care

for Williams and that I couldn't ask anyone in the confirmed ward—people whom he knew well by this point—to take on such a responsibility. And Williams needed help. After a brief exchange I realized that he was more than simply dreading returning inside, as if the post-traumatic stress of moving back into the nightmarish prison from which he was so recently set free was only the beginning of his vexations. I saw that same fear in his eyes that I saw every day with patients in the suspect ward.

But what was he concerned about? He was, after all, cured, possessing Ebola-specific antibodies and lymphocytes, which now made him immune to a repeat infection. But . . . did he know that? As I spoke with him, I sat there puzzling this over. Surely he knew at some intuitive level that he was not at risk of getting sick again while he spent day after day convalescing, although maybe he had thought a reset button had been pressed when he emerged from the decontamination shower. But how to explain a concept like acquired immunity to someone who probably had no formal education beyond grade school?

"Look, George," I said. "You're like Superman." It crossed my mind that he might not be familiar with Superman, but I plowed ahead. "You have . . . *special blood* now. The virus cannot hurt you. You can go back in there and you won't be sick. And your son needs you right now." Some more give-and-take took place, and along with heaping spoonfuls of reassurance, we convinced him to perform the nearly unthinkable act of walking back into the high-risk area and receiving his sick son from his uninfected wife.

In the coming days everyone on the staff, Liberian and expat, followed Williams's progress carefully. Nobody said anything, but it was easy to see when we discussed everyone's status as we ran the boards that we were monitoring Williams with heightened vigilance and had attached special emotional importance to his prospects for survival. We also carefully observed Williams because he had taken a less typical clinical course. Most patients were on a clear trajectory: either up, or down. We could usually tell within about a twenty-four-hour window whether they were getting worse and would likely die, or had weathered the storm and would likely survive.

However, Williams behaved differently: He plateaued, then bounced around. His wet symptoms were not as profound as they were in so many other patients. We would see him on morning rounds inside the ward, lying in bed listless, unable even to sit up and take fluids while his fever raged out of control, the heat draining his small body of the water and electrolytes that would be critical to his survival. Then only hours later George would be seen escorting him by the hand outside to sit on the plastic chairs while he idly munched on some cookies, and the afternoon rounds would include chattering among the staff about how he had turned the corner.

But over this time his clinical picture had become a canvas onto which everyone painted different impressions: The more sanguine among us would view every stirring as an indicator of impending improvement, while those more naturally predisposed to pessimism noted that he wasn't looking like the true survivors, who often had made such progress within twenty-four hours of their worst moments that one didn't need to be a medical professional to see they would leave the unit intact.

I am much more naturally predisposed to pessimism. When I try to think scientifically, I do my best to check this pessimism, along with any other emotions, at the door, lest they interfere with good clinical judgment. For me, in order to understand his prognosis, those emotions had to be corralled, which meant ignoring the small blips of improvement that would get reported and celebrated. Instead, a simple mental equation needed to be performed, and the equation went like this: Fever equaled fluid loss, fluid loss equaled dehydration, and dehydration equaled circulatory collapse. Which, no matter how many ways I turned it over in my head, equaled death. I couldn't explain why he was able to hold on and have moments where he seemed to look, if not well, then definitely better. But unless we could figure out a way to get a lot of fluid into him, I just couldn't see how this would lead to a happy outcome. I didn't say so during rounds, but I wasn't in the mind of putting forth a huzzah just because he was able to hold down a little orange juice. Still, with each passing night, I felt the longer he survived, the more likely it was that he was going home.

Then one morning I came in, and I knew something terrible had happened. Everyone was silent. Steve Whiteley, the most unflappable person in the ETU, hardly made eye contact with anyone. The national staff moved about their tasks quietly, and the expat office space felt oppressive. Sheri Fink had been working through the night on a story, and I searched her bloodshot eyes for an explanation, but none came.

"Sheri, *what happened?*" I asked.

"Williams died last night," she replied in a monotone voice. I blinked, surprised to hear this news, a part of me thinking, *No, that can't be right, he looked good yesterday,* and then was surprised at my surprise, as if the hemispheres of my brain were unhappily squabbling about what to do with this information. I should have surmised instantly why such a pall had been cast over the ETU, and yet it made no sense to me in the moment. I shook my head once as if to rid my ears of what I had just heard, even though I knew not only that it was true but that I had sized it up pretty accurately in the previous days.

What she didn't tell me right away, and I would learn only a few days later, was that after Williams had died, George had stayed up the entire night, wailing for his lost son, speaking to him, entreating him to come back, wishing for him to be alive. His lamentations rang throughout the compound for hours. We all knew that the ETU was a place of hellish misery, for by the time that Williams died, about thirty souls that had come to the Bong ETU had been committed to the earth. And we knew there were more to follow, as we fed one new body each day into the maw of the beast. Despite that knowledge, we were able to keep on with our jobs and not let our spirits flag. Our cheer and hope were among our only weapons in the darkness.

Yet what made the passing of Williams Beyan harder than the others was not only that we had all become deeply emotionally invested in his survival, but that we had asked George to cross back over in order to help achieve this. If there was a literal place that could be called hell on earth, for George Beyan, the confirmed ward was it, and we had willingly cajoled him into returning to that place of his nightmares only to provide him with one even worse. We asked him to make such sacrifices knowing that this might happen. Indeed, *I* was the one who had asked it of him.

Rounds that morning were unlike any other, with the raucous banter that usually accompanied the handoff absent, and the morning meeting a quiet recitation of pertinent items. Everyone silently went about their tasks. I asked Godfrey, who was in charge of burials, when they would inter Williams. He told me it would happen around eleven. I turned to Sambhavi Cheemalapati, who was running the ETU while Sean was on his R & R, and told her that we needed to go. She reluctantly agreed.

George came back out a second time through the decontamination chamber, glistening from the light bleach shower, and Sambhavi, Godfrey, and I formed the back of a small processional led by two members of the burial team, an empty cart, a sprayer, and George. We moved around the peripheral road of the ETU, stopping at the back fence abutting the morgue, and the staff retrieved Williams's body, covered in two shiny white body bags. George began to wail again, and I struggled like mad to stop the tears from flowing down my face, for this was not my loss, and I didn't dare guess whether such a show of emotion would be considered appropriate. Eventually I had to bite the tip of my tongue so hard to prevent my tears that it bled. We put Williams in the ground in a ceremony that lasted no more than two or three minutes. Godfrey, I believe, spoke some official words.

It was the only funeral I attended in the outbreak. Sambhavi, Godfrey, and I had to return to work.

6

BEHOLD, A PALE HORSE

Blessed is he that readeth, and they that hear the words of
this prophecy, and keep those things which are written
therein: for the time is at hand.

—Revelation 1:3

The governments of Liberia, Sierra Leone, and Guinea did what they
could to halt Ebola's spread. Instituting a *cordon sanitaire*, as the
West Point episode had demonstrated, was a dangerous and logisti-
cally nightmarish method of containment. The president of Sierra Leone, Ernest Bai Koroma, instituted a much larger cordon, restricting
the movements of one million of his fellow citizens. International ad-
visors howled in indignation, although not everyone in the West
shared this opinion. Laurie Garrett, who had written the enormously
influential *The Coming Plague*, wrote an opinion piece pointing
out that in the Kikwit outbreak of 1995, the Zairean president
Mobutu Sese Seko cordoned off the entire city, and the first truly large
Ebola outbreak never spread to the rest of the country, or any other.
But the Kikwit cordon may not have been the best model for President Koroma, for the Zairean military was much more organized,
and there was only one road in and out of Kikwit, making it easily
contained, while Koroma was attempting to seal off whole portions
of his country. The debate wasn't really about whether a cordon
would be heartless or not. The debate was about whether it would be
effective, or whether it might even take a critical situation and make
it worse.

At the same time, another solution was being scaled up. Instead
of placing a cordon around an entire community, local communities

could simply construct a miniature cordon and place those requiring quarantine *inside* the facility. In Liberia, they came to be called Community Care Centers, but everyone at the ETU referred to them as holding centers. All that was needed was active community surveillance. If someone had come down with symptoms that required ETU evaluation and was eventually shown to be positive, the people living with that person could be brought to the holding center where they could wait their twenty-one days. If they themselves became ill, they could simply be transferred directly to the ETU. The logistical issues were less complicated by an order of magnitude. You didn't have to think about food and drink for the *whole* community, but just those members at the highest risk. In theory, it seemed a sensible way to at the very least cut down on Ebola's transmission.

In practice, however, holding centers were tricky places. They were often run by local groups who did not completely understand the nuances of risk stratification, so some people could find themselves placed in quarantine on the flimsiest of criteria and had little or no opportunity to appeal their detention once in. In the later months of the outbreak, unsettling rumors were circulating that some politicians held ever-greater numbers of people as proof of the success of their quarantine policies, even though the rate of infection was on a sharp decline throughout the country as 2014 came to an end and the number of cases was approaching zero even in places where nobody was held in quarantine.

Toward the end of my third week, Sean Casey came up to me after the morning staff meeting and pretty much ordered Colin, Steve Whiteley, and me to take a day off. We all gently protested to little avail. I wasn't reluctant to rest for a day—we were all putting in fourteen-hour days, the work was physically grueling, the atmosphere was tense, we still weren't sure whether the social structure was going to implode—but I had no idea what I would *do* with a full day off. Cuttington University was a ghost town, so all I could do there was wander around a picturesque but empty campus. Even if markets were open, it would have been risky in the extreme to go wandering about in a densely packed place, which was why the markets were mostly closed. Everyone I knew and had become friends with was going to work, so there were no social options. I hadn't brought any books in my luggage. I did have my computer with reasonably decent Internet access, but between Facebook and *The New York Times* I might occupy two or maybe three hours of the day. What else was there to do besides sit around and brood?

But Sean is not the type of person to take no for an answer and shrug it off, so while I pondered ways that I could avoid this micro-vacation, a solution presented itself after morning rounds. I had emerged from the decontamination suite in my usual sweat-soaked state and looked up to find Sam Siakor staring back at me. "Doctor Steve," he said, "I would like for you to come to church with me on Sunday. We can get one of the drivers to take you into Gbarnga. Is that okay?" Well, I thought, there's my solution: A big chunk of my day off was going to be spent sitting in the pews of an African church, which from the standpoint of a visitor coming to a new country is awesome. It would be a field trip extraordinaire.

Sunday came and I made the half-hour trek to Gbarnga. Sam and I met, and he walked me around the Grace Baptist compound. Like many substantial structures that dotted the Liberian landscape, Grace Baptist showed the ravages of the Civil War, for it was obviously once a lovely building with a soaring interior, a pitched roof peaking at a height of more than twenty feet. Yet it had become shoddy and threadbare since its heyday, with missing doors, peeling paint, and a few broken windows to complete the picture. But the signs of slow rebirth were apparent as well, as I toured a construction area of what was to become a new elementary school. They were clearly finding their footing with limited financial means.

Eyes followed me everywhere I moved. Sam introduced me to the various dignitaries of the congregation: the assistant pastor, the lead pastor's wife, their family, the Sunday school principal. Children darted about, all stopping for one dumbfounded moment to see their visitor. A few of the more curious ones followed me around. Under normal circumstances I would sweep them up in my arms and turn myself into a one-man amusement-park ride for them, but I was hyper-conscious of the no-touch rule as I made my way amidst the bustle.

It felt especially strange to be offered a formal introduction to my hosts and not offer my hand in thanks and greeting, but I was confident they understood, even if the knowledge provided only a small amount of solace that such a simple gesture of respect had to be trampled upon.

I had arrived midway through the services, and we eventually entered the main chapel during a break in the action. The chapel was big, with sea-green paint illuminating the interior, accommodating enough seating for what I guessed was about three hundred people. Nearly all the pews were full. I was unsurprised to be placed in the front row. Before the service resumed, a thin man approached me with wide eyes and said, "Doctor Steve," expectantly. I had no idea who this was and quickly looked to Sam for help.

"It's Dennis," Sam said.

Dennis?

The Dennis I knew was from two weeks before. His clinical course had been typical for those who survived: He felt lousy for the first few days, then hurtled toward the abyss for the next three or four, and had his "crisis day" to which so many others had succumbed. When we returned the following morning, there he was, lying in bed and blinking at us, saying he actually felt a little better, and we knew he would walk out the front of the ETU instead of being borne out on a litter, shrouded in a body bag, through the back. That was followed by a gradual restoration to health, which included more than a week where he sat in the confirmed ward, perfectly healthy but still with detectable virus in his blood and therefore still potentially infectious, but with very little to do. Dennis had requested a Bible be brought into the ward, and during his convalescence he spent much time reading and preaching to his newfound, and quite captive, flock. Many members of the national staff would also congregate at the psychosocial workers' hut, which sat only feet away from the boundary of the confirmed ward, to hear his message.

So it shouldn't have been surprising for me to witness him here. However, as razor blades were rather frowned upon in the high-risk area, by the time I knew him Dennis had already sported a thick, bushy, white-and-gray beard. During the times when I made rounds while he preached, I couldn't help but think I was looking at Charlton Heston, tending to his flock of Israelites as they stood at the foot of Mount Sinai. Only the encampment was gravel bounded by plastic fencing, and Moses had dark brown skin.

That was the last image I had of Dennis, and in the two weeks that had passed, much had happened in the ETU and I had forgotten his face enough so that I could not process what he might look like without the beard. The Dennis of the ETU was almost prophet-like in his appearance; the Dennis in front of me was a lean, healthy-appearing man with a wide grin. As with the children, I had to stop myself from wrapping my arms around him in a giant bear hug out of the sheer joy of seeing one of my patients truly on the other side, back to something resembling a normal life, no longer tethered to that place of their nightmares, that place where I continued to work.

Dennis and I exchanged some pleasantries for a few moments, and then the service resumed. Unsurprisingly, there was much singing, but the organization of the service and its choral music was initially a curiosity, and then a fascination. For there were *two* choirs, each with its own particular structure and function within the service. To the right of the pulpit stood the English choir: a group of about twenty people, both men and women, dressed in Sunday finery. A young man in his twenties sat in front playing an electronic keyboard that added music through a temperamental speaker, and next to him was the choir director. They sang nineteenth-century hymns that could be found in many mainline Protestant white churches in the United States or the UK. They were sung with an African inflection, but the music was purely Western in structure, and I was able to follow along in the hymnal and sing them without much trouble.

On the opposite side of the pulpit, however, stood an altogether different group known as the Dialect Choir. This smaller group, about twelve in all, was all women and had no director. The service was vibrantly punctuated by their songs, as they turned the words of the Bible into their native Kru, Bassa, and Kpelle languages. Content-wise, it was standard church fare: At one point Sam casually mentioned that one of the leads was telling the story of David and Bathsheba, and I wished that some of my more religious Christian friends from youth could have joined me on this church excursion to witness this choir sing about King David in this particular way.

The music of the Dialect Choir was simply breathtaking. The tonality of the music was completely different, sounding almost but not quite like a minor key that would veer into something else. Usually there was one lead who would "sing" while the other women chanted in the background. Only it wasn't quite singing. It wasn't quite yelling. It was something in between and yet more. I kept searching my brain for a way to describe the not-exactly-singing-not-exactly-speaking quality, and the best I could come up with was the vocal style of someone like Bob Dylan or Tom Waits, but the pitch was much higher. The words, the sounds, the spirit were from somewhere else entirely. I had never heard anything like it. I wouldn't describe it as pleasant, but it definitely wasn't *un*pleasant, and it was most certainly compelling. I resisted the temptation to take out my smartphone and open a recording program.

These two choirs, both in some sense complementary but also in conflict with one another, couldn't have provided a better representation of the kind of split personality that constituted Liberia. It was like watching their history play out over the course of the service, a demonstration of ontogeny-recapitulates-phylogeny as ecumenical exercise. Here was this church, Grace Baptist Church, bearing the exact same name as a church from my hometown of Mansfield, Ohio, with its mission written right into its name, a flock searching for divine favor, deep in its belief of the redemptive power of purification through the immersion of baptism. It was a church in some ways indistinguishable from its Ohio cousin, the worldview of the parishioners shaped by stories compiled long ago in a land far from either congregation. Yet Grace Baptist in Gbarnga was also very much of Africa, and the tribal culture lived on inside this new and alien religion, its animistic DNA incorporating itself into a Western faith that was at once liberating and oppressive. Appreciate these two choirs and the tension inherent in their different aesthetic messages, and you know something essential about Liberia.

After we were treated to David and Bathsheba, the congregation settled itself into the next phase of the service: the reading of the

Gospel, followed by the Pastor O'Malley Moore Segbee's homily. Although I only rarely find myself in a church, I had been to enough services to have a general feel for the flow of the morning, and I eagerly waited to see what part of the Bible was going to be read, since my acquaintance with the New Testament was fairly limited. My enthusiasm quickly turned to shock, however, for the text of the day was from Revelation. We were going to read about the opening of the seven seals.

I *was* familiar with this particular text, because I had read Revelation carefully as a teenager. Growing up Jewish in Mansfield sometimes felt a little like being a six-fingered person: I was for the most part treated just like everyone else, but the recognition that I was *different* would sometimes bubble up as classmates gave voice to a number of misconceptions, most of them trivial, but some of them disturbing—as in, "your people killed Jesus Christ," a fact my Sunday school teachers had neglected to mention, and thus was something of a surprise to me. Trying to understand what made Christian and Jewish theology different became a priority for me in those years, and Revelation seemed a logical place to start.

The portion that they were to read is in the early chapters of the book and describes the unwrapping of a unique scroll held in God's right hand. In order to expose the scroll, seven seals must be opened, a feat accomplished by a seven-eyed, seven-horned lamb. Each successive opening of the seals unleashes a judgment upon the world. These passages provide some of the most vivid visions of Christian apocalyptic language.

They read:

> And I saw when the Lamb opened one of the seals, and I heard, as it were the noise of thunder, one of the four beasts saying, Come and see.
>
> And I saw, and behold, a white horse: and he that sat on him had a bow; and a crown was given unto him: and he went forth conquering, and to conquer.
>
> And when he had opened the second seal, I heard the second beast say, Come and see.
>
> And there went out another horse that was red: and power

*was given to him that sat thereon to take peace from the
earth, and that they should kill one another: and there was
given unto him a great sword.*

*And when he had opened the third seal, I heard the third
beast say, Come and see. And I beheld, and lo a black horse;
and he that sat on him had a pair of balances in his hand.*

*And I heard a voice in the midst of the four beasts say, a
measure of wheat for a penny, and three measures of barley
for a penny; and see thou hurt not the oil and the wine.*

The reading continued through the chapter, and then the pastor
ascended the stage for his homily, during which he reflected on the
passages, occasionally asking the assistant pastor to read back from a
particular verse. Listening to the words of John of Patmos, who had
committed them to parchment nearly two thousand years before, I
gradually became more and more uneasy as I heard the words spill
from the pulpit.

*And when he had opened the fourth seal, I heard the voice of
the fourth beast say, Come and see.*

*And I looked, and behold, a pale horse: and his name that
sat on him was Death, and Hell followed with him. And
power was given unto them over the fourth part of the earth,
to kill with sword, and with hunger, and with death, and with
the beasts of the earth.*

What was the pastor thinking? I could imagine people back in the
States sitting around at some dinner party when talk would turn to
what was happening in Liberia at that very moment, with someone
describing it as "a disaster of biblical proportions," using the phrase
mostly for emphasis and effect. Yet this really *was* a calamity that
many Liberians would instinctively think of in biblical terms, for they
believed in the Bible in a way that all but the most hard-line of funda-
mentalists in the United States did not. As we sat there, Liberia had
been slowly imploding over about four months, and everyone sitting
here knew it. How could these faithful not think of this moment as

anything other than God's wrath visited upon them? A new virus as exotic to them as it was to any American had been unleashed, and now even the most remote villagers knew something novel in its wickedness lurked in the countryside. Some Liberians still didn't believe in Ebola, but by mid-October, more and more people did, and they had a powerful template on which they could interpret the data. How could they not think that perhaps the End of Days was upon them, with the final battle between good and evil to commence?

And *if* those thoughts had flashed through their minds—which, though I am not Liberian and do not claim to be an expert on Liberian thought, seemed an entirely sensible chain of reasoning—then what other evidence could support this view? Could the fire that God was to unleash on Gog and Magog at the Battle of Armageddon really be the burning fever of Ebola? Was not the pale horse at full gallop throughout the Liberian countryside, to say nothing of Sierra Leone and Guinea, taking care to make a special, daily visit to the hilltop where I worked?

And if *that* were true, that people conversant with Scripture and believers in the prophecies of Revelation could infer that the End of Days were indeed upon us, then wasn't it also reasonable to assume that they might no longer be interested in the minutiae of everyday living? We trudge to the markets, throw out our refuse, quarrel with neighbors, perform kindly acts to strangers, and pay our taxes to the government all as part of our routine. This is as true in the tony suburbs of Boston as it is in the far-flung reaches of the interior of a small West African nation.

But if that routine should be so upended—by, say, the end of the world being nigh—then why bother? If the rapture really is around the corner, does it matter much if we follow the rules that create the hive of human activity we call "society"? God will sort 'em all out, and soon we and our loved ones will be in heaven. To hell with the others. Literally.

Surely that's a logical thought process if one truly believes that an unprecedented Ebola outbreak is the manner by which God's Revelation is taking place. These questions were furiously assembling in my head as the pastor churned through the verses and meditated on their meaning. More than once I found myself turning around to see just how this message was being received.

> *And when he had opened the fifth seal, I saw under the altar the souls of them that were slain for the word of God, and for the testimony which they held:*
> *And they cried with a loud voice, saying, How long, O Lord, holy and true, dost thou not judge and avenge our blood on them that dwell on the earth?*
> *And white robes were given unto every one of them; and it was said unto them, that they should rest yet for a little season, until their fellowservants also and their brethren, that should be killed as they were, should be fulfilled.*

Fortunately, the pastor's homily went on *forever*. He passed the ten-minute mark as if he hadn't taken a breath, and seemed as if he was just warming up to his subject at twenty minutes. Combined with the ambient temperature—it was well over ninety degrees Fahrenheit outside, and this was a packed room full of people making it hotter still inside, with only a few ineffectual fans to put any kind of a dent in the mugginess—the congregants started to do what congregants around the world do in such situations: They politely and subtly, but gradually and definitively, tuned him out. I turned to my right to see Sam's eyelids grow heavy. At the half-hour mark, I glanced over my shoulder and surveyed the room to see the vast majority of people in a not-quite-comfortable Sunday late-morning doze. What a picture this must constitute, I thought: a West African pastor talking about the end of the world, his flock at least three hundred strong, all more or less in the midst of a collective nap, while his most keen listener, who was sitting bolt upright with eyes darting from the pulpit to the verses at the end of the King James Bible, happened to be a white, atheist Jew.

> *And I beheld when he had opened the sixth seal, and, lo, there was a great earthquake; and the sun became black as sackcloth of hair, and the moon became as blood;*

And the stars of heaven fell unto the earth, even as a fig tree casteth her untimely figs, when she is shaken of a mighty wind.

And the heaven departed as a scroll when it is rolled together; and every mountain and island were moved out of their places.

And the kings of the earth, and the great men, and the rich men, and the chief captains, and the mighty men, and every bondman, and every free man, hid themselves in the dens and in the rocks of the mountains;

And said to the mountains and rocks, Fall on us, and hide us from the face of him that sitteth on the throne, and from the wrath of the Lamb:

For the great day of his wrath is come; and who shall be able to stand?

It wasn't until the pastor reached the discussion about the sixth seal, nearly an hour into his discursion, that I finally grasped his point. *What* was the great earthquake? Well, he noted, many people thought it was the San Francisco earthquake of 1906—the fact that many people thought this was a bit of a surprise to me—but then a long explanation ensued about how it was actually the Anchorage earthquake of 1964 because it fell on Good Friday. Not much known outside of Alaska, the Anchorage '64 event measured 9.2 on the Richter scale, which was more than one hundred times stronger than the San Francisco 1906 trembler. I had happened to read Simon Winchester's book *A Crack in the Earth* about the San Francisco quake only a few months before, hence my knowledge.

The point he was making, as best I understood, was that because the Anchorage earthquake happened about sixty years after the *supposed* opening of the sixth seal, we've got the chronology all messed up. The breaking of the seventh seal isn't nigh; it's still way off in the future. Ebola, in other words, was not a herald of the end of the world. It was God's judgment, to be sure, just not God's *final* judgment. Everyone: At the end of this service, please go back to your homes, your jobs, your routines, and resume your lives. The message was as Byzantine as the language of the Book of Revelation itself, especially because he never once said the word Ebola in his talk, and this all had to be inferred. But as he reached his conclusion, I found myself comforted by the whole theological exercise.

After the homily, they asked people to give testimonials. I was more than a little surprised when Sam told me to stand up and tell the pastor my name. I dutifully did so, and some nice words were said about me. *Then* they asked me to come forward and talk about Ebola. There I stood, not at all sure what people knew and what they didn't, terrified I was going to say something Very Wrong, hoping I wasn't going to commit some unspeakable faux pas by, say, discussing body fluids, maybe a taboo topic in a church, when mentioning the vomit and diarrhea of Ebola. But that was the disease; how could I not? The only optimistic thought flashing through my head was that, based on my time at the ETU, up-country Liberians find it quite difficult to understand American English, and it was much easier for me to understand them. Maybe I would put them back to sleep, though somehow I doubted this.

I took a gamble and decided to start off by playing to the crowd. "Ladies and gentlemen, I want you to know that we are in the midst of the strongest man in Liberia. Dennis, will you stand up?" I gestured to Dennis, who stood up, and I asked we all acknowledge his bravery. Dennis had spoken earlier in the service, even taking a moment to tease me publicly about how I cajoled him to take his medications when he was in the unit. The fact that he had been embraced by the church leadership and proudly displayed as a survivor, rather than treated with suspicion and contempt, was perhaps the single most impressive display of this group of believers. Other survivors throughout the three countries were not always so lucky. A round of enthusiastic applause ensued.

With the crowd warmed up and, I hoped, open to my message, I told them about how I came to Liberia the year before and met Dr. Borbor, and I felt I had to come back to help once he died. I had no idea how that was received since everyone sat there silent, staring at me. I then told them about very basic infection control: Glove up and protect yourself if someone gets sick and sweats or throws up or has diarrhea, a *lovely* topic to discuss when everyone was dressed in their Sunday best. Though while I said this, I began to wonder, *What if there might not be any gloves to be had since the aid organizations have bought them all up?* I happened to work in a place that could implement maximum infection-control procedures without any thought of cost or availability; what could these parishioners do to protect themselves in Gbarnga, a town that was hours from the capital, in a country where supply lines had been severely stressed by the outbreak? Was I just another clueless American giving pie-in-sky advice?

I had little time to ponder this as the service wrapped up, after which I was ushered outside for a series of pictures with various church leaders. And then, before I could process any of what had just happened, I was whisked back into one of IMC's cars and was on my way back to Cuttington.

The car ride took maybe forty-five minutes, and even across cultural divides I'm typically a chatty person, but I spent that time silently mulling over the implacability with which that congregation had politely absorbed a message about the end of the world. *The end of the world.* The *literal* end. The evidence was all around them. Friends, neighbors, and members of their families had either been sent to our ETU to take their chances or were being rounded up in the holding centers by their own local politicians who were eager to curry favor with the national government, the international media, and the aid organizations. That didn't include those who had *already* died of the disease. The parishioners in Gbarnga would have been more than justified in thinking that every man, woman, and child was going to end up in one of those places eventually. In short, the environment could have easily been described as apocalyptic. How could they have looked around at what was happening to them and bear this cataclysm with such equanimity and gracefully receive one of its white-skinned alien messengers?

The answer, I thought, was that they *already* had witnessed the end of the world, and yet, here they still were. In the West, we call it the Liberian Civil War.

To say that story is a little complicated is an understatement. I'm going to make my best attempt at simplifying it here. Trying to keep track of the three-dimensional chessboard of the myriad groups and players involved in the Civil War makes following internecine political squabbles in the United States feel like a game of checkers. However, without at least a general idea of what the Civil War was about, a critical part of the Ebola story doesn't make any sense.

Traditionally, the date given for the start of the Civil War is December 24, 1989. On that day, a group of a few hundred insurgents belonging to a group known as the National Patriotic Front of Liberia, or NPFL, moved across the river that separates Ivory Coast from Liberia's Nimba County. From there, the fighting expanded outward and raged for the next fifteen years. Each act of war was met with a retaliation even more violent—and, ultimately, savage—leading to an ever-worsening feedback loop that would decimate the country, destroying virtually every part of the infrastructure and ripping apart its social fabric. When Liberians emerged from the generation-long nightmare in the early 2000s, they would be forced to rebuild their entire society almost completely from rubble.

But to get a better sense for what kind of butchery was in store for the country, one might look to events five years before. In 1985 President Samuel Doe had bowed to international pressure to hold elections. The pressure mainly came from the United States, without whose support Doe was finished, so elections it would be. Doe's principal rival was a man named Jackson Doe, of no relation to the president. Jackson Doe was the son of a Gio tribal chief from Nimba County, but because of political connections, he had been raised and supported by wealthy and powerful Americo-Liberians, who paid for his education at the University of Liberia, a degree from which was an exceedingly precious commodity in Liberian society, as it provided the key to open the doors of social advancement. Though not an Americo himself, Jackson Doe nevertheless had ascended through the ranks of the True Whig Party during the 1970s, becoming the country's minister of education, and represented in essence the kind of gradual progress that was taking place under President William Tolbert.

Then came the coup. As a high-ranking member of the now-deposed government, Jackson Doe was initially imprisoned in Monrovia but was later released by now-president Samuel Doe, and he returned to Nimba County. Over the next five years, President Samuel Doe's administration proved itself to be at least as corrupt as and even more ineffectual than the True Whigs who had come before. Embezzlement was endemic. Its most talented purveyor was Charles Taylor, who had been appointed by President Doe to be the director general of the General Services Agency—a position that made him essentially the Liberian government's purchaser in chief. Taylor had skimmed the cash and cooked the books, making deposits in an American bank account estimated to be around $1 million. He was eventually found out and charged, and fled to the States in 1984. By that time, the United States was applying heavy diplomacy to persuade President Doe to hold elections, and he reluctantly agreed.

Because of his experience and education, Jackson Doe was a natural choice for president, and he became Samuel Doe's principal opponent. It was clear, however, that Samuel Doe never intended to relinquish power. In an election universally deemed fraudulent by the international community, the president was reelected, and Jackson Doe remained in Nimba County to take his lumps.

Enter Thomas Quiwonkpa. Quiwonkpa was one of the original members of commandoes who had staged the coup five years before. He was generally seen as a competent soldier, the real orchestrator of the military in the early days of the junta. He was President Samuel Doe's close confidant until Doe started to consolidate power by eliminating rivals. President Doe executed two important members of the People's Redemption Council (the body that had taken over the government from the True Whigs in the aftermath of the coup) and eventually had Quiwonkpa removed from his post as commanding general of the Liberian army. Seeing the writing on the wall, in 1983 Quiwonkpa fled with many of his fellow Gio tribe members who had served as his military protégés.

When the 1985 election was stolen from the challenger, Jackson Doe, Quiwonkpa returned from exile to support Jackson, who was a fellow Gio, and his claim to the presidency by launching a coup against Samuel Doe. The group Quiwonkpa founded to achieve this aim was named the National Patriotic Front of Liberia—the same NPFL that would be headed by Charles Taylor, also a Gio, a few years later. But the coup attempt was botched. The United States, for all its frustration with the president, was not yet prepared to gamble on a new administration that might not be friendly to American interests—the irony being that its support of the corrupt and increasingly inhumane Samuel Doe was sending opposition into the arms of American adversaries on the world stage. Regardless of the lack of long-term wisdom of that calculation, when the NPFL fighters started their uprising in Nimba County, U.S. embassy officials tipped off President Doe, who immediately dispatched his most trusted generals in the Armed Forces of Liberia to crush the rebellion in a swift stroke. They were defeated quickly and with ease.

Two separate but equally important features were on display in the immediate aftermath of the brief, ill-starred Quiwonkpa uprising that would define the depths of the brutality, savagery, and self-destructiveness of what was to come five years later.

The first feature could be seen in what happened to Quiwonkpa himself. Unlike the members of the Tolbert government, who in 1980 were simply executed by a firing squad and were never to be seen again, Quiwonkpa suffered a much more humiliating fate. Although the precise mode of his death is unknown, after his body was retrieved, it was publicly mutilated, with Samuel Doe's troops dragging it through the streets of Monrovia. Parts of his body were hacked off by the men. Some kept them as souvenirs, while others ate them, believing the act of cannibalism of a great warrior's body would increase their own strength. The idea took hold. Because only a scant number of reliable accounts were recorded during the Civil War, nobody knows exactly how frequently various forms of cannibalism were practiced, but what accounts do exist indicate the practice was common and became a matter of routine following "military victories," which were often nothing more than local slaughters with no real military objective.

The second feature involves President Doe's handling of ethnic tensions. Samuel Doe was a Krahn, and Quiwonkpa's coup attempt was seen as the collective act of the Gio tribe, and so the response was directed at the entire group. The reprisals of the Krahn against the Gio in the months that followed were ruthless and widespread. Members of a third tribe, the Mano, immediately became entangled. Both the

Gio and the Mano were subject to various murderous purges in the wake of the rebellion that were designed to discourage in the strongest terms any thought of resistance. Over the next several years, especially once the war began in earnest, each act of violence begat a response increasing in depravity. Moreover, each retaliation would land on more than just its intended target, and another tribe would find itself as collateral damage, leading that next tribe to feel it incumbent upon itself to respond with at least as much viciousness.

For instance, Nimbans of Gio or Mano descent were frozen out of any job involving civil service, and whatever government contracts existed were handed out to other groups. One of the main groups to which Samuel Doe sent the government's business was the Mandingo. The Mandingo weren't exactly a tribe in the same sense as the others but rather formed an ethnic minority throughout Liberia. They were Muslims whose origins aren't firmly established, but they regard themselves as the descendants and living remnants of the Mali Empire that had collapsed nearly four hundred years before. In some ways, the post-empire Mandingo were to West Africa what Jews had been to Europe during the Middle Ages; because of cross-border connections, they served as a minority who were more likely to be traders than farmers and thus performed critical tasks for local communities. The Mandingo served Doe's purposes well enough, but their elevated status under his administration would cost them dearly years later.

In the immediate wake of the 1985 elections, Samuel Doe tightened his grip on power, and the NPFL fighters who escaped the melee in Nimba County crossed back into the territory controlled by Ivory Coast. Five years later, on Christmas Eve, they returned, this time with Charles Taylor at their head. Taylor and his Gio-dominated NPFL subsequently established a base of operations in Nimba among Liberians, many of them Gio and Mano, who after years of repression were all too ready to throw off the yoke of Samuel Doe and his fellow Krahn. As he made his way deeper into Nimba after his Christmas entrance, no doubt carefully selected for maximal effect to a deeply religious populace, Taylor must have seemed like a literal savior to his fellow tribesmen, who hoped that he would chase off Doe and life would settle down again. That hope would be in vain.

Like the Ebola outbreak hitting Guéckédou, Taylor's entry into Liberia's history led to a series of events whose consequences could not have been foreseen, with each additional shockwave careening in some unanticipated direction, exponentially increasing the gloom that had accompanied Doe's reign. When the year 1990 began, Liberia was, however miserable, still a recognizable political entity. But as Taylor's position became stronger and his power increased, a gradual dissolution of even the most rudimentary forms of unity swept across the Liberian countryside.

Within months, signs that Taylor was no less treacherous than Doe began to surface, and the NPFL split. The splinter group was led by a man named Prince Johnson, and the group became known as the IN-PFL, with the additional *I* standing for "independent." Both the NPFL and INPFL moved on Monrovia. Since Doe, who treated other non-Krahn tribes not considerably better than the Gio and Mano, had few allies in the countryside, by September he was reduced to defending only a small portion of the capital, fighting Johnson, who held the North of the city, and Taylor, who held the East. By now, the war had become a serious regional matter, and so the strongest and wealthiest nation, Nigeria, sent the contingent known as ECOMOG to serve as peacekeepers.* For reasons that remain shrouded in mystery, Doe sought a meeting with the general in charge of the ECOMOG troops, but their compound was in territory held by Johnson. Doe may have thought that he was arriving under some form of truce, but Johnson,

---

* ECOMOG stands for Economic Community of West African States Community Monitoring Group. As an aside, among the many aspects of Liberian culture with which I became enamored is their impish and sardonic sense of humor. From what I can tell, Liberians love to be creative in providing alternate interpretations of national organizational acronyms. The military junta that Doe led was named the People's Redemption Council, but on the street this was renamed People Repeat Corruption. As Doe's tenure ended and the Civil War began, a group of exiled Liberian politicians claiming to represent the various Liberian political factions met in the Gambia to develop a power-sharing arrangement. They dubbed the conference Interim Government of National Unity, which cynical Monrovians almost immediately rechristened Imported Government of No Use. When the largely Nigerian forces of ECOMOG arrived, whose troops were only marginally better than the actual Liberian combatants during the Civil War since they displayed a special talent for looting privately owned goods, the locals took to calling them Every Car Or Moveable Object Gone. In the midst of the Ebola outbreak, the International Medical Corps was sometimes wryly referred to as International Money Comes!

described in nearly all accounts of the time as a dangerously erratic man prone to unexpected violent outbursts, did not. From Prince Johnson's point of view, Doe had basically delivered himself up on a silver platter.

Johnson then provided an object lesson to Samuel Doe in what it must have been like to be Thomas Quiwonkpa, to whom Doe's troops had done such unspeakable acts five years before. Doe was kept alive long enough to be mutilated—ears sliced off, shot in the leg, other parts of his flesh cut with knives—while Johnson presided over the event, drunk. Unlike Quiwonkpa's death, whose details are known only in print, Doe's end was recorded for posterity by a cameraman who videotaped the proceeding. In the early portion of the video, as Doe is being stripped of his uniform in the foyer of the ECOMOG headquarters, Johnson bellows at the assemblage, although the audio is too garbled to make out his meaning, while Jesus Christ quietly watches on from a portrait immediately behind him.*

From there, summarizing the plot of the Civil War in a few terse paragraphs is hopeless. By that point there were already three major players carving up Liberia—Taylor's NPFL, Johnson's INPFL, and Nigeria's ECOMOG. The Krahn tribal members who had been loyal to Samuel Doe were still around as well and armed to the teeth; to defend themselves and maintain what control they had over Liberian politics, they formed a group known as ULIMO. ULIMO had gathered the Krahn and the Mandingo under one banner, but the group would quickly split along ethnic lines into ULIMO-J and ULIMO-K. Regardless, both ULIMO groups were aided by tribal and ethnic connections in Sierra Leone, a fact that did not go unnoticed by Charles Taylor, which led to the war spilling over the border. He would sponsor his own group in Sierra Leone that went by the name the Revolutionary United Front, and their creation would beget the Sierra Leone Civil War, which started in 1991 and lasted more than ten years. All these groups would engage in massacres and reprisals that eventually left no tribe or portion of Liberia free from some form of tragedy.

---

* Johnson continues to reside in Liberia and serves as the senior senator from Nimba County.

In contrast to Prince Johnson, Charles Taylor was not an unstable man. He was handsome, articulate, and capable of genuine charm. Videos of him on YouTube giving interviews reveal a man who could easily run for a U.S. congressional seat and give many a politician a good run for their money. In one, he easily bats away a question about the circumstances of his detention in the United States in 1984 after fleeing from Doe's justice on the charge of embezzlement. "Oh, I was not held in the United States for any crime," he says with a wave of his hand—and it's a convincing performance, despite being a completely preposterous claim, as he was arrested in the States for extradition back to Liberia. (He would later escape custody, and he resurfaced in Libya to begin his military training that paved the way for him to take control of the NPFL.) The reporter eagerly swallows this answer without even a hint of skepticism. It's like watching a CNBC interview of some uber-wealthy business executive spouting complete nonsense about his company.

But whatever his charms, Taylor was calculating and ruthless. As the war dragged on into the mid-1990s and tens of thousands of people, especially adults, fell victim to the fighting, an enormous group of orphaned children began to appear throughout the countryside. Taylor saw this effect not as a lamentable by-product of war but as a material advantage from which he could leverage his power. The NPFL increasingly sought out these children and incorporated them into their structure, providing them the stability of a family that they no longer had and the comfort of having a purpose in life, the purpose being advancing Charles Taylor's interests.

They became known as the Charles Taylor Boys, and there were thousands of them. He fed them fufu, ganja, and alcohol. Because they grew up knowing only war, and an exceptionally horrific one at that, where atrocity lost its ability to shock and instead became part of the daily humdrum routine, these boys had been conditioned to show little respect for the value for life, theirs or anyone else's. They were often in charge of manning roadblocks in the highly partitioned countryside, where they would kill on the most trivial of pretexts, without hesitation or remorse. One of the Taylor Boys, a soldier who went by the "name" of Young Killer, manned a checkpoint and distributed the most severe and arbitrary justice imaginable. Once he lined up a group of people seeking to pass, said, "I like the number twenty," and started counting from the back of the line, shooting the twentieth person dead on the spot and letting the others pass. The checkpoints themselves often displayed trophies of skulls stacked atop one another, and at least one report surfaced that a checkpoint "rope," used to indicate the vehicle should stop or face severe consequences, was made of human intestine. There were thousands of Taylor Boys, and those who survived would be mostly in their thirties today.

The Charles Taylor Boys were only one small part of this generation-long nightmare. Indeed, Taylor himself was only one piece of the puzzle. All of the groups competing with Taylor's NPFL for control of Liberia were savage in equal measure; Taylor was merely the most successful and most calculating of the various faction leaders in the Civil War. But the international media, especially the U.S. media, needed to find a simple story line for Americans who would be distracted and annoyed by all the complexities. Thus, to economize the plot, Taylor was cast as chief villain, especially by the end of the bloody conflict in the early 2000s. That Taylor had, for instance, managed to accrue and maintain his power by a quiet but mutually beneficial arrangement with Firestone Corporation to keep the rubber flowing out of Liberia did not make front-page news, although eventually that story got told.*

So for anyone who was casually following headlines from this part of the world, the story was Taylor=monster=Civil War, which meant that his removal would quickly resolve all of Liberia's ugly conflicts. That was how I would have described it if pressed. It's true that Taylor really was a greater menace than his adversaries, but it wasn't because of his propensity for cruelty. Rather, Taylor was simply a better manager than the other warlords, equipped with the predisposition of an MBA in the implementation of devastation. (Had he stayed in the United States, where such instincts might have been channeled toward more productive ends, one wonders whether he'd be sitting at

---

* A useful hour can be spent watching *Frontline*'s special "Firestone and the Warlord," made in conjunction with ProPublica. It is wise not to eat prior to the screening.

the end of an oak-paneled boardroom as a CEO of a Fortune 500 company.)

One other point about Taylor: Prior to his occupation of the presidential palace in Monrovia, his headquarters were located in Gbarnga, the unexciting little provincial town in which I found myself that morning. Gbarnga served as a staging point for military thrusts to the south on Monrovia, as well as to the north into Sierra Leone, whose supply of arms and diamonds was bringing it deeper into the conflict. Cuttington University, which had closed down, was frequently used as a training base. I knew none of this the first time I was in Gbarnga, but was beginning to understand it by the time I returned several months later.

If you had found yourself nervously moving through an airport concourse in the fall of 2014, wondering whether you might be taking your chances by brushing past some people incubating a deadly virus, perhaps an African family, en route to your gate, or if you had lived in the Dallas area, or if you had lived in Ohio, the state to which one of the nurses that Thomas Eric Duncan had infected had flown home for a visit, or if you were among the tens of millions living in metropolitan New York in the days following the discovery of an Ebola case there—in short, if you fit *any* of these descriptions, your anxieties were due to events taking place in Africa that had gotten out of control in no small part because of the repercussions of the Civil War, an event the U.S. government, however unbenign in its motivations, had clearly not intended but had nevertheless fomented and exacerbated. There was almost no running water for the average Liberian following the Civil War, there was little health-care and surveillance infrastructure following the Civil War, there was exceedingly little trust in government announcements following the Civil War, and no functioning professional press corps who could serve as an alternate source of news to word of mouth.

All of these were critical ingredients that fed the growing conflagration of the Ebola crisis, so even a cursory examination of the war's consequences might help frame the events taking place in late 2014. I have begged the reader to indulge me in this brief detour into the Civil

War, which I have massively oversimplified here in just a few dense paragraphs, for a few reasons.

The first is that by specifically demonizing Taylor, the impression that Liberia had rid itself of evil and been taken over by angels, in effect just picking itself up and carrying none of the baggage from that event, is naïve in the extreme. But that is to some extent how the story was portrayed. Taylor may have been the war's poster child for inhumanity, but he was not its instigator and does not represent its last breath. Moreover, his NPFL lived on, and the remnants of that party still hold much sway in the current government.

The Nobel Peace Prize–winning Ellen Johnson Sirleaf, Liberia's current president and long a darling of the international community for serving as the only democratically elected female African head of state, was a high-ranking member of the NPFL during the run-up to the Civil War. She would eventually break with Taylor before the worst of the atrocities began, but it's not clear precisely how many abominable acts she had been aware of during her time with NPFL. None of which is to take away from President Sirleaf's accomplishments. For instance, after the West Point disaster, Sirleaf herself went to visit the mother of the boy who had been shot by the soldiers, a bold move that helped calm Monrovia in its most desperate hour, which indicates the woman's mettle and leadership. But the circumstances of Sirleaf's rise to power helps to contextualize her accomplishments and gives a sense of the environment in which she continues to work.

The second is that the barbarism, of which I have related a miniscule amount, was beyond anything by which we typically measure human suffering in war. Even the most notorious industrial-grade genocides of the twentieth century—about which my people know a thing or two—lacked a viciousness that was commonplace during these years. So many of the killings that took place seemed to be exercises in one-upmanship in just how outrageous the snuffing of a human life could be. *Snuff* seems an apt word, for indeed some of the descriptions of murder simply defy belief. One of the more colorful figures from the Civil War was General Butt Naked, whose given name is Joshua Milton Blahyi. He earned his name by launching himself and his followers into battle entirely nude except for shoes and weaponry in the belief that this would make them impervious to bullets. To prepare for battle, the general typically would abduct children, often young girls, to be sacrificed for their blood, which was then drunk for its magical properties.

Blahyi, who is a year or two younger than me, lives today in greater Monrovia and is a Christian preacher with hundreds of followers. His notoriety in the West, in the electronic age, has brought a constant stream of vociferous criticism, which leads to a daily exercise in truth and reconciliation on his part. "Most of the time they get me on Facebook, they see me on Facebook. They ask me to be their friends, only to insult me," he said to the television crew of VICE News in 2013. "And I keep telling them that they would have never known if I never said it. There are a lot of people today who did worse than me, and they are in the government. They are holding national seats. And the nation accepts them like that. And they see them as heroes." It is not merely the nation that accepts such a simplified version of the story. It is much of the world community.

The third, and perhaps most important, consequence of the Civil War is that almost every person in my midst on that Sunday in Gbarnga had seen those days. What did they do to survive? What did they do to *others* to survive?

And how would that affect their interpretation of Pastor Segbee's homily, and of the Book of Revelation itself?

During the time I had been contemplating the meaning of Revelation in Gbarnga, a more hopeful event was taking place at the ETU. Over the weeks that I had been working there, a host of dignitaries, from prominent Liberian politicians to U.S. Army generals and Navy admirals to leaders in global health, to say nothing of a bevy of journalists from around the world, had visited the Bong facility, meeting with Sean and Pranav to discuss the manner by which they had gotten the ETU up and running, and thus far had been doing so with a fair amount of success. But that Sunday, the biggest VIP of all showed up for a tour: Samantha Power, the U.S. ambassador to the United Nations. It was going to be a *big* media day for IMC. I was perfectly happy to avoid the circus, although I did feel more than a little regret at not being able to meet Power, for she had become something of a hero to me over the preceding few months.

At a moment when world leaders were all running for political cover, Power was using her soapbox at the UN to urge the international community to step up its response, saying that they weren't just losing the race to Ebola but were getting lapped. At the time, such frank pronouncements showed real courage—especially by someone working for an administration that had had some difficulties convincing a shockingly substantial portion of the electorate that the president was not a practicing Muslim and citizen of Kenya. I hardly knew Power's name before the outbreak, but after watching a few interviews and reading a few articles on her work on forcing the UN to respond to the Ebola crisis, I had become a fan.

And now she was really putting her money where her mouth was: She had hopped a plane and flown right into the jaws of the beast, setting out on a breakneck four-day, three-country tour. From where I stood, one couldn't learn much in that stretch of time, given that it almost takes a full day just to recover from the jet lag. Then again, just *seeing* the place improves one's understanding by an order of magnitude, so perhaps her already keen insight became even better informed.

But the real value of having someone of Power's caliber on the ground was the media entourage, and especially its television cameras, for which I felt skepticism or even outright hostility. The truth was that cameras would follow a person of this stature and would become part of the larger Ebola story, serving as a counterweight to the stories of fear and death. And for that, I was more than pleased that she had come.

The next day was back to work, but during the late morning lull a few people had checked their laptops to see how the Power visit was playing back home. Not everyone from the ETU had been pleased by her presence. She had come to the unit, that much was true. But she and her staff had made the decision not to enter the work area proper—I don't mean the Hot Zone, which was obviously out, but rather the low-risk area that was no more or less dangerous than standing where she stood at the outer wooden fence. Among other things, it meant that she could not get anywhere close to the patients to find out how they were doing and ask them directly what was being done for them, how they regarded their experience, and generally hear whatever thoughts they cared to offer. By not entering the work area, the closest she could get to the Hot Zone was about half the length of a basketball court; had she entered, she could have casually conversed with actual patients at a distance of her choosing, as close as about four feet.

To at least a few of the staff who were present, Power's decision to stand at the outer fence seemed more than faintly ridiculous, since it increased her risk of Ebola infection by approximately zero, but just the *perception* back home that she was being cavalier about her travel was enough to keep her at an unfortunate remove from the action and created the idea that this substantive visit was a bit of a farce. Politicians of the Republican persuasion back home had been sharpening their knives for weeks, and any misstep by Power during such a bold move could add to the president's woes as the Democrats tried to hold on to the Senate and contain what were sure to be losses to the Republican majority in the House. They did lose control of the Senate a few weeks later, a reversal that allowed me to write one of my finest status updates ever on Facebook: "The realization that you are happier to be in the midst of an Ebola outbreak in West Africa than in the U.S. the day after midterm elections."

From where I stood, her hypocrisy seemed a very small price to pay for the big benefit of changing the tone of the news coverage, but it rankled some. One nurse quipped with more than a touch of bitterness about what appeared at first glance to be a touching moment. Power had seen one of our young boys in the confirmed ward saluting this important American who had come to visit, and delighted, she returned the salute. Only it wasn't a salute. "He was squinting and shading his eyes to see what all the commotion was," the nurse said. "He was just keeping the sun out of his eyes." And there, I thought, was a metaphor for our self-perception of our good intentions, and I wondered what signals I had similarly misconstrued over the course of my time here.

The ETU had opened for business right around September 15, and the first two physicians to staff the place were Pranav and an ER doc who worked at Brown University named Adam Levine. They had not only overseen the medical operations during the first two weeks but had been around throughout September overseeing the construction, the staff training, and all the other details that would go into running our little hospital on the hill. Colin came at the end of Adam's stint, and Steve and I arrived just after his departure. Since the day we arrived, we had informally agreed to a schedule where Steve took the nights and Colin and I staggered the time we arrived during the days, usually with Colin working a swing shift that overlapped the two. To the best of my knowledge, everyone was content with that plan, and we never had any long discussions about changing things around. The nurses, by contrast, staggered their shifts into morning/afternoon–evening/night blocks. They would rotate with one another, working three or four days at one time, taking a well-earned day off to recharge, and then advancing to the next shift. Though theirs was a different system, it seemed like a happy arrangement.

Sean, however, wanted to make sure that everyone got the full experience and announced that we would be swinging our shifts so that we could observe the ETU operations at all hours. It is also possible that Pranav had a hand in this policy. By late October, he had returned from his R & R to resume his work, which in addition to running the medical staff at the Bong ETU was increasingly consumed with setting up IMC's second ETU about three hours away in the town of Kakata, in Margibi County. As with our enforced day off, we protested to little avail. But we didn't care that much because we trusted the judgment of these guys with our lives.

So the three of us sat down to figure out how to spell one another while we made the switch without having to work a twenty-four-hour shift. I happen to *like* working twenty-four-hour shifts or even longer ones, at least once in a while, and always have since my medical school days. At the end of such a period, there's a euphoric feeling that I assume is not altogether different from a runner's high. It's one of the reasons I kept moonlighting well beyond my residency years, as it provides an odd feeling of accomplishment after having become symbiotic with a hospital for one full cycle. But working twenty-four consecutive hours here was out of the question. Walking into the Hot

Zone even a little groggy could quickly prove to be a lethal mistake, and so we performed some complicated scheduling algebra to switch ourselves around, and with a little more than a week to go in my deployment, I was about to show up for work after the sun had already gone down.

7

NIGHT

An ancient English law made it a crime to witness a murder or discover a corpse and not raise a "hue and cry." But we live in a world of corpses, and only about some of them is there a hue and cry.

—Adam Hochschild, *King Leopold's Ghost*

When I had returned from my little Gbarnga adventure, I was not quite refreshed, but I did feel as if a small weight had been lifted from my soul. I tend to assume the worst is going to happen, but by the end of the day, I realized that, at least with respect to one aspect of the West African Ebola outbreak, the worst *wasn't* going to happen. The worst would have been a Womey-style massacre in every major city across the region by the end of 2014. But I had gone to Gbarnga and sat through an orderly and sedate church service, in which a discussion about the End of Days was received with about as much anxiety as one devoted to Tupperware, yet no machetes were produced. I had concluded back in September that the fast track to a million deaths would much more likely involve the collapse of society, as the countries lost their collective faith in their institutions and one another, than from actual infections. However limited, there was evidence right in front of me that Liberia wasn't going to descend into that kind of anarchy.

As I began my night shifts a few days later, some news was filtering in that suggested optimism on other fronts might not be completely ridiculous either. Sheri Fink had returned to Monrovia to continue her reporting there, and she wrote a story noting a phenomenon that seemed too good to be true: There were fewer cases of Ebola being reported throughout Liberia. The Liberian Ministry of Health, the

World Health Organization, and the Centers for Disease Control—
each of which had by now imported small armies of personnel to
engage in detailed surveillance of the outbreak—could see ETU beds
only opening up, without replacements waiting in the wings to fill
them. The article reflected the tense balance of cautious optimism and
skepticism, noting that this downturn was either a very good sign, or,
mindful of what had taken place earlier in March, a very bad one. In
Bong County, our slightly smaller census appeared to be due to the
ambulance fleet requiring a one-day sabbatical for maintenance rather
than want of patients, and so I assumed this was some kind of epidemiologic optical illusion. The opinion among the rest of the staff was
divided.

That was the mood of the place when I began work the night shift.
Similar to the hospitals back in the States, the ETU at night had an
entirely different personality. The frenetic pace disappeared. The an-
cillary staff, performing all their essential but nonmedical duties, were
almost completely absent, though a few members of the sanitation
staff continued to work, mainly doing all of the laundering of the
scrubs that the staff wore during the day. The patients, most of whom
had struggled to maintain some form of normalcy in their daytime
existence, drifted off to sleep. Nearly everything fell into a lull.

Only the jungle's insects asserted themselves, as the night lit up
with chirps and clicks and clacks of dozens of species of African ar-
thropods. The electric lighting of the ETU proved an irresistible lure
for the winged insects. We tended to walk around the periphery of the
light to avoid having our heads assaulted by the various creatures,
ranging in size from that of a common gnat to a small bird. There was
a moth so large it could easily have been mistaken for a bat, and indeed the first night I spent some time watching the creature, finally
ruling that it was *not* actually a bat, although Pranav had given me a
preparatory course with one very emphatic roll of his eyes and the following quip when I told him that I'd soon be on nights: "Yeah. Watch
out for those moths."

The moth, however, was small fry compared to the real nighttime
terror, the flying rhinoceros beetle. Picture an insect with the subtlety
of a Sherman tank and the mobility of a B-29, and you've got an idea

of it. It was at least twice the size of the stag beetles that I encountered in my youth, with a third horn emerging from its head in addition to the two pincers that came from its jaws, making it look a little like a miniature triceratops. With wings, because it, you know, like, *flew*. Its spindly legs along its length had small claws that allowed it to hold onto trees in a vertical position despite its significant weight, which meant that it could also find a perch on just about anything—say, the scrubs on a human's leg. The discovery of one of these creatures attached to me proved an event sufficiently traumatic that I would gladly have run into the arms of a patient infected with Ebola to avoid it. Everyone found my little-girl screeches amusing when these bugs flew around the staff quarters. One of the expat nurses, a Kenyan named Perris Tabby, grabbed one of them one evening and placed it on top of the paperwork I was doing, with a sheet underneath it bearing the message, "Hi Steve! I missed you." A smiley face accompanied it. Mirth ensued.

Rounds lasted longer and had an easier pace to them, for dehydration was not a concern in the cooler nighttime temperatures. That meant I had more time to assess patients with greater care, to observe their bodies and pay attention to their diarrhea and their vomit. I had more time to talk to the patients, and I had more time to think about them. Which meant almost by definition that I had more time to brood.

Nighttime brought special challenges, however. It was *dark*. The lightbulbs threw little light, and the dark blue tarp seemed to soak up what light there was like a sponge takes up water, so moving about the high-risk area required even more attention and deliberation than it did during the day shift. Finding items in the stockroom could be an exercise in folly. Moreover, although donning PPE didn't induce the river of sweat that coated my eyeglasses and goggles during daytime hours, it was still warm enough that a hazy mist was produced, so everything appeared as if I was living inside a dark Monet painting. It certainly made hooking and unhooking the IV lines tricky.

We worked a skeleton crew: There were fewer nurse aides, which meant that there was more to be done in the way of basic care for the patients. One of the first nights on, I worked with a lead expat nurse named Kelly Suter. Kelly had come from Michigan with the most impressive health-care résumé imaginable for someone who hadn't yet turned thirty. She had done disaster response work during the Haiti earthquake as well as the ensuing cholera epidemic, had seen action in war-torn Southern Sudan, aided in the postwar rebuilding efforts in East Timor, and had a job at a tough city hospital in Pontiac, Michigan, all before coming to Bong County. Yet she still worked with as gentle and caring a manner as could be envisioned. You would want Kelly Suter to be your nurse.

Her cholera experience was perhaps the most amazing of these accomplishments. "I was sent to the northwest corner of Haiti with a manual about cholera and instructions to build a team to respond to the crisis," she told me when we shared our experiences to help pass the night hours. "There wasn't any training. I had to learn everything about cholera from that manual, and I had to learn everything about running a team just by doing it." This being asked of a woman in her mid-twenties who had never been to Haiti before the earthquake. It was there that she met Godfrey Oryem, where she supervised him and his WASH team. Now she was in the middle of something even deadlier than cholera.

We entered one night, just the two of us, to work in the suspect ward. There was a family, a mother with two children, one of them a toddler running a temperature of nearly 39 degrees (about 102 degrees Fahrenheit). Kelly was determined to get an IV line placed in this child so that we could hydrate her. A fever means fluid loss, and children lose a greater percentage of fluids than adults when they run a fever, so staying hydrated in such a situation is critical. Since I don't throw IV lines as part of my work and haven't done so for many years, there wasn't any point in me trying to attempt what Kelly could not accomplish, for it would be cruel to the child and dangerous to me and perhaps Kelly as well. So I held the child while she tried to get access, and the girl wailed so loud that I wondered if she could be heard in Monrovia. Because she had so much energy, and because her mother said that she had been holding down some fluids, we decided to leave it be after two attempts and would try again in the morning. Even in failure, given the dangers of trying to find a vein from an apoplectic and confused child bucking about in the dark, when one errant twitch could potentially lead to a needle stick injury with Ebola, it was a remarkable piece of nursing. Moreover, we did at least get enough blood to send off for the test the next day.

Then we were on to the next patient: a man in his forties who was obtunded. That's doctorspeak for confused and mentally altered. His loose pants were soiled with semisolid excrement, and he had moved about his bed, soiling the mattress as well. I didn't know what was causing his delirium, but I was reasonably confident that whatever it was, it wasn't Ebola, for an Ebola patient this sick should have been pouring out watery diarrhea instead of the brown paste that we needed to clean up. He would die the next day, the test negative, of what disease God only knows. At any rate, Kelly and I went about cleaning him, taking time to wash him down with care, soothing him in whatever ways we could as he loosed his grip on life. It took perhaps thirty minutes; during the day, I would never have had the chance to provide this kind of sustained attention to a patient's body and still make rounds, and the work would have gone to one of the national staff. Here it was a privilege. Strangely, this was among the happiest half hours of my time in the Hot Zone.

Next it was time for distributing medications to the patients. I approached a man in the adjacent room, about the same age, and this time I was fairly confident that I was looking at someone infected with Ebola and that his test would come back positive the next day. (I was right.) He had already gone into the throes of the wet symptoms, when diarrhea and vomiting come in wave after wave of wretchedness. I handed him his evening medications, a veritable pill bonanza. As he looked at the drugs I held in my hand I could feel his nausea, although he clearly wanted to prove that he would do anything to not be overtaken by this illness. I got into a catcher's stance to encourage him as best I could to take the meds. I held a large plastic bottle of water in one hand, almost spooning the meds into his mouth while I put the water to his lips to help him wash the pills down. Down they went, where they stayed for all of maybe ten seconds before coming back up in a miserable heave.

After medications, it was time for cleaning the commode buckets. I took them one by one, sloshing liquid filled with filoviral particles, to the latrines, where I would carefully dump them so as to avoid splatter, then slowly wash them in the bleach solution multiple times before returning them to their owners. I took the broom and swept the hallway before moving over to the confirmed ward for the same process. We emerged about three hours later, having not only worked with the patients but also having conversed with one another through the work just as we would have done at any typical hospital. Indeed, much of what I know about Kelly's life I learned that night.

I like being a doctor: I like the complex reasoning of differential diagnosis, the blending of physiology and molecular biology, the dove-tailing of cold, hard science with warm, soft pastoral care. I like it when I make good decisions and think through a difficult case, emerging on the other side with some ideas that make a difference for the better in the real world. This was just as true of my time at the Bong ETU as it was in all the years that preceded it.

That being said, I think one of my proudest accomplishments in my career thus far was the night I held a child who needed an IV line, cleaned up the shit of a confused man at the end of his life, handed out medications, and just tried to comfort my patients as best I could. One of my finest moments as a doctor was the night I was Kelly Suter's nurse's aide.

The night also brought one unexpected boon: The Internet access was flawless. By late October, the ETU information technology people had succeeded in installing a satellite dish. It looked quite impressive, though during the daytime the huge amount of data traffic streaming out of Liberia to the rest of the world made checking even the most low-bandwidth websites, such as those without graphics or streaming video, an exercise in tedium waiting for the page to load. But at night, as the electronic squawking of the nation settled into a dull hum and the airwave congestion dissipated, my laptop again became a window on the world. I caught up on all my work e-mail, wrote friends, was able to peruse Facebook. I devoured the online *New York Times*, finally reading about something *other* than Ebola, which was a delight and relief but was balanced by the annoyance that much of what I read was about the impending tidal wave of Republican know-nothings sweeping into power based in part on stoking the nativist hysteria that the West African outbreak had induced.

One night just past midnight I even had such a good connection that I managed to catch some face time with my children on Skype. A few hours before I did this, I had been sitting around with members of the national staff in the main workplace, a structure little more than twice the size of the medical staff offices that were about ten meters away. One of the pharmacists had started a discussion about salaries and ranks of pharmacists—and, by extension she argued, all professionals with advanced training. She complained that Liberian academic degrees, like those offered by Cuttington University, were considered inferior to those acquired abroad, especially degrees obtained in the United States. Why, she wondered, would the Ministry of Health treat people who had shown faith in the Liberian system of education with less respect than those who had fled? She was tired of Liberians being treated as second-class citizens, and it was high time that the government institute some policies designed to encourage and promote home-grown higher education.

The counterpoint was offered up by one or two members of the staff whom I did not know. They pointed out that the reason why education abroad was treated as something superior was because it *was* something superior, and would be for the foreseeable future. Only after a generation of Liberian professionals obtained their training at some of the better systems of higher education in the world would they have enough intellectual capital to reinvigorate Liberian colleges with highly skilled professors and deans. In the meantime, they argued, a Liberian degree wasn't up to snuff, and those going to a school like Cuttington or Dogliotti (Liberia's sole medical school) were just not coming out as thoroughly prepared for their jobs.

I watched the conversation proceed as it morphed from conjecture to discussion to argument, voices becoming raised with each response, the cadence of the language more emphatic, the gestures more assertive. I did something rather out of character; rather than insert myself directly in the conversation and offer up various ideas both for and against, instead I just sat and listened, trying to absorb not only the worldview of those involved but also how they interacted so that I understood at least a little of the culture of Liberian political discourse. My role was to be the pupil, and I stayed on the periphery, trying to remain as unobtrusive as possible—a feat that for me requires heroic levels of self-control—and quietly exited after I'd learned a little but before I was perceived as being something akin to a white spy.

I was there perhaps fifteen minutes and then I made my way across the compound to the medical staff quarters where I sat down with my laptop and got on Skype. It was the first time I had seen my family since coming to Liberia. I had mostly remained in radio silence save for a few one-way e-mails. I remained out of touch for the simple reason that I didn't want the distraction. Here I was treating kids and watching them die, and I wasn't sure how I would handle talking to my own kids or how such a conversation might affect the difficult work I was performing in the unit. I feared that my emotions would get the best of me, and above all else I was determined to remain as focused as possible during my deployment. But as I neared the end of five weeks, with little more than one week to go before jumping on a plane headed back Stateside, I figured a quick hello wouldn't compromise me.

The connection was so good it even allowed, at least for a few minutes, a video feed, and I swung the laptop around in my hands so that my daughter, Ariella, could go on a virtual tour of one small corner of the ETU. I spoke with my son, Erez, about what had been going on in school. The conversation proceeded over the next several minutes as we caught up on the events of the past month. They asked me a few questions about my work, and I asked them what the talk was like among their classmates about Ebola.

When I had left the national staff, the conversation had become fairly animated as each person tried to deliver the final, irrefutable argument that would bring the discussion to a QED close. As I made the call home, I thought I heard a lull but wasn't sure if I was just tuning it out. At any rate, as my conversation with my kids continued, it felt like the volume and the intensity of the other discussion suddenly made a quantum leap, and disagreement turned into outright yelling. I made a distracted face for a moment, briefly raised my head from the laptop to survey the noise, and then sighed as I went back to my electronic world.

But then, moments after returning to my family, I realized that the ever-rising volume had indeed turned to yelling. At first I was irritated, thinking, *Is it* really *that important to settle the question of Liberian postgraduate education once and for all while the worst Ebola out-break in history is still on, guys?* But then I listened more, and I realized it wasn't angry yelling but *frightened* yelling. A second later Perris came rushing in and said, "Johnson! He's on the road!" and ran right back out.

Johnson was one of the younger patients on the confirmed ward. All of eleven years, the wet symptoms had hit him hard. Usually the kids on the confirmed side, sometimes despite being quite ill, never-theless managed to rouse themselves each day to come out and sit in the plastic lawn chairs and watch the activity of the ETU. If they weren't seen outside, it was usually a predictor of their course, and many of them would die. When Johnson's test had first come back as positive, he was healthy enough to join his playmates, but as the days passed, his energy flagged, and he was seen less and less often, retreat-ing to his bed for ever-increasing amounts of the day.

Bleeding may be the manifestation that has earned Ebola its fear-some reputation, but after working in the ETU for weeks, we noticed two different signs that were more likely to occur in patients and held great predictive power. Just to see a patient with either of these symp-toms was enough to know their chances for survival were slim. The first was hiccups. We had long conversations about what this meant and why it was happening, but most patients who showed up hiccup-ping were not going to walk out the ETU front door.

The second sign was delirium. This happened usually right before the end. I saw maybe ten patients with delirium, and they all died. If you came in to round and asked a patient how they were feeling and received a nonsensical reply, it probably meant they had less than twenty-four hours to live. The most unnerving case of delirium I wit-nessed happened during my second week, when we admitted a man named Ballah. He was in his mid-thirties and had one of the most rapid deteriorations of all the patients we cared for, dying four days after his admission.

But the four days were eventful. After being sent to the confirmed ward, he began to behave erratically. He would wander around the hallway in a daze, telling the staff that he was going to kill himself, something no other patient did while I worked there. The disturbing quality of his behavior, however, morphed into alarm two days later when I walked in to find him dead. His body was at the end of the bed, legs planted on the ground, as if he was about to get up and walk around. While I was examining him, I noticed an object lodged in between the mattress and the frame. I reached for it and a moment later found myself holding the handle of a twelve-inch blade. We later concluded that the knife had accompanied him on admission to help him pare the rinds of the fruit his family had given him for sustenance. Tucked away in his plastic bag, nobody noticed it at the triage area. Had Ballah been cognizant that he possessed this weapon in his final days, he might have attacked any of the patients and staff. It was a sober reminder of the ways in which we could not anticipate the complications that might kill our patients or us.

By the time Perris came running in, Johnson had become equally delirious. I had seen him on rounds just before the Liberians' debate, and he was unable to respond when I talked to him, just staring back at me with wide eyes. As I headed back out to the low-risk area, I figured that I would find his body when I performed my early-morning rounds just before the day shift arrived.

Now Perris was informing me in the most urgent tones possible that Johnson in his delirium had summoned the energy to get up and go wandering through the compound. His path followed the precise opposite order by which we moved through the high-risk area, drifting his way back through the one-meter boundary and into the suspect ward area, turning to the triage hut instead of weaving into the suspect ward's hallway, Jesus be praised. From there he opened the swinging door to the fenced-in road where the ambulances brought patients, and was stumbling toward the beginning of the road where the one fuzzy boundary between Hot and Not existed at the ETU. He was within about three meters of being completely out in the open, within five meters of several of the staff, who until then had been hanging out in various shanties at the ETU's entrance used for guard duty.

I hastily finished my Skype conversation (*"Sorry, guys, something's up, gotta go!"*), slammed the laptop shut, and headed outside. The only advantage we had over Johnson was that he was barely strong enough to stand up by that point, much less walk, the physical act of having journeyed that far consuming most of his reserves of energy. I ran out to the end of the road, ordered everyone inside the main work building except for one or two staff who were to stand at the entrance and await further instructions, and told Perris to go suit up and walk through to the access road so that she could retrieve him from the inside. Johnson lurched forward another step, enough to convince everyone remaining that my instructions made a whole lotta sense, and I asked the lone remaining person to get me some gloves and goggles. "Before you go, do you guys have any kind of object that I could use to keep him away if I had to?" I asked. "Like a stick or something? Anything like that?" I kept my eye on Johnson, who had been looking at me the whole time. He took one more step. He was now a little more than a tall person's body length from being completely out of the Hot Zone.

"Johnson! *Don't* you walk out now!" I said to him like a mother scolding her naughty son. A second later, I finally had my object: a square wooden shaft that seemed the length of a pole vault. There would be no problem keeping Johnson at bay, as long as I could hold the unwieldy object properly. I started to plant myself in a stance that would force him backward with the pole, but he never moved a step further. A few minutes later, Perris emerged from behind him and slowly entreated him to take her hand and allow her to walk him back down the road, through the triage area, across the suspect ward, and back to his bed. Thirty minutes later, he was lying down, the episode seemed to be over, and my pulse fell back below 120.

After the sun had come up and the day shift began, I made a passing reference to the incident in the morning meeting but downplayed its importance because I wanted to have a chance to give Pranav the full rundown, as Johnson's little jaunt had clearly exposed some structural flaws that needed to be addressed as soon as possible. The knife incident with Ballah might have been a weird one-off that wasn't likely to happen again, but not only was there a decent chance that another delirious patient might have a wandering episode, there could just as

easily be someone who was pissed off, perhaps by the tedium of waiting around for a positive test, who would march out of their own ac-
cord. The ETU operated on an entirely voluntary basis: No patient was
ever held against their will, and confirmed patients were free to leave
against our medical advice, though none did.* But I wanted to point
out to Pranav that it might be worth considering where the soft spots
were so that we could make alterations that would physically discourage such patients from getting on the loose.

We talked in the open part of the compound, the geographic center
of all the action, because it was the noisiest place with all the post-
meeting commotion, and therefore paradoxically the most private.
The conversation quickly turned to identifying these soft spots and
what would be the most useful changes—mainly to be implemented
by Jean-Francois Baptiste, a Frenchman who had some formal title but
I basically thought of as the Everything Fix-It Man. As Pranav and I
were having this conversation, we turned to see something at our feet.
To drive the point home, there was Johnson, who instead of walking
toward the suspect ward as he had done the night before, had walked
straight out through the decontamination chambers and into the
middle of the compound, and was maybe two feet away from us. The
effort to travel that far had depleted him, and he rocked back and
forth on his hands and knees. Somehow in all the commotion, we
were the first to notice, but within a few seconds all the staff had scattered to the periphery, like a drop of dishwashing liquid in a greasy
water-filled frying pan.

When we looked at how Johnson had once again managed to leave
the confirmed ward, the lack of a door to the decon chamber seemed
like such an obvious oversight. It wasn't, really; it was simply that the
circumstances were producing contingencies that required improvisa-

---

* In terms of the patients who had recovered, there was one major incentive to remain, so
powerful that, however bored or annoyed they might have gotten, none dared leave the
ETU even when they were fully restored to health. When patients had finally cleared the
virus, they were given a stamped and signed certificate saying that we at IMC vouched for
their recovery and that they were no longer contagious. Patients were perfectly able to
walk right out of the ETU whenever they wanted, but without that certificate, the chance
that they would be shunned by their neighbors, and quite possibly attacked to the point of
death, were quite high. They all seemed to know this, and so nobody ever hinted that they
were going to leave.

tion. The events of the past eight hours suggested, however, that it was high time to improvise. We repeated our strategy of trying to contain his movements while someone suited up, and he was led back in to his room. Now thoroughly exhausted, I went home for some sleep. When I returned, there were now swinging doors to the decon chambers that needed to be unlatched, something a delirious person would be hard pressed to accomplish. The presence of these barriers solved one problem but created another, as the hooks to the latches were simply large nails sticking out and could easily tear the PPE of someone who wasn't careful while they unhooked the contraption. That could not only lead to an Ebola infection if the outside of the PPE was coated in virus but could just as easily lead to tetanus from a scratch of the rusty nail.

Johnson died that afternoon.

The night brought other features of the daily rhythm of the unit. While I was still working days, Sambhavi had been on a mini-warpath to make the Bong County facility "the happiest ETU in Liberia." At first I made some snarky asides about this to Colin, but as usual, the joke was on me, as several of her improvements really *did* keep morale high, not only among the staff, but even more importantly, among the patients as well. The most important of these tweaks was to have movie night. Somehow she managed to procure a digital projector from Monrovia, and staff people provided copies of movies that they had kept on their memory sticks, allowing for a small Ebola Cineplex to be operated for several days. It took some time to work out the logistics of showing the movies since the projector could not move into the Hot Zone behind the audience and project *forward* onto a screen, but instead had to be rigged so that it was presenting an image in reverse so that when it hit the screen it would appear correctly. The screen itself was a sheet that had been strung up in one of the no-man's-land boundaries between the high- and low-risk areas, which technically made it Hot, so any adjustments had to be done from the inside in full PPE.

The first of these movies, screened when I was still working the day shift, was *The Lion King*. After some false starts, we finally got the picture set up and the movie started; we all stood next to the exit area of the decontamination chambers and watched almost every member of the confirmed ward watch the movie. Those on the suspect ward who were interested brought their lawn chairs to the edge of the boundary and craned their necks to see what part of the screen they could.

Virtually everyone stopped to participate in the same activity, like we were all a family sitting around a very large dinner table at a special holiday gathering. You could touch the joy in the ETU that night. I did marvel at the choice of movie: Here we were, in *real* Africa, watching *real* Africans watching a movie about a most *unreal* Africa dreamed up by people who were on the whole very *un-African*.

Postcolonial critiques of Disney be damned, the audience was rapt from start to finish, and demanded a rescreening as soon as possible. Watching this whole bizarre event take place, I felt the same sensation I had at church, when the words of Revelation had started to cascade down from the pulpit: You really can't make this stuff up—or if you did, you'd be accused of importing the most transparent and shallow of metaphors. But there we were.

By the time I had taken up my work on the night shift, however, we had cycled through the popular movies. I had stopped paying attention to them while I was working days, especially as the movies often started to play only as we were headed home. But now I was rounding between nine o'clock and midnight, and so I basically couldn't avoid movie night. The popularity of the activity had diminished, and it was mainly the children whom I would find sitting outside, spellbound. By that point, the cache of movies owned by the expats had been exhausted, and so some members of the national staff working for the WASH team had brought their movies in. But like the adult patients, I paid little attention to them and stayed inside the building, able to actually spend some quality time with my patients.

One night, as I was making my way over from the suspect ward, I rounded the corner, hardly paying attention to the screen, when I heard a *pop!* come from one of the movie speakers and caught a glimpse of red splashing at the periphery of my eye. I turned back to the screen to see what was happening. A man was lying on a table, shot and bleeding, and another man was over him. I tried to process this scene. A war film? It was some kind of foreign movie. I kept watching, and although I never did learn the actual name of the movie or what country it came from, it appeared to be about Middle East-ern terrorists settling their ideological differences with methods best described as medieval. And the kids were watching this—*my* kids were watching this, for I had suddenly found myself transforming into Doc-tor In-Loco-Parentis, charging up to the boundary and giving in no uncertain terms instructions to the WASH staff that these movies were Capital-O Out, and I would be having a conversation with their mothers—ahem, Godfrey—in the morning. "Show's over, kids," I said to the three boys, who looked crestfallen at the news. Hadn't this country seen enough senseless violence?

Other elements of life in the ETU, of which I had been only dimly aware, became featured during the night. Graft is a complicated sub-ject in as impoverished a place as Liberia. Stealing from the ETU was commonplace. The thefts were generally petty, and I was only pe-ripherally cognizant of them for the most part. For instance, I had a rude awakening to the practice my first day there, when I went to the communal locker room to change into scrubs. The cubby holes did not have locks, and I tucked away the clothes that I had hastily donned in Monrovia hours before, clothes that included a wallet stuffed with cash. Later that afternoon as I was driving to my flat in Cuttington, I noticed that the wallet was still there, but more than two hundred dol-lars of my money had vanished.

The pickpocket was kind enough to take only the cash, so all the truly important items, including various forms of identity and electronic credit, remained unmolested. They were even kind enough to leave me a little cash in the form of Liberian currency, with former President Samuel Doe, a man with a gift for the related art of embezzle-ment, staring up at me, almost winking, from the front of a fifty-Liberian-dollar banknote, which could just about purchase a can of Coke. Although irritated, I took it as a lesson learned and became extremely careful about my valuables after that, especially since IMC doled out our monthly allotment of petty cash in a lump sum at the beginning of each month, leading me to squirrel away small amounts in hidden corners of various parts of my flat so that a repeat episode would not prove to be financially devastating.

But I never paused to develop any moral outrage over the matter.

Dating back to its modern origins, Liberia has always been a place where plunder of some sort had taken place—mainly the plunder instigated by corporate America through the intermediaries of the Americo-Liberians. We were, in some important sense, the thieves: Americans coming to this country and looting the land of its natural resources, walking away with palm oil and bauxite and, above all else, rubber. We just had developed the nicety of calling it *trade* to provide it with an air of civilization. But if trade was the great win-win scenario that gets those who claim to have read Adam Smith so jiggy, why, after more than a century of Liberia providing rubber and other valuable commodities to the United States, was Liberia still so appallingly impoverished? What had become of the wealth of *this* nation, other than to find its way onto the tires of my Toyota back in Massachusetts? There seemed to me to be a logic inherent in the theft, a small settling of accounts that had historically become wildly unbalanced on a massive scale.

But I did come to see that there was something of a Catch-22 about an amoral approach to private property and ownership in a place like this. It's true that Liberia had been plundered by the West for hundreds of years, setting in motion a system that hardly looks equitable and for which its penurious masses might be justified for thinking themselves entitled to institute on-the-fly policies regarding wealth redistribution. But if that was so, and people felt no sense of shame about pilfering from the international aid organizations or those who worked for them, how would an economy in a place like Liberia ever become anything beyond a corrupt mess? The aid organizations would continue with their work despite the graft, but that didn't mean that small businesses would want to sign up for risky ventures if they believed their products had a high probability of being stolen. There was a highly determined group of Lebanese merchants in the country, bless them, but there wasn't much beyond that. The problem of government corruption and the prospect of having to deal with a culture of bribery must also be forcing legitimate businesspeople, even those genuinely interested in doing work in a place like Liberia, to remain at a wary distance.

Therefore, this cultural attitude probably kept all but the most ruthless of organizations from starting work in Liberia in the first place, and these outfits were the least likely to care about such trivialities as equitable pay and increasing the standard of living for the average Liberian. From my vantage point, as long as the status quo remained, the cycle wouldn't stop. Though I had no idea how many people were stealing—and America is hardly without corruption itself—I did know from the grumblings of the logistics team members that the problem was widespread.

IMC eventually handled the problem by locking away everything that could be locked away. The storerooms became increasingly secure, with fewer and fewer people having access to the keys to retrieve items except under carefully controlled situations. This dramatically cut down on theft, but theft never completely dissipated. A few items in the medical and general storerooms always seemed to be lower than the inventory would suggest. Every few days, someone would complain about it. In general, I shrugged my shoulders, thinking that this was the cost of doing business in a place like this, and tried to avoid simple moral judgments given the convoluted history of this nation. Yes, graft was a technical problem to be solved, but paternalistic lectures from mostly white people weren't going to help matters in the long run, or even the short.

But working nights changed my view of the matter, at least to a degree. The days were hot, but the nights had a coolness that reminded me of summer camp in August in a place like the Poconos. The temperatures would drop to the low seventies or high sixties, and when combined with the damp, it meant that two layers of clothing were needed to stay comfortable. We would round in full PPE before midnight, and the gear brought a comforting warmth. My longest spin in PPE happened this week, when I once spent four hours, in no real hurry to finish my work since I was comfortably, thermally neutral.

It was a different matter for the patients. We could not wash their clothes, because every object in the high-risk area had to be incinerated, so the stockrooms were always supplied with donated clothes so that we could offer something new to patients every few days. We plowed through an astonishing amount of clothing. Sometimes it meant that someone was wearing pants five inches too long, or a man would wear a frilly pink taffeta shirt obviously intended for a woman, but I never heard anyone complain about such indignities.

But trousers, a T-shirt, and flip-flops were not enough to keep one warm in the confirmed ward. What was plainly, desperately needed were *blankets*. Yet blankets remained among the few items apparently so precious that whoever was stealing stuff would try to circumvent every roadblock the leadership threw up in order to take them, whether for personal or business—that is, black market—ends, I cannot say.

I can go along with the notion that property and theft is a good deal more complicated in Liberia than it appears at first glance. I can offer up any number of justifications for why it behooves Americans or Europeans not to reflexively judge their Liberian cousins who might swipe some goods from what they perceive to be an organization with endless supplies and limitless resources. All this I can do and be genuine when I say it, but all that becomes intellectual claptrap when I am forced to watch my patients, the most vulnerable people on earth, suffering one of the worst diseases imaginable, sitting there *shivering* because one or two of their fellow Liberians think it's okay to steal a blanket knowing full well the consequences it has for these people—people who could just as easily have been *them* were it not for chance alone. *So quit taking the motherfucking blankets!* Good grief, these are *your* people! I am still furious as I write this.

My final night shift took place on Halloween. There was some talk of a gathering of expats that night, which would have been one of the only times we socialized as a group after hours, since everyone worked long days and nobody wanted to come to the ETU groggy from a late night, but I couldn't come. Over the course of the week, the moon had been waxing, so maneuvering around the ETU had gotten progressively easier, and by then there was a half-moon lighting up the night. I moved into the donning station to take my last nighttime spin.

Just before I put my leg into the Tychem suit to start the process of gowning, one of the staff came to tell me that we had a problem. In the suspect ward were a father and his six-year-old daughter. Their test results had returned negative earlier in the afternoon, but due to a variety of logistical glitches as well as a big bolus of new patients, nobody had dealt with their discharge planning until now. It was late, and there weren't exactly evening buses running on the Gbarnga express, especially two miles up a dirt road into the jungle, so there was no way they could get home. Normally, getting our negatives out of the suspect ward was the highest priority for obvious reasons, as nobody wanted them to remain in a Biosafety Level 4 environment for an additional twelve to sixteen hours. But what to do?

On the corner of the campus we had constructed a visitor's center, but it was almost never used, owing to the stigma involved with the place. Even the love of family wasn't enough to convince people that it would be safe—or that their neighbors wouldn't shun them after they had visited. We made a plan to set up a couple of mattresses and provide sheets and blankets in the visitor's center, which, needless to say, was *outside* the high-risk area, so that they could sleep the night away no longer inside the ward. All we had to do was decontaminate them and take them there.

The path to the visitor's center had to be accessed by walking the entire way around the compound from the opposite side. Because of the manner by which the Hot / Not Hot boundaries had been constructed, there was no direct route from the suspect ward to the visitor's center, even though a visitor would have looked across a mesh divide to their loved ones only feet away. The problem was that one side of the ETU is nestled up right against the rainforest; the small part of clearing that skirted that side was occupied by the ambulance path, which means that part was still high risk. Thus, to get to this structure, visitors were forced to walk nearly the entire perimeter in the opposite direction.

This would have been nothing more than tedious, but as the ETU's needs changed over the course of the outbreak, there was additional construction at the far edge of the compound. Weeks before, when the epidemic was still raging at full tilt (and still was, for all we knew), plans were in place for more beds on the confirmed side. The back of the ETU was the only place where this new structure could go, so what was originally a clearly demarcated path had been torn up, with piles of dirt, wooden beams, corrugated tin roofing, and nails lying all over the place. I learned all of this as I accompanied this pair through the dark, with a cheap flashlight that I had to keep banging to get the current to flow.

So I began Halloween by taking a terrified girl and her father all the way around our Little Shop of Horrors, after she had already endured one otherworldly experience, and walking her through a post-apocalyptic landscape, only to deposit her on a cold, damp bed. The maneuver was meant for their safety, but good luck explaining that to a six-year-old unfamiliar with the subtleties of filovirus transmission and the need for strange forms of infection control.

It was damp that night, and by the time I returned a half hour later, I was a yucky muck of dirt and sweat. Going into PPE already schvitzy is not fun, especially since my sweaty skin always became irritated from rubbing against the PPE, so that night I was giving my eczema a head start. But I was a soldier, so off I went into PPE without complaint. By the time I had made it over to the confirmed ward, I was not surprised to find one of our patients, Joe, had passed away. At the evening hand-off, the team said that they didn't believe he would survive the night. He must have died not long after he was last seen in the afternoon, for by the time I arrived, he was in rigor. His daughter, who was recovering from the worst, was three doors down and blissfully unaware of this; we decided to let her sleep the night and inform her in the morning.

By this point it was just shy of eleven, and Kelly and I found the two young men from the WASH team who were spraying down the surfaces of the confirmed ward, a nightly practice, to tell them we needed to prepare Joe for transfer to the morgue. They looked at each other quickly and then at us, hoping that they hadn't actually heard it right. "Oh, we can leave this until morning," one of them said casually, trying to inform me of the standard operating procedures on the night shift that I, a mere greenhorn, had failed to grasp.

I looked at them and said, "No, there's plenty of us, we can do this," and although they were masked, I could sense their faces fall. There was simply no way we were going to leave this kind of work for ten more hours. Certainly the patients did not want a dead body in their midst, even if that body posed no physical threat.

I went to get two body bags for the move: The first bag, after being zipped up, is then sprayed down from the outside and placed in the second, where another round of spraying takes place for maximum infection control. We placed Joe into the first bag. He was heavy and stiff as a board, with one arm held out crooked. Because the room had tight corners, simply moving him into the bag involved contorting ourselves just so.

We eventually succeeded, and then got the second bag in place and zipped up. We then placed him onto a stretcher and sprayed everything a third time, which included ourselves. At that point the WASH staff were backpedaling, hoping that they would not be asked to perform any further tasks, but I pointed at one and said, "Okay, it's you and me who are gonna take him to the morgue." Because I had spent the better part of four weeks among the national staff managing the tricky maneuver of acting like a goof while also simultaneously being deadly serious about the work, I felt that I had earned their goodwill, so by then most of the staff who knew me would do what I asked of them without protest. While he raised no objections and stayed behind to help me bear Joe on the stretcher to the morgue, you could tell he hoped this highly unpleasant activity would end as soon as possible, or that some other staff member would magically materialize in front of us to take over his duties.

We picked up Joe and headed out the back. The entry and exit points to the high-risk area were basically flat, but this part of the ETU was where the hillside sloped back down into the valley and was the steepest decline in the Hot Zone proper, the one place where one could easily stumble, especially while wearing rubber boots that didn't quite fit. The back stairs were tricky, for not only were the steps themselves not perfectly flat, tending to slant downward, but the distance between the risers of each step was wildly variable, some being inches apart and others more than a half foot, so that one could not ascend or descend these few stairs without carefully looking down. That, however, was obviously out as we carried Joe, so we moved slowly and deliberately. I did not want either of us to fall down and tear our PPE on the rocks while bearing Joe, who in such a stumble could land on us, or we on him.

Even with the moonlight, it was dark between the buildings, as the shadows of the latrines were cast on the back exit of the confirmed ward. And, per usual, I still couldn't see anything through my misted-up eyewear. Carrying Joe to the morgue proved to be the most adventurous thirty-foot walk of my time in the ETU, which given my recent misadventures escorting the father and his daughter to the visitor's center only hours before, was saying something. After this brief journey, we arrived at the morgue. Effectively, the morgue was just a concrete platform over which a framed tent of tarp was draped since it hadn't been intended to be used as anything other than a place to put the bodies prior to burial. The entrance was a tarp flap rather than a door, so pulling it aside while keeping the stretcher steady proved to be, like everything else associated with this move, awkward.

The morgue didn't possess electrical wiring, and so once inside it was pitch black. I couldn't see a foot in front of my face. The phrase "dark as hell" leapt to mind, and I comforted myself by the fact that I didn't actually *believe* in hell. But my WASH companion would have felt otherwise. Fortunately, since there were no other bodies in the morgue at that time, we walked into the center of it without being able to see and lowered Joe to the floor. As soon as the stretcher touched the concrete and Joe's temporary resting place was secured, my colleague bolted for the flap, scurrying out as fast as his legs could safely take him, leaving me in the absolute darkness.

I decided to linger there for a few moments and soak the moment in. It was midnight of Halloween, and I was standing in the middle of a morgue, in complete darkness, over a body that had just succumbed to one of the most frightening viruses known to humans. *Who needs a ghost story?* I thought. *I'm living in one!* I stood there and, with apologies to Joe, started to laugh.

It was then that I was hit with a sudden, powerful, and inexplicable feeling. I couldn't explain why, but at that moment, I had the realization that I was probably going to get out of this thing alive after all.

8

PURGATORY

For reasons which can certainly use close psychological inquiry the West seems to suffer deep anxieties about the precariousness of its civilization and to have a need for constant reassurance by comparison with Africa. If Europe, advancing in civilization, could cast a backward glance periodically at Africa trapped in primordial barbarity it could say with faith and feeling: There go I but for the grace of God.

—Chinua Achebe, "An Image of Africa:
Racism in Conrad's Heart of Darkness"

I left the Bong ETU for Monrovia late in the morning the first Thursday in November, dropping by one last time to say my good-byes both to patients and staff. In a preview of coming attractions, during the morning staff meeting I was given a few minutes for a valedictory speech where my voice quavered over three octaves while I praised the nurses in particular and spoke of the honor I had in working with the national staff.

Tears flowed easily for me as others looked on, not altogether comfortably, for the staff meeting was a place to get business done. As we wrapped up, people moved about quickly in anticipation of the myriad activities that were required to keep the place running. There was, after all, a catastrophic outbreak still going on, and the virus wasn't pausing to dry its eyes after my address. Nor were the patients, who would die over the next few days and likewise wouldn't be comforted by my words. I dabbed my face with the industrial-grade toilet paper that served as our Kleenex and strode to the men's locker area for one last change into scrubs, and then PPE, to make my last rounds, at least for this deployment.

I especially wanted to see what had become of the Kollie family—the *entire* family, all of whom were now in the firm grasp of the virus. Their story had begun in a remote village a few hours walk from Ganta, the capital of neighboring Nimba County. There, a few weeks before, the patriarch of the family, a man named Jeremiah, had helped his friend and neighbor Matthew carry Matthew's wife to a clinic several miles distant. A second man had also helped, and they took turns carrying the frail woman to the clinic. She died not long after reaching medical attention. Having done what he could, Jeremiah had returned to his wife and three children.

Matthew was the first of this sad group to arrive in Bong County after the eight-hour journey from his home. He had arrived a few days before I started working the night shift, and this was the story as we knew it upon his arrival. By the time I had returned to working days, he had weathered Ebola's storm and was now, like so many of the other survivors, pacing the halls, bored stiff. But as I neared the end of my time in the ETU, we admitted a woman and her three children to the suspect ward, and they all looked ill. By then we had the clinical instincts to guess with reasonable accuracy which patients had Ebola and which did not even before we drew their blood, and it looked like all of them were infected. As we gathered the story from the mother, she said that she had come from this village, and that there was a man here whose wife had died. We realized that she was speaking about Matthew and that this was Jeremiah Kollie's wife, Lorpu. "Where is Jeremiah?" we asked. And then, almost as soon as the question left our lips, we wished we hadn't. Not only had Jeremiah died but so had the other man. These two men, in turn, had transmitted the infection to each of their families. The Kollie family was now before us; the other family had been taken to a different ETU, to what fate I would never know.

I cannot imagine what must have gone through Matthew's mind at the sight of Lorpu Kollie accompanying her three young children to the confirmed ward. I cannot imagine *anyone* imagining this. But I can try to provide words, feeble though they are, to at least approach his state of mind in that terrible moment, words like *anguish*, *remorse*, *horror*, *guilt*, and *fury*. This man had loved his wife and only asked his neighbors a simple favor to help restore her to health. Now that decision had ended up killing them. This simple and touching gesture of assistance, a deed of kindness and solidarity that requires no prolonged explanation of particular cultural mores, was now threatening the lives of anyone associated with this universally compassionate act. And now, he had to face the woman who never had a say in what had happened but was now feeling its brunt. Can you imagine what might have going through *her* mind at the sight of a recovering Matthew? All words fail. There is an empty, dark, dreadful nothing to summarize that moment. I was glad I wasn't there when it happened.

The Kollie children did not fare well. On my penultimate day in the unit, I came in to find Peter, Lorpu's middle child at two years old, lying on the cot. She must have known, for she had left the room by the time we arrived and he was alone, not in rigor but clearly dead. I quickly found Fredericka Feuchte, the head of the psychosocial team who happened to be rounding in the confirmed ward that day, and asked her to relay the news. I took what seemed like the much easier job of preparing little Peter's body for burial. Bridget Mulrooney, the nurse working that shift, had gone to retrieve the spray contraption, which she hoisted on her back, spraying down the child along with all the surfaces he had touched, while I went to get the body bags from the storage room. I was unaware that there were special, smaller body bags for children, so when I arrived with these huge, adult-sized bags, Bridget took the opportunity to mirthlessly tease me for a few moments. Neither of us laughed, but the insertion of something that could at least pass for a kind of humor helped us move through the grim business that was upon us. After I sealed the second bag, I didn't need to find a stretcher, and I gathered the child in my arms to carry him to the morgue. Carrying children was one of my favorite things to do in the unit, for it provided the joy of human contact, something strictly forbidden outside the Hot Zone. Every few days I would look for some excuse to pick up one of the kids and twirl them around, to their happiness as well. Peter would be the last child I would carry in the ETU.

So that following day I needed to see the other two children for myself. Though ill, they still lived, while Lorpu Kollie maintained a mask of flat affect that didn't even hint at the suffering that she must have felt. I moved on to see other patients and bid my farewells, especially to those who had been there for weeks and were waiting around for their ticket to freedom to be punched, which they knew would come eventually.

I climbed into the SUV and headed down the long dirt road, unsure whether I would ever see this place again. Similar to the biblical Lot, I didn't look back. We were at my flat at Cuttington within ten minutes, where I retrieved my luggage, and before I knew it I was on the road to Monrovia. We made a stop halfway there just outside the town of Kakata to drop off some supplies and documents at the next ETU that IMC was building. Because they hadn't yet finished construction—it was due to open in mid-November—I was able to walk around without having to suit up.

If the Bong ETU was a blue world, then the Kakata ETU was most definitely a *white* world. Compared to the hastily constructed facility in Bong, the Kakata ETU was a massive complex whose structural advantages were immediately evident. Unlike our hilly ETU, the ground here was even so the risks of stumbling or falling were minimized. It was obviously designed to accommodate many more patients, easily twice as many, yet there was plenty of space for workers to maneuver. Both the suspect and confirmed wards were massive, about one hundred feet in length, each with a steel-ribbed skeleton that rose twenty feet into the air to form a pitched roof. Exhaust fans with the circumference of a truck tire were placed at each end of the building, just below the roof peak, to keep the air circulating and the temperature at least reasonably cool, in marked contrast to snug ovens that characterized the interiors of the wards in Bong County. The advantages for patient and health-care worker alike were clear, but I couldn't help but think, as I watched the makeshift yurts of our ETU transform into semipermanent buildings of Kakata, that we were witnessing the industrialization of the virus. The epidemic had gone on so long and had infected so many that frantic improvisation had yielded to careful and deliberate planning, a mixed blessing if ever there was one.

But as we left Kakata for the final two-hour push into Monrovia, my mind turned to what awaited me in the next few days, and far from feeling a sense of euphoria or relief from having made it through the experience, at best I felt anxiety and at worst dread. For although I had not become infected, I could still be incubating the virus and wouldn't know that I was truly in the clear until I had been away from the patients at the ETU for twenty-one consecutive days. The clock was starting to run, but the next few weeks were likely going to be a trying time rather than a triumphant return. That was largely due to events that had taken place in New York City only two weeks before.

On Thursday, October 23, a doctor named Craig Spencer started to run a fever. Spencer had just returned the week before from Sierra Leone after working a six-week stint for MSF in one of their ETUs doing pretty much the same thing that I had been doing. According to later reports, he started to feel fatigued a day or two earlier, but on Thursday his thermometer read 100.3 degrees Fahrenheit, and he immediately isolated himself and called the local public health authorities. The next day, in full Biosafety Level 4 isolation and with obvious signs of illness, his blood test was positive for Ebola.

And that Friday the 24th, we all sat in front of our laptops at the ETU and watched America become totally unhinged, even worse than when Thomas Eric Duncan had died in Dallas the month before. Every detail of Spencer's life since his arrival became known and dissected by the media in short order. He went running. He went bowling. He had eaten with his fiancée at an Italian restaurant. The twenty-four-hour network news channels had turned Spencer's infection into wall-to-wall coverage.

A responsible version of the story would look something like this: He was a threat to no one before his fever, he's isolated now, a few people in close contact need to take some special precautions, but otherwise it wasn't a big deal from a public health standpoint. It was obviously a *big* deal for Craig Spencer himself. But Fox News and CNN among others couldn't resist the lure, Fox especially, given its advanced training in fearology. Just because of the sheer volume of coverage devoted to the most idiotic minutiae of Spencer's recent life—he had taken the subway, crowded with people, for goodness sake!—there was no way a layperson could conclude anything other than that an act of biological terrorism had just been committed on American soil, and for the second time in two months.

Yet it was that *other* act that should have given Americans some sense that Ebola wasn't quite the public health calamity that its portrayal suggested. Thomas Eric Duncan's story was instructive. Everything that could have gone wrong with his initial evaluation and subsequent care did go wrong. The screening questions designed to identify potential Ebola patients somehow failed to pick him up, so he remained out in the community for three extra days. The isolation procedures were hastily and incorrectly performed. The PPE wasn't adequate. The Dallas situation was, in short, *fubar*—the word that GIs from World War II had invented to describe a mess like this: *fucked up beyond all recognition*. By the time he died, the Texas Department of Public Health identified 168 people requiring careful monitoring, of which 120 were exposed at the hospital, while the other 48 were personal or professional contacts that Duncan had made before his hospitalization.

After this mostly man-made disaster played out, how many people did he infect?

Two.

Even though the people that Duncan had exposed were still a moving target by the time that Craig Spencer had become infected and it would not be known for many weeks that the outbreak that he caused really would stop at two, it should have been apparent by the end of October that there weren't *dozens* of Ebola patients suddenly cropping up in the Dallas area. If the members of the media so breathlessly pursuing every detail of Spencer's life had stopped to think about this, they might have concluded that Stateside Ebola was certainly something to cause *concern* but not perhaps *alarm*, much less *panic*. But the exercise in sophistry that constitutes television news makes no allowance for turning the temperature down or helping to calm the populace, so the idea that Spencer's infection was going to be met with a measured response by the news media was placing hope far above experience.

Given the timbre of the news reports about Spencer, the political reaction was swift and severe. Within hours, governors of various states were cobbling together hastily considered policies for what to do with anyone returning from the three affected countries, and they were either doing this without the input of their own public health experts or were ignoring them altogether. *Quarantine* became the watchword. It didn't help that the state in which Spencer resided was being governed by Andrew Cuomo, who was eyeballing a run for the White House, depending on the political fortunes of the early prohibitive nominee, Hillary Clinton. For Cuomo, the chance to look statesmanlike, especially on an issue concerning international policy, could be an unexpected gift if he was going to make the argument that he was as qualified to be commander in chief as someone who had served as secretary of state.

But Cuomo wasn't the biggest beneficiary of Craig Spencer's rising temperature. The real political windfall came to New Jersey's governor Chris Christie, who could distinguish himself by appearing tough and competent within what was looking to be a crowded field for the Republican presidential race by isolating the African hordes in whatever way possible. Given that Newark airport was the entry point for many such returning travelers, he would almost immediately get his wish, for within twenty-four hours of the news of Spencer's infection a woman named Kaci Hickox, herself also returning from Sierra Leone, had been pulled aside by New Jersey authorities when she mentioned that she had been working with Ebola patients. Hickox was using Newark only as a transit point to return to her home state of Maine, but suddenly found herself as Exhibit A in Christie's tough-guy agenda.

She was whisked out of the airport against her will and stuck in a makeshift tent set up in one of the parking lots on the campus of University Hospital Newark a few miles away. The news of Hickox's detention spread quickly, and the story went international within hours. Christie's office tweeted that she had a fever and was "being evaluated" that evening. But Hickox was for the moment without recourse, and instead of starting a quiet weekend at her home in Maine where she could begin to unwind and process a difficult experience, she had become a captive of the State of New Jersey.

It's not hard to see the appeal of Christie's gamble: If she got sick, he would not only get to claim that his administration was not merely more competent but less reckless than the one in Washington, and he could use New York's alleged mishandling of Spencer as a perfect counterexample of how the overly sensitive limousine liberals of the Democratic Party could threaten the populace with their bleeding-heart policies. And this would all be happening when the largest number of registered voters was paying attention to the issue.

Even Bobby Jindal, the governor of Louisiana and also a White House hopeful, tried to use the outbreak to muscle his way to some free publicity. Since Jindal didn't have the benefit of an international airport to use as a prop, he had to wait his turn until the following week, when he vowed not to let in anyone from West Africa to the meeting of the American Society of Tropical Medicine and Hygiene in New Orleans. The conference annually hosts more than 3,500 attendees from more than a hundred countries, many from sub-Saharan Africa. You couldn't have found a better place to concentrate some of the most important minds currently working on Ebola in order to hash out a coherent strategy for what could be done moving forward, but Jindal, not surprisingly, couldn't see beyond his own narrow interests. By that point, however, the quarantine story was starting to fade from the front page, and the only people who were paying close attention to the outrage of the ASTMH convention freezeout were the very public health experts to whom few politicians were listening.

If Chris Christie was right and Kaci Hickox had Ebola, he might be able to leverage the whole affair to upgrade his candidacy for president; if he was wrong and she didn't, he still had a decent chance of using the event to his own political advantage by showing he was a Serious Man, willing to take swift action when called for. Needless to say, I'm not a political strategist, but I wouldn't be surprised if someone in his inner sanctum opined early on that, whatever happened to her, it was a win-win situation.

But in his bungling lust for power, Christie overreached. At best, what could be said about her physiologic state was that the forehead thermometer used to check her temperature did indeed register a fever, while the more accurate oral thermometer that was used simultaneously clocked in at a pedestrian 98.6 (Hickox claimed that the discrepancy was due to her being flushed because she was upset). Christie's team, however, selectively interpreted the data, expanding the errant measurement into full-blown illness. The following day, Christie doubled down on his bet at a campaign stop in Iowa. "When I left this morning she still had a fever and she's being tested for other illnesses after the Ebola test came back negative," he said. "*There's no question that the woman is ill,* the question is what is her illness" (my emphasis). This kind of pronouncement came in spite of his receiving status updates from physicians and nurses charged with her care, who saw nothing of the sort.

Hickox swiftly proved to be ready and willing to tangle with the governor on the biggest of stages. Despite being exhausted, scared, cold, and unwashed, she channeled her rage and eloquence into an op-ed that ran in the *Dallas Morning News* that Saturday morning, and she gave an interview to Candy Crowley of CNN the following day. She portrayed herself, accurately, as a clean-as-a-whistle professional— who had, after all, just returned from some incredibly dangerous volunteer work for which the word "heroic" might not have seemed out of place—yet was being treated little better than a felon by the governor. She also had a quick comeback to Governor Christie's inflated assessment of her "obvious" illness. "First of all, I don't think he's a doctor; secondly, he's never laid eyes on me; and thirdly, I've been asymptomatic since I've been here," she said.

As it became clear that Christie was at a high risk of being perceived by the voting public as a crass bully—which is what he really is—the administration quickly pivoted, and less than seventy-two hours after the start of the brouhaha, Hickox was granted leave to become someone else's problem and was allowed to catch a jet to Maine. There she would find an entirely new circus to contend with and a conflict with a governor far less predisposed to care about the opinions of voters in Iowa, or for that matter even of the voters in Maine: Paul LePage.

But those three days, from our vantage point in Liberia, had already done substantial damage to what we saw as the necessary work to bring the outbreak to heel. We were all going to need replacements, and the Americans were leading the call. It wasn't merely an impulse toward tree-hugging humanitarianism that provided a sound rationale for doctors and nurses and sanitation engineers to come over; it was a desire to prevent a biomedical disaster in the United States. If the wealthy countries turned their backs on West Africa, there was an excellent chance the epidemic would spread unchecked and the virus would start to run over borders into Senegal, Mali, Ivory Coast, and beyond.

The more the disease was feared and stigmatized, the more likely that people with means to do so would flee, which in turn meant the more likely the virus was to spread. Moreover, potentially infected people would minimize their symptoms and lie about them to authorities. The more punitive the policies, the better the chance would be that the virus, driven underground, might pop up in unexpected places. And finally, if those very policies did lead to the spread of the virus back to other countries in West Africa such as Nigeria, the northern hub of all sub-Saharan African travel that had just contained its own outbreak, it could lead to a shutdown of any international travel through Africa, turning what was already a multibillion-dollar problem into a multi*trillion*-dollar problem.

So with Christie and LePage and Jindal all instituting draconian policies designed to punish the very people who were most willing to risk the danger of coming to help, we all fretted that the volunteer well would dry up. All of the aid organizations rallied and did a media blitz to try to counter the fear that was now running rampant in the United States. IMC asked me to do a spot on *Good Morning America* just before we knew that Hickox would be allowed to leave New Jersey. I didn't like the idea of doing a television interview—you might be under the impression by this point that I don't care much for TV news—especially on a fluffy show like *GMA* that provides a product that can be only generously described as "news," geared as it is to avoid the complexities of a story. And the Ebola story had become quite complex by that point. At first I balked, but it was made clear that IMC considered this a priority not merely for itself but as part of a unified response by the aid organizations in defense of public health, and so I agreed to the interview. What I feared was that *GMA*, in a quest for simple and undemanding story lines, would try to enlist me in turning this into a referendum on Chris Christie. I suspected that I'd be baited into talking trash.

This proved true almost the moment the interview started. It was about 4:30 a.m. in New York when I got onto Skype to talk to one of the show's producers, as the interview was being recorded for later viewing. I was first asked what I thought of Christie's policy. Without mentioning Christie by name, I replied that if we discouraged volunteers from coming to Africa, we might make the problem worse and that might have unintended consequences. *But Christie is taking a policy stand like this because people in the States were scared—was I saying that people were* foolish *to be scared?* No, I was saying that we need to consider the optimal way to try to contain this outbreak, and that involves fighting it at its source. *So, wait,* came the reply, *was I saying that* I *knew more about public policy than the governor of a large state who is running for the presidency of the United States?* Well, no sir, that's not what I said. And gotcha questions like this continued on for several more minutes.

Then came some personal questions. "So when will you be coming home?" he asked.

"Soon," I replied.

"How soon?"

Was he *really* asking me, just days after I had watched Craig Spencer's every movement since he had come home tracked to within a millimeter, with Kaci Hickox still lingering in a makeshift tent in a parking lot in New Jersey, to divulge my travel plans in front of five million people? "Soon," was my sing-songy response as if he had asked me about how the weather was here in Liberia. I desperately hoped the answer managed not to sound testy to viewers, while simultaneously sending a clear message to this guy to back the hell off.

And on it went. Each question felt like a little electronic noose was being thrown over my head, and each time I wiggled out of it, not giving the producer that sound bite he seemed to covet in which I made some crack about what an ass Christie had been or how hysterical the

American people had become over Ebola. I considered both of those sentiments perfectly true, but the last thing that we needed in the public dialogue was more shouting and needless distraction.

The message wasn't complicated: We need people over here. Treat people like Kaci Hickox poorly, and we won't get people over here. Run away from the problem here, and God only knows where this thing goes. But none of my pronouncements was juicy enough, and after about ten minutes of this cat-and-mouse game, I could sense the producer in New York had lost interest. "Do you have any last thoughts?" he offered.

"Actually, I do," I said. "You need to understand that I've been working here in Liberia for the past four weeks, right here with the virus, every single day. I think it's ironic that I'm actually much more anxious about going *back* to the United States than I am about working *here* in an Ebola Treatment Unit, in a country where the epidemic is still out of control."*

That was the only line that made it to the report, and it appeared during a montage of Ebola B-footage showing the usual scenes of people milling about in protective gear, with no context for where that statement came from and no explanation that it was even an interview conducted by *GMA*'s producers or the question to which I was responding. I didn't see the piece until weeks after I had arrived home, and when I watched it, I felt like I was looking at a Dada art exhibit.

But as I finished the interview and returned to work, I realized it was true: Liberia was going to be a much safer, or at least less anxiety-provoking, place than what awaited me. And because of the events that had just taken place with Spencer and Hickox, I had about twelve days to figure out my game plan.

When I first came over, I hadn't given much thought to what life would be like upon return. First, I wasn't all that concerned, because I figured there was a more than reasonable chance I wasn't coming home anyway. Second, I had what I now realize was an overly simplistic view of how the federal and state governments would treat returning volunteers. This was, after all, a *world* health crisis, the likes

---

* Or that's at least more or less what I said. I can't find the damned clip on the Internet anymore.

of which hadn't ever really been seen before. You could make all sorts of historical comparisons to various pandemics—SARS in 2003, the Great Influenza of 1918, the Black Death—as an exercise in compare-and-contrast to highlight just how different this was.

Surely, I thought, our enlightened leaders will figure out a way of quarantining us in a place where we can have relative freedom and pose no threat to the populace. There was much talk about this at our training course in Alabama. I am now embarrassed to say that I actually thought there was a real chance that, assuming I hadn't been chopped to little Stevie-pieces by a terrified and enraged Liberian populace or melted into an Ebola goo by a microscopic virus, I would find myself riding out November at a U.S. Army base canteen on some far-flung island like Diego Garcia with fellow volunteers and writing about the experience on my laptop. (Diego Garcia is a Navy rather than Army base, but whatever.)

To say this was hopelessly naïve on a variety of levels is to understate the case. The confusion caused by a situation that was shifting by the hour, the fact that all our political leaders were under intense scrutiny, augmented by the unfortunate coincidence of a midterm congressional election and the stirrings of a Republican presidential primary, to say nothing of the labyrinthine complexities of governmental bureaucracies, and no clear indicator of which sectors of government would be responsible for suggesting or instituting such a plan, meant that there was no way there would be some kind of decent civilian-return policy anytime soon. But I didn't work in government, and so a part of me thought that we might all be taken care of by a few strokes of a pen of some well-meaning public official, like a governor or, oh, say, a president of the United States. That notion was in for a big splash of cold water.

To get a sense of what I might expect, a few days before the Craig Spencer story broke I asked some colleagues back at UMass who might be a good person to contact about this. I was eventually given the name of someone who worked at the Massachusetts Department of Public Health, and I shot off an e-mail asking what the policy would be for me upon my return. Although I wasn't even remotely the first person to be returning to Massachusetts from one of the affected countries, or even the first health-care worker in an Ebola Treatment

Unit, I might well be the first one to return after Craig Spencer had developed Ebola.

So I had more than a few questions: Was I going to be subject to the kinds of unsavory restrictions that had been cooked up in New Jersey and Maine? Would any housing be provided for me? Would I be allowed to return to work? The last question was of particular importance because I had no vacation time left; I had entirely used up my fiscal 2015 allotment during October—yes, my time in Liberia was considered a *vacation* by the hospital administration, a long story we don't have time for in this book—and would cease to draw a paycheck even before I got back. Another twenty-one days out of commission was going to be a major financial blow.

I didn't hear anything from the DPH contact for another few days, then Craig Spencer came down with Ebola, and I sent another more urgent e-mail asking whether any policy was in effect.

"We're working on it," was the terse reply that came.

With not much more than a week to go, I had to make some choices. Every option came with risks, and the risks in turn dealt with how my return would be perceived by people back in Massachusetts.

The first and most obvious option was to simply return to my home. But I had two children in seventh grade, each in a different school. I figured that most parents would be split into about three different groups, each with a distinct reaction to my presence. The majority of them wouldn't really care or think it an especially big deal in terms of their families' risk. A sliver of parents would think that this was a really cool thing and it would be a teachable moment for their kids.

It was, however, the *third* group about whom I was most concerned: the paranoid parents who would think that by cohabitating with my children after my journey, I was potentially putting *their* children at risk of catching Ebola by sending my potentially infected kids to school. Every school has a mother or father like this.* I knew that there wouldn't be many such parents, but I also knew that all it would take was one determined mother or father to make a poten-

---

* My daughter's idiotic math tutor had already backed out even before I returned home, despite multiple reassurances that I would never even *touch* her during the monitoring period. The silver lining was we got a much better math tutor out of the process.

tially huge issue out of this, and I worried that my children might be shunned by classmates out of fear and that the entire situation would place the school administration in an uncomfortable position. Indeed, I had already needed to fire a warning shot to the schools when, looking at the schedule, my wife, Miriam, and I realized that my daughter's parent-teacher conference had been scheduled for mid-November, when I would still be in the midst of my twenty-one-day waiting period. We sent an e-mail to the school leadership and said we should reschedule.

The reply was heartwarming: No, Steven, we think what you've been doing is remarkable and we want to show our support. We'll practically *parade* you around to show how special this is. I wrote them back and said that while I was touched, they needed to consider what this might do to their recruitment efforts for the following year if the news got out about how cavalier they were with the safety of the children by allowing a biological threat to wander about the school. *That* got their attention, and we rescheduled.

School issues were only the beginning of my concerns when I went back home. How would my neighbors perceive me? What would happen if a local TV station—let's say, one belonging to a network that might be known at a national level for doing journalism based in part on fearmongering—decided to show up outside my door one day to report that the Ebola doctor had plotzed himself down right in the middle of one of the more idyllic suburbs of Boston?

And what would happen if I *did* develop symptoms? That was, of course, a real possibility. My house would turn to bleach as scores of workers in hazmat suits sterilized every surface of my living space. Our furniture, paintings, and other objects would be ruined. Coupled with the school problems and the potential media circus, the loss of family heirlooms seemed to put the nail in that coffin. Going home was definitely not Option #1.

Finding somewhere *else* to go presented similar problems. At first we had a promising lead from a friend of a friend who owned a getaway cabin in the woods in central Massachusetts. It seemed too good to be true: I'd be away from people but still close enough that I could commute to Worcester. It turned out that it *was* too good to be true.

As the Spencer/Hickox story grew, we received word that the people who made the offer suddenly realized—*oops!*—that they had rented the cabin to someone else during that period. Their excuse seemed fishy, but there wasn't much point in expressing disappointment. And so it was back to the drawing board.

Staying at a hotel posed a host of public relations issues: What would happen if one of the guests or staff found out who I was? Would they kick me out? And what if that TV news crew I was worried about showed up here? This time I would be outside stuffing my belongings into my car after I had been tossed out by the management. I considered the small minority of people who were in a frenzy about Ebola, and thought that it takes only one nut with a gun and an overdeveloped sense of vengeance for me to end up in a pool of blood in a parking lot.

The hardest part was that I was trying to make decisions based on two variables: how my actions would be viewed in retrospect if I became a public figure and what would happen if I did actually become sick with Ebola. Maybe it was paranoia, but watching what had happened to Craig Spencer, I thought that some contingency planning was in order. And I had no idea what new events would unfold over the next several days as I made plans.

With less than a week to go, I still had heard nothing about what the state would require of me, and so I sent a follow-up e-mail, which was met with the same short, and not especially friendly, reply. Whatever was going to happen, the Commonwealth of Massachusetts was effectively saying to me that I was on my own. I therefore made the decision to reserve a room at a hotel in the vicinity of Worcester. I'd get in from the airport, find a local hotel and crash, get up the next morning and pick up my stuff from the house once the kids had cleared out, as I didn't want anyone to think I'd be so cavalier as to have physical contact with them, and drive toward Worcester to set up temporary shop for twenty-one days.

Which brings me back to my ride into Monrovia that Thursday, as I was to spend one night in the capital before making my way back home. I had been couriered into town by the IMC driver over a five-hour drive, during which most of the time I sat quietly, pondering how

I arrived at that precise moment, not quite believing I was still alive, with no real plan for how to cope with the waves of emotion that were now crashing at the shores of my consciousness. Even in my most subdued moments, I am an extremely emotionally intense person, so much so that many people find me either off-putting or intimidating or both. And the turbulence my soul was experiencing on that car ride, and for some time to come, was especially intense. To say it would have some repercussions in my personal life is to understate the case. So I used the drive to try to map out a mental plan of what the next several days would look like, slowly becoming aware as we approached Monrovia's outskirts that there was this huge surge of humanity whose central preoccupation wasn't a ramshackle set of tarps in a split of jungle more than a hundred miles to the north. I had either traveled several hours, or several light-years, depending on how you measured these journeys.

The IMC apartments were in a compound in the Congo Town neighborhood, about a half hour's walk east on Tubman Boulevard from JFK Hospital, and we got there in midafternoon. Having seen them for only a few minutes when I had first arrived about five weeks before, I had forgotten how nice the accommodations were: The floor was a polished stone, with comfortable couches in a large living room and a wide-screen television mounted on the wall. Tubman's bustling traffic could be heard outside. I sat for a few minutes in stunned silence as I soaked in a world that seemed to be going about its business, blithely unaware that apocalyptic events were still transpiring throughout the countryside, and indeed in the city limits. The normality of life felt like an electric shock.

That evening I had dinner with Sheri Fink, who was still working in Monrovia. We ate at a seafood restaurant called Anglers not far from the central government buildings. Anglers was popular among the expat crowd; it was located on the beach, so that if you got there early enough you were treated to a beautiful sunset scene over the Atlantic. We sat on the outside deck eating delicious food, a luxury that seemed obscene to both of us. And for the third time that day, I wept uncontrollably, with Sheri having to suspend her work for *The New York Times* to take on the temporary role of crisis psychotherapist.

The next day, hours before my departure, I walked over to the IMC headquarters to debrief with Sean. Like the rest of Monrovia, the IMC offices provided a scene of a city on the move, with easily a dozen people, a mix of expats and Liberian staff, all engaged in the humdrum work of accomplishing administrative tasks. I was being ushered back into a world not only with a different pace but a lower temperature, lacking the fevered sense of dour purpose that was the ETU's essence. It was the beginning of a series of jolts that would last for the next few weeks as I gradually, and not altogether successfully, returned to my previous life.

Three of the IMC staff were headed back Stateside: Zach Ilan Page, a full-time IMC employee who had come for about two weeks to supervise the security of the ETU; Stu Sia, our communications expert who was taking a ten-day R & R break before another tour; and me. After a small comedy of errors in which our drivers belatedly realized they didn't have enough gas for the trip, leading to a breakneck scramble to find another car, we set off for Roberts airport with about ninety minutes to spare. Somehow we avoided the worst of the outbound traffic, making it to Roberts with a little more than a half hour before boarding time, tapping our fingers in the tiny airport lounge as we waited for the Brussels Air flight to take us away. I made my way over to the Liberian tchotchkeria and bought a few trinkets for my family. I hadn't even left the ground, and I was already assuming my previous identity of American tourist.

The plane out was nearly empty, and the flight uneventful. We got into the Brussels airport early in the morning with several hours to wait, and the three of us took up residence in a booth in a café, checking e-mail and browsing Facebook. I found the synagogue chapel, where I sat alone and wept again for good measure, apparently engaging in this rite on every continent available to me on my way back. Being liberal in my ecumenicism, I stopped to visit all the chapels before boarding, but the only place I shed my tears was in the small room where my people gathered as they shuffled from one country to the next.

We landed at Washington Dulles airport at about four on Saturday afternoon, and as we made our way through the maze of concourses that would take us to Immigration and Customs, I knew I had about a five-and-a-half-hour layover, which seemed like more than enough time to grab my baggage and get to the next part of the airport. I knew that I was probably going to be asked a few questions about my work in some special screening area for West African travelers, but I didn't think that should take more than an hour. As I got to the head of the line at Immigration, I decided to try a line that Colin Bucks had said he used when he returned two weeks before. I presented my passport to the officer.

"Are you traveling from any of the following countries: Guinea, Sierra Leone, or Liberia?" he asked.

"Um, I'm the guy you're looking for," I replied.

He looked up. "Sorry?"

"*I'm the one you're looking for,*" I repeated. "I'm going to light up like a Christmas tree on all these questions."

Silence.

"You a doc?"

"Yep."

"You worked with patients?"

"Yyyyep."

"With Ebola?"

"*Yyyyyyyep.*"

And then, something shocking: A smile flashed across his face. He was as entertained by this as I was, and thank goodness for that. He explained that he had screened a few people like me since the hubbub had gone into full swing, during which time he heard several explanations of the risks of Ebola transmission, so he was far less anxious than many of his fellow workers. "Okay, doc," he said. "I think you know what comes next."

"A visit to our friends at the CDC?"

"*Yyyyyyyep.*"

Consistent with being a federal government operation, the CDC's screening process was not a model of efficiency. Tasked with having to invent a process by which to screen travelers out of the affected countries and set up a system of risk based on the types of exposures they had encountered during their travel, and then coordinate with health officials in each of the fifty states, each with its own particular policies, the CDC had a huge number of logistical hurdles to over-come in a compressed time frame. I understood all of that; the only question was how long the process would take. I also had figured that I was a pretty easy case: I had been working in an ETU directly with patients, after all, which should theoretically put me in the highest-risk category. Someone like Stu or Zach would be harder to triage, since they did work in an ETU—harder to get any closer to the virus than that, after all—but they never had any contact with anyone while there, which from a scientific standpoint means that they're about as much of a risk as someone who just came back from a little vacay in Zurich. I thought that Stu and Zach would be the ones that would hold me up, but since mine was the last flight out (Zach actually dis-embarked in Washington), I didn't think my having to wait for them would pose problems.

Because we sat toward the head of the plane, we disembarked first and were first in line, and therefore were among the first to be screened, ushered into a cramped room near the baggage claim as we waited our turn. Disembarking early proved to be advantageous because while we waited to be called, more than a dozen others, mainly Libe-rian expats, came to wait their turn as well. After maybe a half hour the CDC guys performed the initial screen, then ushered Stu and me into an office down the hall while they processed everyone else (as Zach had already left). "We just need to check a few things," said the man in charge of the screening. "We're really sorry to make you wait." "Nah, no, that's okay," Stu and I both said. "We think you guys are great. We really appreciate what you're doing."

"Well, you guys are heroes," he said.

"No, *you* guys are heroes," came our reply. It was a warm and fuzzy moment.

An hour and a half later, the warmth was starting to fade—almost literally because the office temperature was about sixty degrees and I was wearing clothing suited for the heat of Monrovia rather than a chilly office in Washington, D.C., in November. About that time our luggage arrived, along with the screener, who once again apologized, with the *no, you guys are great* exchange, which was beginning to feel obligatory rather than genuine. At least I could put on a fleece.

We sat there idly checking e-mail and texting people as we waited. We chatted intermittently; although Stu and I had always had great conversations in the ETU and I had come to savor his company, by that point both of us were ready to move on to the next chapter in this saga, and each of us served as a reminder to the other that we hadn't yet finished the current one. Stu, in fact, could have left, for we found out the holdup was *me*. But he stood fast, going above and beyond the call of duty in an act of kindness for which I will ever be thankful.

The problem on my end was that the CDC didn't apparently have anyone they could get hold of from Mass DPH on a Saturday night. They said they couldn't release me on that flight unless a health authority knew I would be arriving. By the time we understood that this was the problem, two and a half hours had passed, and I was starting to become concerned about making my connection. Once I understood this, I showed them the e-mails on my cell phone where I had been trying to tell them for days about my arrival date and asking what more I should do, along with their noncommittal replies. The DPH people had given phone numbers ("Please call us if you have any questions when you arrive"), and so the CDC officer called the number. He got a voice mail since he was calling on the weekend, and they hadn't given an after-hours line even though I had told them I was coming in on a Saturday. I found myself gritting my teeth. *I want to like the Mass DPH people, who are the good guys*, I thought to myself, *but rilly effing pissed at them right now*.

At any rate, I pointed out to the officer, they *knew* I was coming, and they knew when. Now could I please go? "We'll get back to you," came the reply.

As we were approaching the end of our fourth hour, I had had enough and finally walked outside the office into the long hallway that ferried passengers to the main terminal, a place that had been emptied of people for two hours. One of the airport security officers saw me and, apparently thinking that someone was casually tossing polonium in her direction, got off her chair and started excitedly squawking like an enraged hen. "Sir, you are to *return* to that room *right now!*" she growled.

"Officer, *you* will find someone from the CDC *right now*, or so help me God I will call the White House and ask why I am being detained!" I waved my phone. It was double bluff. First, I wasn't going to do anything of the sort unless things got completely out of hand as opposed to merely annoying, and more importantly, I had no signal.

"Get back in that room!"

Then, deus ex machina, the gentleman from the CDC reappears, saying, "Thank you, you are free to leave." Stu and I made our way through the baggage transfer. We zipped through the security screens since no one had been there for hours and we had a line of one, and within a few minutes we found ourselves truly back in the United States. We killed an hour over fast food and bade each other farewell as we walked to our gates that would whisk us home.

I arrived a bit past midnight on Saturday night, headed for a hotel, woke up in the morning to drop by home to pick up some belongings to get me through the pseudo-quarantine. I still hadn't heard anything explicit from the people at DPH concerning what the rules of engagement would be, so I drove out to the next hotel in the Worcester area, spent the afternoon taking a long walk, and *finally* heard from someone at DPH.

Their game plan was mostly simple. They were going to follow the CDC guidelines: I would be required to check in with a DPH representative twice a day (once in person, once over the phone) and report my temperature; if I developed any symptoms, I would obviously need to take myself out of circulation and contact DPH immediately (and was given, this time, an after-hours cell phone to call); I was not allowed to cross state lines unless the authorities in the other state were aware of and approved my visit; and I was *strongly encouraged* to avoid being in crowded public areas like shops and restaurants. Except for the slightly fuzzy area about what constituted a "crowded" area—I was, after all, going to need to retrieve food for myself over the next three weeks—the guidelines seemed logical enough to me. I settled in for a night of long sleep before returning to the UMass campus on Monday morning.

The following morning was mainly a blur. I went to the division office to find out whether my personal office had been moved during my absence as had been planned, which it had. I made a phone call to Ann Moorman, a researcher whose main work dealt with malaria and Burkitt's lymphoma in Kenya, but because of the outbreak had been coordinating a huge effort by UMass to stabilize the laboratory infrastructure in Liberia. She was also working to create a personnel pipeline so that people like me could temporarily leave their positions at academic institutions and go work in the affected countries, and I called her to find out what work I would need to do for the Ebola crisis group. I looked for Rick Forster, the UMass internal medicine residency director, to see what help he could use, as our interview season for the new applicants was just under way.

While wandering through the hallways I ran into a variety of people, and the reactions spanned a wide range from pleased to fearful, but no matter where on the spectrum it fell, I did become aware that eyes were upon me. In retrospect, I suppose that I should have seen it coming, but it was one in an ongoing series of surprises that showed no signs of abating. At the ETU, I was just another person; here, I had the sense that I would be an object of intense fascination and scrutiny for the next several weeks.

When heading down one corridor, I noticed maybe a dozen or more people milling about. I heard my name called and turned to see a former student, Emily Bouley, dressed in a business suit, in the middle of a group of applicants for residency. "Bones!" I shouted. (Emily's maiden name was McCoy. Since I thought she would be a future Doctor McCoy before she changed her name, from the moment I met her, I had always referred to her as *Bones* in homage to the *Star Trek* character.) She rushed at me and we hugged each other in the middle of the hallway, and I took great comfort in someone elated to see me and without any fear whatsoever of my touch. It wasn't just the best moment of that day but would turn out to be among the best moments of the next month.

But it came at a price.

A few hours later I got another call from my contact at DPH. This time I could sense some anxiety on the other end of the line. "Um, Steven, uh, so . . . you're back at work?" was the opener, which came as a surprise since I had had this conversation less than twenty-four hours before with the same person.

"Ummm . . . *yeah*, I am. As you know, I don't have any more vacation time to take off."

"Well, do you *have* to be on the campus?"

I had two instantaneous reactions. The first was emotional, deep within the reptilian portion of my brain, and the second was of pure rage: I didn't like to be reminded that I was back at work only four days after putting a two-year-old into an oversized body bag and spraying him down with 0.5 percent chlorine bleach while his mother comforted her two remaining children a few rooms away, and I was expected to resume my duties as if I had been sipping mojitos on a Caribbean shore for the past several weeks. Did I *have* to be on campus? Well, in fact I *did*, as I had already stopped drawing a paycheck because my vacation time had run out. If DPH wanted to *strongly suggest* that it would be a great idea for me to be paid by the hospital while I did basket weaving, or became a basket case, in some hotel room, that would be fine with me. But I wasn't about to initiate that conversation with them myself.

My second reaction was one of mystification: Though subtle, his speech was pressured. He was nervous about something. I suddenly had an inkling that there was a series of frantic phone calls being made between UMass administrators and the DPH, and perhaps between the DPH and the governor's office. I wondered if they were scrambling. But why? What had happened in the intervening twenty-four hours? I had, after all, given them a pretty decent lead time to think about this, reaching out to them even before Craig Spencer turned into, well, Craig Spencer. So what was up?

I'll probably never know this unless someone inside DPH or in the UMass administration spills the beans, but my guess is that my name became an item on the governor's Monday morning agenda once people saw me prowling the halls of UMass—an action that I had thought of as this thing called "going to work." I also wouldn't be surprised if some senior staffer in Governor Patrick's administration learned to his or her surprise that the Ebola volunteer about whom they had been hearing reports just made a brief appearance on *60 Minutes* the night before and was identified as being from Massachusetts.

If I were the governor, after watching what had just happened to Andrew Cuomo and Chris Christie, I would want to know more than just the whereabouts of the Ebola doctor and make damned sure he wasn't running amok so that some political egg didn't end up on my face. Especially if, just as an outside chance, I might be thinking about making a run for the presidency of the United States someday. It seems reasonable that *lots* of phone calls were made that morning, and possibly for the next few days afterward, while people in high places figured every angle in case damage control was necessary.

This analysis could be paranoid: I have no idea whether Deval Patrick even wanted to return to political life once his two terms as governor were over. The analysis could be narcissistic: After all the media coverage, maybe I had acquired a warped perception of my own importance in the larger story. But it may, however, also have some validity. The phone call ended with the plan that DPH would talk to people at UMass, and they would try to find for me a temporary office as far away from the *hospital* as possible. It was repeated in a variety of guises a few times in this tense conversation: *Just please stay away from the hospital, Steven.*

I puzzled over this for a time, for I had never drawn a sharp distinction between the hospital and the medical school. To me, they were always the same thing, sharing a large building, even if they had distinct wings. But in fact the two institutions have different missions. The school is broad in its focus and thinks about itself as a player on an international stage, while the hospital has a local mission, serving the needs of the people living within about a sixty-mile radius of Worcester.

Those two separate sets of priorities normally don't conflict with one another, but the Ebola outbreak posed some peculiar challenges. The school, because of its long-standing relationship with Liberia, had a vested interest in staking out a leadership position in the international aid effort. The Paul G. Allen Family Foundation had given UMass an $8 million grant to parlay our strengths based on our contacts and experience working there to assist the aid organizations and help rebuild the medical-scientific infrastructure of the country. Although I was only peripherally involved with the grant, as the group had begun its work while I was in Liberia, I was at least marginally publicly associated with the group's work, and it would have seemed logical for the school to see me as an asset for public relations.

The hospital, by contrast, saw me as a liability. That's only my guess, but look at it from, say, a CEO's perspective: The lifeblood of the hospital is patient volume. *Any* negative press coverage associating the UMass hospital with an Ebola scare could lead to a huge downturn in visits. At Dallas Presbyterian Hospital, where Thomas Eric Duncan had been seen, the total number of visits had declined by a significant percentage, as much as 60 to 70 percent in some divisions of the hospital. That could mean tens of millions of dollars of lost revenue in a worst-case scenario. If I turned into a bad story, even if I never developed Ebola, that was the kind of hazard the hospital faced.

And unbeknownst to practically everybody, I was on the verge of turning into a bad story.

The following evening, as I sat in my hotel room quietly trying to process all that had been going on over the past two months, my cell phone rang with a number I didn't recognize. Normally I let these calls go to voice mail, but I had a premonition that something important was about to be said on the other end of that line, so I picked it up.

"Steven, hi, I'm Jennifer Berryman," the voice began. Jennifer was the head of the school's communications division. She got straight to the point. "We need you to be aware that a writer from the *Worcester Telegram & Gazette* is writing a story about you, saying that you violated the CDC guidelines upon your return to campus."

"I did *what?!*"

"Steven, I hope you don't mind my asking, but did you . . . *hug* somebody on Monday morning? In a public place?"

"Oh my goodness." I suddenly pictured the following morning's above-the-fold headline in forty-point lettering: "Ebola Hugging Doctor Wreaks Havoc at University Campus."

"Well, apparently several employees called this reporter and they have been reading the CDC guidelines, and they are under the impression that this violates the guidelines in a fairly dramatic fashion," she said. She went on to say that they were currently trying to find out what they could and that she would let me know anything, especially if they wanted to ask me any questions before going to press.

But there I was in a hotel room, suddenly feeling like a sitting duck, wondering what would happen over the next several hours. Would the *T&G*, as it is known locally, want to keep the Ebola-Hugging Doctor story to itself as a scoop, or would it try to notify a TV station who could show up at the front desk asking questions anytime between now and tomorrow morning? After I hung up the phone with Jen, I broke into a cold sweat, called Miriam, and told her that I would be home within the hour. If a reporter showed up at our house, at least I could hunker down and weather the storm in my own bed. We were going to have to roll the dice with the kids and how they would be received at school. I gathered up my belongings, throwing them into the car as quickly as possible, and drove home, about seventy-two hours after I had arrived.

The next morning it was time to read up on the CDC guidelines. The source of the misunderstanding became immediately apparent and revolved around the concept of what constituted high risk. Normally a health-care worker in the United States would consider direct contact with a patient who had a serious communicable disease to be a high-risk situation. But the CDC guidelines regarded people who had known direct contact with Ebola *without* protective gear to be high risk, while anyone who had known contact with Ebola patients while wearing PPE to be at *some* risk, and even a casual reading made clear that I fell into this category. Whoever had been calling the *T&G* reporter hadn't bothered to read the criteria carefully and instead went directly to the recommendations on what to do with these people, having placed me in the wrong category.

No article appeared in that morning's edition, and I spent much of the day—now safely tucked away in a new office in a research building, far from the corridors of the hospital, as I had been explicitly enjoined from venturing there—reviewing drafts of press releases by both the school and the hospital about my return, as both institutions felt compelled to make some announcement so as to get ahead of the story. Why there needed to be a "story" at all, of course, was a question only I was turning over in my mind. Or at least it felt that way; everyone else was in damage-control mode, and I was a radioactive particle that someone needed to demonstrate UMass was taking care to seal in a lead-lined chamber for the next three weeks.

It wasn't that people from within the institution, even at the highest levels, weren't proud of what I had done and wanted to support me. My boss, Bob Finberg, had given me a temporary posh parking spot adjacent to the building of my temporary office (which had the added advantage of preventing me from walking the quarter mile to the building and randomly hugging whomever I happened to encounter at a given moment) and had indicated he would support any ongoing work I would do while the outbreak continued. Katherine Luzuriaga's group, which had received the funding from the Paul G. Allen Family Foundation, was prepared to sketch out what role I might play in their grant. And various colleagues dropped by to make sure I was being fed, since I wasn't allowed to go to the cafeteria. They also came to ask about my experiences, about which I both desperately wanted to talk, and felt guilt for talking about at all.

On the following day, while driving into Worcester from the Boston suburbs, my cell phone rang. I answered through the car speaker system and heard a voice saying, "Doctor Hatch? The chancellor would like to speak with you. Can you please hold for a second?" And then, the chancellor's voice.

"Listen, Steven, I know this must be a very stressful time with all of this paranoia," he said. "I can't believe what's been going on with a news story about you being dangerous by hugging people. So I want to make an offer. Why don't you come in here to my office today, and we'll get our photographer to come by, and I can give you a hug, and we can put that picture up on the school's website so that everyone knows you're perfectly safe to be around?"

This from a man I've not only never met, but never even conceived of meeting. "Well, thank you, chancellor, that's a very kind offer," I said. "I think at the moment I'm going to take a pass only because I'd like to keep my face out of public view."

One brief pause, exquisitely timed to convey total disbelief, followed by his reply, "It's an interesting policy for someone who was just featured on a *60 Minutes* story that was seen by thirteen million people."

I had no snappy comeback for that except that my concerns were local: The UMass employees that I was most concerned about probably *hadn't* seen me on *60 Minutes*, which I was on for a scant twenty seconds anyway, and weren't likely to see it either. So I could still move about the campus as a reasonably anonymous figure. Not that I was really moving anywhere at all; I went to my office and stayed there most of the day before going home. But if we posted a photograph of me on the school website, whatever anonymity I still possessed would vanish, and from my point of view, that was just begging for trouble.

That afternoon both the school and the hospital issued a press release, saying that I was a doctor who had been to Liberia to work with Ebola patients and had now returned, and that I wouldn't be seeing any patients or come *anywhere* near the hospital in the immediate aftermath of my return. You could hear the press release practically shout this last point. The Ebola Hugging Doctor story never materialized, and a different reporter from *T&G* followed up on the press release in a story that would run the following morning.

The local anxieties were addressed in a headline that must have been music to the ears of the hospital administrators: "Back from Liberia, UMass Memorial Doctor Will Not Treat Patients for 21 Days." You could almost hear someone in an office in the hospital add, *See? It's still okay to come to our medical center!* The picture that ran was one of me from the ETU in full gear, my face covered in a mask, and that was music to *my* ears, so to speak. Anyone wishing to recognize me on campus was going to have to go to the trouble of an Internet search. Moreover, no story materialized in the Boston area, and no neighbors or parents of my children's classmates seemed to be assembling outside my doorstep bearing pitchforks and torches. It looked like I would get through the monitoring phase without a major event, provided I didn't come down with Ebola.

The three weeks of pseudo-isolation, and the daily tension that came along with each new development, served the purpose of keeping me mentally and emotionally occupied. My daily temperature had to be taken in front of a public health official to prove that I was not running a fever, and after several days I learned to my surprise just how low I could run, with the thermometer consistently hitting 35.5 degrees (or just about 96 degrees Fahrenheit). Neither the official nor I believed it initially, but repeated measurements with different thermometers seemed to confirm it. The lowest I ran was an astonishing 35.3 degrees Celsius, or 95.5 degrees Fahrenheit. That was more than a curiosity, since low body temperatures are *also* associated with severe infections just as much as a fever, and again I fretted about what might happen if a reporter got hold of these numbers.

Then there was my left elbow, which presented an entirely new dilemma. Five straight weeks of wearing PPE had been brutal on my skin, especially my legs and arms. In my final week at the ETU, my skin had become so raw on that part of my body that I was forced to raid the supply closet so that I could wrap my elbows in gauze bandages. More than a week later, the left elbow was getting red and sore. I knew that it was, at worst, bursitis, an annoying but not deadly problem.

But what would happen if I got a fever, which could easily happen in a bad case of bursitis? Normally I'd just call a colleague and ask for a prescription of antibiotics, and when I warned the weekend on-call ID physician about my situation, that's exactly what he offered to do. I pointed out that if I was given medical help without a formal evaluation, there would be many questions asked in retrospect that might prove to be thoroughly unpleasant for both of us if I did develop Ebola. But getting a formal evaluation for a fairly trivial matter was asking for a different kind of trouble, since the evaluation would by necessity require Biosafety Level 4 procedures, and rumors of the Ebola doctor requiring medical attention would become almost instantaneously exaggerated. Even *mentioning* the matter to my colleague put us both at risk. This kind of second-guessing activity kept me busy for hours at a stretch.

Sooner or later, though, I knew that the excitement would abate and that I was going to need to process what I had just lived through and, given that I had now become enmeshed with the outbreak, figure out what my next move would be. I could not simply walk away from it until it was over, but I wasn't sure what I was going to do.

9

MAWAH

Community leaders needed to be convinced that the disease was real. During the current Ebola epidemic, earning community trust and confidence in response efforts has at times been challenging. In Mawah, community members might only have been willing to accept the proposed quarantine after witnessing the devastating effect Ebola had on the village. . . . [T]he appropriate isolation of sick persons and comprehensive contact tracing remain essential components of an Ebola response, irrespective of decisions on community quarantine.

—Centers for Disease Control, "Morbidity and Mortality Weekly Report," *February 27, 2015*

While I fretted about my elbow in mid-November 2014, Dr. Trish Henwood had shifted her work from the IMC ambulance service to the wards. By that point, a crush of patients from Gbarpolu County had been absorbed. Gbarpolu, which lies to the northwest of Bong County, is Liberia's most remote area, with essentially two roads into its interior. The limited access proved a valuable asset in keeping Ebola at bay, since it was difficult for an infected person to bring the disease into such an isolated area. The WHO situation reports would show a map of Liberia, shading the counties that had seen Ebola cases. Nearly every county in Sierra Leone and Liberia was colored, although Gbarpolu remained pristine white until October 8, when it finally saw its first case. Once Ebola came to Gbarpolu, however, that inaccessibility served as a trap, and bringing patients to ETUs became a dangerous and demanding exercise. It was not unusual for the ambulance team to have to drive three hours, then get in a canoe for another hour, and walk on foot for another still in order to retrieve patients. Then there was the trip back.

The Gbarpolu patients practically overran the ETU. Our confirmed ward had been designed to hold, at its maximum, forty-five patients. While I worked there, we came within range of that number only rarely. But combined with the influx of patients who were still coming in from Bong and Nimba counties, the Gbarpolu bolus stretched the ETU beyond capacity. On the confirmed side, there weren't enough beds, and patients had to sleep on the floor. To make matters worse, the Gbarpolu patients had one other unusual feature: They *bled*. For the first time in the Bong County ETU, patients began to present just like Richard Preston had described them. Trish said that their clinical behavior was different, the bleeding out of proportion to anything we had seen before. She wondered whether generations of isolation led to small genetic changes that could account for the differences she and the rest of the staff were observing. It would be a question that could be answered with only speculation, for the outbreak was still on and that level of scientific research would have to wait.

While the Bong ETU was coping with this massive surge in its census, other ETUs were quietly continuing their steady decline. The article that Sheri Fink had written suggesting that the worst might be over was now starting to look like a real possibility. By the time that I completed my monitoring period, Liberia recorded only sixty-seven newly confirmed cases—a number that we wouldn't have dared dream about while at Camp Ebola in mid-September. When combined with Sierra Leone and Guinea, the total number of new cases stood at six hundred. The trends looked encouraging, although this number from one single week in the West African outbreak was, all by itself, still substantially larger than what had previously been the second-largest Ebola outbreak, which had lasted more than an entire year.

As the initial excitement from all of the distractions of homecoming finally died down and my first month back gave way to the second, I finally let the tide of grief that I had tried to keep at bay overwhelm me. Mainly I sat in my office and stared out the window. Massachusetts in December is a depressing scene to begin with, as the hard frosts and bracing winds come along with a sun that almost testily insists on starting its decline not long after three o'clock. To match the out-side weather, my mood willingly turned dark. I withdrew from people, wandered about in a daze, and avoided public gatherings. When I did venture out, I carried myself in a completely different manner than I had before in my life. As a friend remarked to Miriam after observing me at a luncheon, while I sat there quiet as a mouse, "It's like he's lost a layer of skin."

That I was able to get up in the morning and eke out a day at work without raising too much alarm among my colleagues, including giv-ing a reasonably decent Grand Rounds presentation on my experi-ences to my department, might have been the greatest trick I pulled off during this stretch. But I was reeling, and I couldn't fully explain why that was so.

The simple explanation was that I had post-traumatic stress dis-order, and a few people, including some whose job it is to make such diagnoses, thought this to be true. But that diagnosis rankled me on more than one level. For starters, I felt that showed incredible disre-spect to the Afghanistan and Iraq War veterans who had genuine and unambiguous PTSD. I have seen some of those people in my work, and to compare my experience to theirs is to significantly discount their suffering or inflate my own. They were routinely jarred, without any warning whatsoever, by bombs, bullets, and flashes of all manner, often for months at a stretch, watching perhaps dozens of friends or civilians get blown up. What did I do? I went to work, slept in a com-fortable bed, showered every day, and got an op-ed published in *The New York Times*. That's hardly deserving of the word "trauma."

Moreover, what everyone else thought so difficult—watching people die—is what I do in part for a living, and I had long acclimated to that aspect of my work. As Nahid Bhadelia, the doctor who had worked in even grimmer circumstances in Sierra Leone at the height of the outbreak, had noted, people who died of Ebola were just dying of sepsis brought on by a severe viral illness. About thirty-five people died on my watch while I worked in Bong County, which is a lot, but it was nothing compared to what the MSF doctors had seen in the huge Monrovia ETUs, where at its worst it wasn't out of the question to witness that many die in a *day*. Of those thirty-five, I personally found about six or seven of those patients after they had died. None of them had died in an especially grisly manner, Richard Preston and his *Hot Zone* descriptions be damned.

True, it wasn't a hell of a lot of fun to place a toddler in a body bag, especially with his mother a few rooms away. I could, however, recall the event in my mind without being emotionally overwhelmed, but also just as importantly I was able to still experience emotions about it, feeling appropriately somber. I just didn't feel traumatized.

Nevertheless, I was in a state of turmoil, some of which had to do with the actual experience, but most of which involved the unfortunate mind-set by which I had launched myself into the epidemic a few months before. I had had many conversations with the other expats who made the decision to come over, and everyone talked about "making their peace." That is, they knew that losing their lives in one form or another was a *risk* that they were willing to take in the name of some higher purpose. I did something different: I just *assumed* I was a dead man walking and that I wasn't coming out of Liberia alive.

I hadn't formulated the idea fully as I was headed over there, but it became clear that's how I viewed things when people back home were writing me and asking me about my fear, of which I had none at all. I offhandedly mentioned this to Sheri at one point, saying the reason I wasn't scared was because I knew I was, in some important sense, already dead, so what was the point in having any fear? She rolled her eyes, having already grown a bit weary of some of my more melodramatic pronouncements.

What I *did* share with many other volunteers was a sense that I didn't belong in the States, for the work in West Africa was far from over. I desperately wanted to return, and almost within days of coming home I was trying to figure out how I could get back to an ETU. What I missed was the profound sense of purpose that such work had provided, and I slowly realized why people talked of "missing the war," a phrase that always seemed discordant to my ears. You *miss* being in the midst of senseless butchery? *Great*. But I belatedly realized it was that purposefulness, the sense that you were doing something that was deeply and truly meaningful, that drove people back to such unstable situations.

It was also during this time that I thought in a more organized way about why patients had died. I thought a lot about fluids—in particular, intravenous fluids. If, as my own two eyes had shown me, Ebola was a disease closer in appearance to severe gastroenteritis than it was to a river of blood being unleashed, then giving back as much fluid as possible might take a disease with a 50 to 70 percent mortality and turn it into one with a 10 to 20 percent mortality.

The evidence to support this had been accumulating while I was doing my work. During the week I returned home in November, *The New England Journal of Medicine* published an issue almost exclusively devoted to Ebola. One of the articles dealt with a German expat who had been working as an epidemiologist for the WHO and had gotten infected in the course of his duties. He was eventually flown home and cared for in an intensive care unit, where he had the misfortune of having a bacterial bloodstream infection on top of his Ebola. Being in a Western facility, the team caring for him was able to quantify precisely how much fluid he was losing, how much fluid he was receiving, his body temperature, his weight, basic laboratory values—as many variables as could be mustered for the article.

While his fluid losses seemed consistent with everything I had witnessed in Bong County, looking at the data on the printed page nevertheless shocked me. He had arrived in Germany ten days into his illness, and *still* fluid was pouring out of him. On the eleventh and twelfth days, he lost nearly ten liters through diarrhea and vomit each day. Ten liters is more than two and a half *gallons* of fluid. Moreover, these measurements didn't take into account how much fluid he was losing from the fever, which was also substantial. Based on what I had seen, the worst of these "wet symptoms" started around day eight, give or take. If these numbers were to be extrapolated, that meant that over the course of an infection, a patient could lose something in the vicinity of three dozen liters of body fluid, or nearly ten gallons. Most Liberians are small or lean or both, so a reasonable guess is that many or most of our patients weighed somewhere in the range of 150 to 170 pounds. Ten gallons is equivalent to half that weight, which is so much that it can't be believed, but whatever the real number, it gives a sense of just how severe this illness could be. No wonder so many people were dying. Bleeding wasn't the biggest problem; fluid loss was.

All that was required to turn this tide, at least in theory, was aggressive IV hydration. Everyone back in the States was obsessed with space-age drugs like ZMapp, but the answer might have been something much more mundane—and easily available for distribution within West Africa. Phebe, the hospital a mile down the road from the ETU, had an IV saline production plant that supplied much of Liberia with this critical product. Steve Whiteley had always advocated aggressive hydration as the optimal approach, and he used his time during the quieter night shift to hang as many bags of fluid as possible. Even before I left in November I could see the compelling logic, but I started to think about fluid replacement in new ways.

For instance, we spent a fair amount of time gathering, distributing, and recording a number of medications given to patients, many of which were likely to have a limited impact on actually saving their lives. The problem with that approach was that it chewed up precious work time in the Hot Zone, which was always a race against the clock due to the physical stresses of wearing PPE. If fluids were the key, and we only had so much time, why were we prioritizing the less effective interventions? This was pure speculation on my part, but I wondered about the mortality impact of an ETU that had specialized "fluid brigades," whose sole job would be to distribute nearly round-the-clock bags of IV saline or its equivalent. All that was needed was a good deal more labor, which is cheap in a place like Liberia, and more bags of fluid, which didn't seem to have a supply issue (unlike, say, PPE suits, which were becoming increasingly more difficult to obtain given the huge increase in demand in the United States as every hospital cobbled together an "Ebola preparedness plan" for cases that they were incredibly unlikely to see).

So I thought that if I could get back to an ETU, I might be able to make a difference, and I started to scheme ways in which I could return as soon as possible. I spoke with some people from the International Rescue Committee about working in a large ETU in Sierra Leone, and I continued to talk with Sean about how I might be incorporated back into IMC's overall plans. It seemed like I had promising leads, and my hope that I would be back in Africa kept the despair at bay, at least in part.

As before, getting my goals to align with the institutional imperatives of UMass proved challenging, and also as before, the details to explain the conflicts are tedious. But by mid-January, I had decided that I was headed back over there one way or another, even if it meant that I wasn't in a position to mount my attack on Ebola with my fluid brigades. For by that time, there were plenty of volunteers for ETU work in the pipeline, and so I wasn't needed for that kind of work, even if it was what I most wanted to do. What they *didn't* have in full supply were trainers—people who not only had ETU experience but actually knew something about the virus, its history, its physiology, the purpose of infection control, and so on. They were looking to add another teacher to prepare this vast pipeline of volunteers for the ETUs that were belatedly popping up now across the country, and that played to my strengths.

Bong County had proven an ideal site for the training, since not only was there an ETU in which genuine "hot training" could take place, but the campus of Cuttington University allowed for everything else that such training would require: dorms, classrooms, and a large-scale kitchen to feed the dozens of people in each training class. "Ebola University" was in its infancy as I was leaving, but it was fully developed by January, and I would be its scholar-in-residence for another five-week spin.

When I got back to Cuttington, I found a completely transformed site. In October 2014, it was a ghost town, populated only by the IMC volunteers who numbered one or two dozen, as well as a skeleton crew. But the students had begun to return, at first in small numbers, but eventually it looked very much like what a college campus should. IMC, which had had complete run of the place previously, was now confined to one corner of the campus, occupying the dorms and classrooms of the Agriculture School that had yet to open. When the IMC staff, most of whom were white Americans or Europeans, ventured around the central portion of the university, we were greeted by curious stares from young, black Liberians. It was *their* campus and we

were its oddball guests. I took it as a sign that normalcy was returning to life in Liberia, and that gave me great comfort.

We ran weeklong sessions for cohorts of twenty or more trainees.
The on-campus training was a split of classroom time and "cold training" where people learned to don and doff PPE and simulate basic
tasks required for care of patients with Ebola right on campus in a
mock ETU. That was followed by the hot training where they went to
the Bong ETU and tended to the patients there under careful supervision of the existing IMC staff. Mainly my job was to provide three or
four lectures about the epidemiology, science, and clinical aspects of
Ebola, and help out during the cold-training exercises. I had no hand
in their hot training, although I did usually accompany the trainees at
least once or twice to the ETU, in part because I wanted to make sure
they transitioned nicely, in part because the wireless there was perfect.
Either way, it meant that I had a lot of downtime, and although I was
a good deal happier to be back in Liberia, I still had some difficulty
pushing back the darkness that seemed to have ingrained itself into
my outlook.

I don't think I was the only one. The after-hours socializing among
the staff, who unlike me had mostly *not* returned to their home countries for a prolonged convalescence but had been gritting it out for three
or four months, almost always involved a moderate to heavy amount
of alcohol consumption. There was never any real drinking in October and November, with alcohol being used sparingly, nothing more
than a social lubricant, with one glass of wine per person on the rare
occasion when everyone got together for a group dinner. By February,
a river of gin and tonic water was flowing through Gbarnga, and the
local merchants must have been delighted supplying the newfound
demand. Fortunately for me, gin is among the few types of alcohol I
really don't like, and so I kept my drinking to not especially tasty
Liberian beer and only the occasional desperate binge, during which
times I did enjoy myself immensely.

In particular, I suspect that the team tasked with witnessing the
devastation the virus had wrought in the community was coping with
an absurd amount of grief. During the ETU's heady days in September through December 2014, the psychosocial support staff had tried

to find answers to such heartrending questions as what to do with a child who had survived the infection but now would not be accepted back by her village or had no family to return to because they were all dead. They also tackled issues such as helping adult survivors find jobs, encouraging villages to accept survivors back into the community, and simply figuring out how to get patients from the ETU back to their homes, which could often be several hours away. These were among the issues they dealt with on a daily basis. It was clear to me not long after I had arrived in October that the psychosocial support staff had the *hardest* job in the ETU, for while the medical staff tended to the destruction of the body, their team saw the damage of the outbreak through the lens of human connection and loss and suffering and grief.

Now in January the outbreak was nearly over: There were no cases in Bong County or its neighbors, and only a few suspect cases trickled in each day to the ETU. But the psychosocial support team was still hard at work dealing with the aftermath, as the entire country was in the midst of a *genuine* post-traumatic stress disorder. Liberians had faced what they thought would be the end of the world, and now they were trying to piece their lives back together. The psychosocial support staff, or "PSS" as we called it, of which about half were Liberian but the rest of whom came from all corners of the globe, were going to try to bridge a huge number of cultural barriers to aid in this transformative process. It was a tall order.

When I was doing my ETU work, I never had the time to do anything other than work in the Hot Zone and tend to the patients. There was a sufficient amount of paperwork that needed to be done during the downtime, and that meant that I had little chance to see the other workings of the operation or to witness the work of the PSS team up close. PSS was led by a German expat, Dr. Fredericka Feuchte. Fredericka had been living in Monrovia for a few years prior to the outbreak; she came here as part of a research project on the psychological health of the Liberian community in the wake of the Civil War and quickly realized that such work could not be done, or at least done well, by bouncing back and forth to Germany. So she had set up shop in Liberia, doing her research and collaborating with colleagues back home.

Then Ebola came and everything changed, and she found herself running a crisis response to the innumerable social and psychological problems that the outbreak had introduced. During September and October she worked with a staff of about ten nationals, some but not all of whom had formal training in psychology or social work. Despite these rather harrowing working conditions, Fredericka somehow managed to maintain the brightest smile in all of Bong County, one so pleasant that I would actively seek it out on especially rough days.

One of the nationals that worked in the psychosocial support team was Garmai Cyrus, the woman I became friends with during my previous deployment. When I first came back to the ETU, within a day or two I wandered over to the psychosocial hut to find her. The outbreak was still technically on, and the rules regarding not touching anyone were still in force. We looked at one another when I came to the door, and I thought, *To hell with the rules*, and wrapped my arms around her, the first moment I had touched anyone in Liberia since this whole mess began. Let 'em send me home if they have to. Nobody seemed to care as we held each other for a few moments, trying to use that time to process what we had seen together.

Because there was downtime in February, I wanted to take the opportunity to see what they did. As IMC's Liberian operations had expanded to include the Kakata ETU, Fredericka's work likewise grew, and she came to oversee two separate staffs, splitting time between Bong and Kakata in addition to returning to her apartment in Monrovia. And unlike the rest of the workers in the ETU, the PSS team was still very busy, although obviously its work had shifted from sorting out immediate matters for patients and their families to assessing the psychological impact of the outbreak on some of the harder-hit communities and helping those communities process some of the loss. But that required poring over the records to see which communities were hardest hit, organizing trips to those places, establishing rapport with the locals, and maintaining those ties over time. They had become, at least partly, a traveling psychotherapy outfit, making weekly stops at some of the more deeply affected villages.

When I showed up asking questions about sitting in with the PSS team, I met a young Irishman, Eoin Ó Riain, who had been in Bong since early December, along with Marco Morelli, a somewhat free-spirited American who was working on his Ph.D. in psychology in California and came to Liberia to help out while organizing his thesis materials. I ended up living with both of them in the dorms at Cuttington, and when I inquired about joining them, they said, "Hey, we're going to Mawah on Saturday. Garmai herself is running one of the group sessions, she'd love to have you come. We're going to stop off at the Kakata ETU for the night and drive to Mawah at first light. What do you think?"

That was a no-brainer, so I packed up my belongings on Friday the 13th of February (yes, truly) and took the exceedingly bumpy, dirty, hot, and long car ride into Margibi County. As we drove on one patch of dirt road adjacent to a stretch of the highway that was under construction, we finally made the turnoff to the Kakata ETU just past five in the afternoon.

The living quarters for the Kakata ETU staff were immediately adjacent to the patient care areas, housed in a building originally intended to be a county outpost of the Liberian Ministry of Health. The permanent construction was two stories and made of concrete, with the medical and staff offices on the first floor, and what amounted to dorm rooms on the second. In Bong, the staff were scattered across various residences on the Cuttington University campus, but here many of the staff, including all of the expats, were concentrated on the second floor of this building as well as in a few satellite cottages within a hundred meters or so. The conditions were clean and, in relative terms, luxurious; a lounge sat in the middle of the building and had an enormous flat-screen TV with a satellite hookup, and a well-stocked fridge stood nearby. I took to calling it Hotel Kakata during my brief stay.

Though somewhat haggard from the bumpy and dirty ride, the PSS team immediately arranged a debriefing in anticipation of the following day's events in Mawah, so that everyone knew the plan. The five members of the Bong PSS team were joined by three of the PSS staff from Kakata. Because the other office space was occupied, we convened the meeting in a small but well-lit storage room that held the toiletries for the ETU, making space amid cubbies filled with soap bars and toothbrushes, and large, trash-barrel-sized bins that contained clothes for patients, since they would have to leave their current ones behind to be burned as they left the high-risk area.

Mawah had been one of the main villages the PSS team targeted early on as being in special need of help. About eight hundred people live in Mawah, a typical Liberian village tucked into the jungle about an hour's drive from Kakata and roughly a five-mile walk to Hinde, the first community on the paved road. On the last day of August 2014, the virus crept into the village in the form of a young man who had lived in Kakata. He was twenty-two and was a student but had fallen ill days before and had ventured to Mawah to seek help from his mother's family, as she hailed from the tiny village. He stayed briefly before returning to the town of Bong Mines, halfway to Kakata, where he died and was buried by other family members on September 4. From there, the nurse aid who had cared for the patient himself fell ill and traveled to two other villages named Monokparga and Kalikata Meca, where at least nine other people became infected, though what became of them and whether it spread further, I do not know. The events of the Mawah cluster, which included the information about the other two villages affected by this ill-fated young man, were being reported by the CDC in its "Morbidity and Mortality Weekly Report" at almost the exact moment I was walking around the village.

Once Ebola had made its entrance to Mawah, it started to pick off the villagers one by one. By the time the virus vanished, more than twenty people had become infected and nearly all of them died. Everyone in the village was linked to the dead by blood or friendship or mutual work. Nobody could escape anguish of some sort. Now, four months later, they were beginning to process some of that grief. IMC's team had been busy, making weekly visits and running group sessions of about twenty people per group lasting two hours or more.

Each of the leaders of the four group-therapy sessions reviewed the main topics of discussion from the previous week and what they anticipated was likely to happen in the next session. Garmai sketched out the particulars of her group: There was to be a bit of a "truth and reconciliation" moment, and she wanted everyone to be alert to the potential for explosiveness.

The matter related to the death of one of the villagers, whom we'll call Alex. Alex's best friend was Elijah. Elijah was from Monrovia and had come to the village a few years ago after having met and married Alex's sister Esther. It must have been a huge adjustment to come from the bustle and density of Monrovia to the isolation and quietude of Mawah, but Elijah settled in, helping the family with planting the crops and gathering the fish from the river that ran beside the village. He and Alex became close, and as I heard this part of the story, I was struck by how Elijah's story was a Liberian version of an archetypal tale often told in the United States or Britain, that of the grizzled city dweller who came to find peace and happiness in the sleepy countryside, though instead of some quaint little hamlet lush with grass and maple trees, this was a complex of mud-brick houses with dirt floors and palm trees.

But you know that this story doesn't end happily. Alex got infected sometime in September and died not long thereafter. For reasons that weren't yet clear to me, Alex's mother—that is, Elijah's mother-in-law, Matta—apparently held Elijah responsible for Alex's death.

"Wait. I'm not getting something," I said to Garmai. "Why does she think he's responsible? Do we know how he got infected?"

"Yeah—Alex took his nephews to the clinic in Hinde," she said. "They both had Ebola and died." Which meant that Matta had not only lost her son, she lost two grandchildren on top of that. So I could see that Matta had gone through some horrible psychological trauma, but I still didn't understand why she was targeting Elijah as the cause of Alex's death.

"What happened to the parents of those children?" I asked.

"Oh, they were the children of Alex's brother, and he got infected too," she replied. And then, almost offhandedly: "You know, *he* was treated in our ETU."

"Really? When?"

"He came in the end of September."

"What was his name?"

"Aaron Singbeh."

Oh good Lord, I thought. Aaron Singbeh was the man I encountered lying in the hallway of the suspect ward during my first few moments in the high-risk area.

We were told to be up and ready to go at 7:00 a.m., but Liberian time has a way of seeing deadlines come and then watching them drift by, so we didn't leave the Kakata ETU until just before eight. During the lull, I sat in front of the entrance to the living quarters, watching the activity as the night shift finished its work and the day shift came on, eating a breakfast of hard-boiled egg whites, which I used to scoop up some sausages in Liberian red sauce. I also saw a few alumni from the Bong ETU and was glad to hear their greetings.

The ride to Mawah took a little more than an hour. The road to the village goes from Kakata through Bong Mines. You take a right in the town center and proceed on a dirt road until you reach Hinde, where a large holding center had been constructed for isolating contacts of Ebola patients. By February, Ebola had nearly vanished, but that didn't stop local politicians from rounding up anyone who could be remotely considered at risk. As patients were turned away from the international aid organization ETUs because they did not meet the strict definition of suspected cases, the holding centers maintained a steady business, for the funding to keep such centers open proved irresistible to local politicians, the strangest form of governmental pork project ever known. The ongoing detention of Liberians in holding centers like the one in Hinde once again indicated that Ebola could spread its horrors beyond those who were merely unlucky enough to become infected.

The road to Mawah is found by taking a left off the main road just past the holding center. Almost instantly the jungle embraces you, as the road narrows to one lane surrounded by high palm trees. We were in the height of the dry season when we drove, but the ruts in the dirt road suggested that the village was isolated from nearly all forms of motorized travel when the rains came. Just to get to Hinde must have been an all-day affair during the rainy season, making transporting bulk supplies a logistical nightmare. In all likelihood, the village had to be self-sufficient for months at a stretch.

We finally arrived and, unsurprisingly, were greeted like illustrious dignitaries. The PSS team had been coming to Mawah weekly for more than a month at that point, and the villagers had appeared enthusiastic, not only because the IMC staff were offering a chance to formally process some of the horrible events that had befallen them, but also I suspected because of reasons why villagers everywhere, in every age, enjoy receiving visitors: It breaks up the tedium. That and the eight or so cases of Coca-Cola we brought.

After an hour of milling about, perhaps a hundred or more villagers gathered in the main meeting area for lunch and a brief program before splitting off into discussion groups, each led by a member of the staff. As part of the program, the assembly had begun singing various songs. Just as I had reacted in Grace Baptist Church in Gbarnga months before, I was thunderstruck by the magnificence of the tonality as well as the joy and urgency spurred on by a simple rattle composed of beads surrounding a hollow gourd. As much as I loved hearing the morning devotional at the ETU, that was Western music, hymns written by some German or Briton one hundred years ago and had since become adapted to the cadences of Liberia. But the singing I was hearing in Mawah was entirely different. This time I pulled out my phone without any shame whatsoever and started to record the proceedings.

A circle formed, and various leaders went to the middle and started to dance, progressing in what I assumed was some form of hierarchy, starting with the most important villager and proceeding down through those who possessed some kind of rank. Maybe a half-dozen people in all had performed for the group. Eventually the IMC staff started to take their turns, each performing their own idiosyncratic moves—some of which, to be as charitable as possible, were not especially consistent with traditional African dancing. I supposed the juxtaposition of odd Western moves to the ambient music might have been taken for normal behavior at the Burning Man festival, but it might not have been what the villagers were accustomed to witnessing on a daily basis. I could see where this was headed, so when all eyes fell upon me I immediately moved to the center and decided to inject my own bit of ethnic background into this fast-agglomerating cultural goulash, improvising some Mayim steps from Israeli folk dancing into a rural Liberian Flying Hora. It may not have been pretty, but it seemed to earn goodwill, which was my only goal at that moment.

We adjourned to a series of classrooms a few hundred meters away in a school that hadn't seen any capital improvements in many years.

They were rooms with floors and walls and a roof over the entire structure, but not much else except some old and very tight desks. As we were at the height of the dry season, the interiors were baking, even hotter than the ETU on a bad day, although this time I wasn't wearing PPE. When the heat of the place combined with the lunch now digesting itself in my stomach, I found I had to fight myself from sliding into a postprandial coma, especially as the meeting was being conducted almost exclusively in Kpelleh.

But fireworks soon ensued. Matta, the mother of Alex Singbeh, who had died of Ebola in Mawah, had declined to come to the meeting. I was partly relieved and partly disappointed, since she was *also* the mother of Aaron Singbeh, my first patient in the ETU, and I both sought and dreaded some form of closure by encountering her. In her absence she had sent her daughter to do the talking to Elijah, Alex's best friend. And talk she did. Whatever drowsiness I had experienced as the meeting began and the pleasantries were still being exchanged quickly evaporated as Matta's daughter, perhaps fifteen minutes into the meeting, launched into a verbal explosion that lasted no less than a half hour and was interrupted by nobody at all, including the village elders, who clearly believed they had the right to interrupt whenever they pleased. Not one word of it was in English, and while I cannot describe the content as a consequence, there was no missing the urgency.

She finished. Then, silence.

Elijah then spoke, mostly quietly, and again I was plunged back into a state of cultural and linguistic illiteracy. All I could do was try to read the body language of those around me, which wasn't much of a guide. Finally, and mercifully, the IMC staff began to explain to me that Elijah was explaining his side of the story.

Elijah had seen Alex take his ailing niece and nephew to the clinic in Hinde. They would not return. When Alex took to fever, enough had transpired in the village for Elijah to know what had happened, as did Alex himself. At that point, Alex made the fateful decision to transport himself by boat across the river that ran alongside Mawah, to an island that had some temporary structures used for fishing but was not fully inhabited, in effect creating a self-imposed isolation zone. The shores of the island were far enough away that Alex could communicate, perhaps fifty yards or so.

But the virus began to tear Alex apart as it did most, and soon his visits to the shore to reassure his family and friends became smaller in number and shorter in duration. After several days, he simply didn't come. At which point, Elijah faced the decision of whether he should help his friend or just leave him to his fate.

It was just as this heartbreaking account was being relayed to me that I realized everyone was looking at me, for while I was listening to the translation, another member of the staff was telling everyone that the doctor would speak. Given that my moment in church four months before had been a dry run for this moment, I at least had an idea of what I would say on the spot. And unlike my moment in Gbarnga, I had a firmer sense of what needed to be said, even if I had missed the vast majority of the nuances of why there was so much discord.

I first apologized for having to speak in English, and American English at that, so that even those who were fairly conversant in what they thought was English were going to have a hard time with my accent. I went slowly and asked one of the IMC staff to translate into Kpelleh, and I halted every few sentences.

"This virus is transmitted by touch," I said. "People who touch those with the disease can become infected, but not everyone who touches the sick becomes infected.

"When people become more sick, they are more likely to pass along the infection. When Alex got sick on the island, anyone who touched him and tried to care for him was at the highest risk of becoming infected."

I then looked straight at Elijah and stopped talking for a moment. I did not understand anything of the social rules in this village, knew nothing of their worldview, and could only remotely grasp the kind of trauma they had survived. But I was willing to risk all the potential misunderstandings in making a simple declaration out of the belief that some motivations, and regrets, are universal. I have no idea whether this is true now, but I said it then, with the hope that I was bridging the divides that separated me from this community.

"Elijah," I said, "it isn't your fault that Alex died. He was going to die no matter what you did. And all you would have done by going over to be with him is that you probably would have gotten sick yourself, and died as well. I'm sorry to say all of this. I am a doctor, and I can tell you that anyone who cared for Alex probably would have gotten sick. This is why Alex isolated himself. He knew. None of this is your fault."

At roughly the same time as I was ambling around Mawah doing what I could to support the psychosocial team, in the United States an outbreak of a different sort was under way. In California, a minor sensation occurred when a few dozen cases of measles came to medical attention. The spread was mainly due to unvaccinated children roaming around Disneyland. Although it is not clear which child was Patient Zero, the parents of that child probably brought the family to the park, either unaware or unconcerned about their child's sniffles and sneezes. That child would expose other children, spreading the disease predominantly to those who had also not been vaccinated. By the time the outbreak was over, public health authorities in a half-dozen states were involved, and nearly 150 cases had been diagnosed.

The fact that none had died might have led parents who refuse to vaccinate their children to raise their fists in mighty triumph against the Medical Machine of Moloch that would jab their offspring into autism or God knows what other fate in their insatiable greed for profits. All of the warnings of public health officials about measles had proven, unsurprisingly they would contend, to be wild exaggeration. Not only had nobody died, no child suffered any serious complications at all. Given the reaction by the medical establishment, the anti-vaccination parents could wag their fingers at the authorities with a righteous air of I-told-you-so.

Indeed, there was almost a poetic irony in the fact that the epicenter of the measles outbreak was Disneyland. Measles might even be described by the anti-vaccine advocates as a Mickey Mouse virus: cuddly, warm, and inviting. By eschewing vaccination, they believe they are allowing children to come and introduce themselves to the world in a safe and comforting manner, surrounded by people whose principal concern was their development, an event that would take place by exposing them to nature. The executives at Disneyland, however, were not amused by the whole affair. They offered testing and vaccination to their employees and publicly declared that parents whose children were vaccinated were perfectly safe to come—an indirect but unmistakable rebuke to the parents whose children weren't.

The California measles outbreak served as a curious counterpoint to the horrors that were finally abating in West Africa. The self-righteous, and largely willfully ignorant, parents of the children who came down with measles may have derived a measure of emotional satisfaction from having demonstrated that measles wasn't deadly at all. Their children had gotten the rash and felt lousy but were now the better for it, with "heightened" immunity, more ready and able to face the world. Instead, what they had unwittingly demonstrated was that when one plays Russian roulette with a one-thousand-chamber gun, odds are pretty good that you can pull the trigger once without consequence. The problem with measles is that it forces the gun into the *next* person's hand—quickly—and makes them play the same game as well, and so on.

For measles is, in critical ways, almost a perfect mirror image of Ebola. Measles spreads like wildfire; the epidemiologic estimate is that one unvaccinated person can spread the virus on average to *eighteen* other unvaccinated people. Ebola, by contrast, is relatively hard to spread, as one sick person has been estimated to spread infection on average to only *two* people—so that if you institute the proper infection-control precautions, including isolating sick patients, you could stop the virus in its tracks.

But those transmission dynamics carry a hidden truth about just how lethal these diseases are. Ebola is deadly to *you* if you have the misfortune of contracting the disease, but within populations it isn't especially deadly. It lumbers along, and while the daily business of more than twenty million people in West Africa had ground to a standstill because of this killer, it had become clear that the 1.4 million infected worst-case scenario envisioned months before was not going to take place. By contrast, measles appears at first glance to be laughably un-lethal, with a mortality rate of about one in one thousand or so.

But because it spreads so much more efficiently than Ebola, it is no less dangerous in an unvaccinated population. Measles isn't deadly to a *child*, but it is certainly deadly to *children*.

And because the entire medical infrastructure had been shut down for the better part of a year in Guinea, Sierra Leone, and Liberia, with hospitals shuttered and clinics closed, the practice of routine vaccination had vanished. While I wandered around the Liberian countryside contemplating the aftermath of this transformative epidemic, a number-crunching doctoral candidate from Princeton named Saki Takahashi, along with colleagues from other universities in the United States and Europe, wrote a paper that was published in *Science* magazine trying to make some estimates about the effect of the vaccination hiatus. Estimating a 75 percent reduction in the overall vaccination rate in West Africa due to the shutdown of the medical system, Takahashi and her colleagues took into account published data about both the mortality rate of measles and the efficiency by which it spreads. Although their work accounted for a wide range of possibilities, the upper range of their estimates was that as many as sixteen thousand children could die from measles as a direct consequence of Ebola's effect on health infrastructure. At that point in time, the official tally of people dead from Ebola infection was just over ten thousand.

While that latter number was almost certainly an undercount by some unknown quantity, possibly in the thousands, the fact that the estimated measles mortality was even in the same *range* served as an object lesson in what constitutes a virus's lethality. It would turn out that the terror a given virus induces in people is but one factor among many, and may not even be the most important. The measles data also showed that Ebola created ripples well beyond those in whom the virus took up residence. The case fatalities in the WHO situation reports included only those dead from Ebola, but the actual death toll would need to account not only for unvaccinated measles victims but those who could not be treated for, and ultimately succumbed to, typhoid fever, malaria, tuberculosis, pneumococcal pneumonia, and all the other maladies that went untreated while millions were left to fend for themselves.

———

After Mawah, I went back to Cuttington to finish training two more cohorts and then returned home. The landing in Massachusetts was easier, and I was no longer of major interest to anyone. Many people from UMass had gone back and forth by this point, and I had started to ease myself back into my clinical and teaching duties. But one more opportunity opened up, and I returned to Liberia in late June of 2015. This time I was going to stay in Monrovia and resume the work I had started when I first set foot here in 2013: help the residency program get back on its feet. Over the four months I had been away, the medical system in West Africa had slowly started to reboot itself, like a decade-old desktop computer that you should probably scrap, but you hang on to because it remains functional even though it is slow and has only the most basic programs. This meant that residency training would officially resume on July 1, and the Liberian College of Physicians would get back to the business of certifying specialists. Once again, by sheer dumb luck, I managed to return at a critical moment, and also at a time when my own academic and clinical responsibilities back in Massachusetts could be paused.

I would be back at JFK Hospital doing what I love to do, which is teach residents. I would be staying in the Congo Town neighborhood, where most of the embassies were located, as well as a good number of offices of the international aid groups. I was, in fact, a two-block stroll away from the IMC headquarters, and I drifted there from time to time over the next month to socialize.

Compared to my housing in Bong County, I was living in almost obscenely luxurious accommodations. The apartment, which could house up to five or six doctors, nurses, and other professionals from around the globe, had been rented by a consortium known as ACCEL (the Academic Consortium for Combating Ebola in Liberia), one of the many aid groups now flush with cash and putting it to use by sending personnel and equipment to Monrovia for the purpose of getting Liberia back on its feet. Its interiors were clean, and each room had its own air conditioner, the showers had hot water, and there was a fully equipped communal kitchen with a gas stove. It was what anyone would expect from a rudimentary apartment in the West, or even in Monrovia for that matter, if they were living there to work. Indeed, it wasn't especially fancy. But after the cabin-like conditions that I had experienced in February at Cuttington, this was a big step up.

On my first morning back, I made the half-hour walk from my flat to JFK in the pouring rain, for the rainy season was well under way and drenching squalls were now part of the daily routine. I wandered the corridors on my way to the Internal Medicine floor, and it looked much the same as it did when I had first arrived. The commotion of the place was unchanged. The first floor, which housed the outpatient clinics, was thick with people crammed onto rickety benches waiting to see doctors with the same kinds of complaints that can be found in the States, ranging from the mundane to the life-threatening. People wandered about the hallways, hand in hand with loved ones. *Touching*. People in Liberia were touching one another again, and the hospital was back in business.

But no Dr. Borbor this time.

The sole remaining internist on staff at JFK was a Nigerian who had long lived in Liberia named Joseph Njoh, but the residency leadership had been temporarily aided by a Rwandan doctor named Ignace Nzayisenga. He was returning to Rwanda for his wedding and a brief honeymoon soon after I arrived, and I was tasked with covering him during his absence. Joining me was a young Ethiopian doctor, Kidist Tarekegn. I take pride in correctly pronouncing the names of those from other cultures and have what is for me a subversively formal streak, in that I like to always refer to my colleagues as Doctor So-and-So. But Kidist's last name was hopeless, and mastering her first name was difficult enough, for it is harder to get right than it appears on the printed page because of a click in the first syllable. Kidist was new to Liberia, and after a few days I could see the same shock on her face that I had registered on mine when I had first worked here. Experiencing culture shock is predictable whenever you take on a task like this, but going through that in a country that has suffered as Liberia had over the past year could potentially leave scars. I worried about her.

A huge surprise for me was in store the first day I was back, when

I walked into the residents' lounge and saw Phil Ireland standing there. We embraced one another as if after a long journey, each of us knowing that the other had gone to extreme places and had been altered by the experience. Somehow circumstances had placed us in exactly the same position in which we had found ourselves a year and a half before. It was a teacher-student arrangement: I was the teacher of Internal Medicine and Infectious Disease; I was the pupil of Liberian history and its social structure and, above all else, the experience of living through the epidemic when there was nothing but chaos and then becoming infected. We spent a lot of time talking over the next several weeks.

During the first days I often spent some time just wandering around the hospital. One morning I was changing corridors at a brisk pace and stopped dead when I saw a woman named Sia Kammara staring back at me. Sia was one of the key faculty at JFK working in the pediatrics division. Although I had only been at JFK for such a short time before, and had met many Liberians since, I immediately recognized Dr. Kammara for the simple fact that—Lord, and Betty Friedan, forgive me for saying this—she is a stunningly beautiful woman. There was simply no forgetting her face. But she did not appear amused to see me despite my glow in her presence.

Sia had been in the room that day the previous November when I gave the lecture on hemorrhagic fever and had made my little sort-of joke about the Taï Forest Ebolavirus being not too far from Monrovia. It had registered. "Doctor Hatch," she said an instant after confirming that my presence was not apparently that of an apparition. "The last time I saw you, you were making jokes about Ebola being not too far from Monrovia. A few months later, we have the largest Ebola outbreak ever. Then we get rid of Ebola. Now, you have come back, and there are new cases in the country. I think you should leave our country!" Her eyes were pure Betty Davis. I nervously chuckled but wasn't sure whether she was teasing.

She wasn't kidding about the new Ebola case, however. Almost within hours of my touching down at Roberts airport, a young man in Margibi County, in a village known as Nedowein, about a ninety-minute drive from the center of Monrovia, fell ill. He had a fever and body aches. With the Ebola outbreak over, this would almost surely be malaria. After all, the outbreak had been declared over on May 9, and another forty-six days had passed since. But it wasn't malaria. It was Ebola. I found out the news after coming home from work that first day. When weeks before I had made arrangements to return to JFK, I assumed that Ebola would finally be starting its long fade into the Liberian memory. Yet when I arrived home that first night, I was stunned to receive a message from a friend linking to a BBC story describing confirmation of the index case in Margibi.

After reading the story, I was befuddled, since I could not understand *how* Liberia could suddenly have a new case on its hands. Nearly three months had passed since the last case of Ebola, and the longest known incubation time was twenty-one days. Years ago, the World Health Organization had more or less arbitrarily decided that it would double that number as a hedge against premature decreased vigilance, which was how the forty-two-day countdown to declaring an outbreak over came to be. This case, however, was so far past the incubation period that there was no way it was a statistical outlier. At first blush, it made no sense.

I also realized that I had signed up to work at a hospital, to evaluate patients in an emergency room, without the protections of PPE, in a country that now had a new Ebola outbreak on its hands. This was how Borbor himself got infected almost exactly a year ago. Now it could be happening again, and I wasn't working in an ETU but was on the front lines. True, there was now a screening process in place at JFK designed to flag potential cases. Yet when I toured Phebe Hospital in Bong County in February, I had seen firsthand how peoples' vigilance had flagged as the outbreak abated and there were suddenly no more cases to be found. All the paranoid precautions seemed like overkill, and the screeners at the intake areas slacked. We had watched this happen at the time, and I had several conversations with the IMC training staff, who expressed their frustration. Now, months later, there was at least one case, and who knew whether that meant there were others out there, perhaps sick and on their way to JFK at that very moment—or, indeed, already lying on a bed in the inpatient wards? Without protection, I stood a chance of getting infected, and now I had no way of knowing whether that was a highly unlikely scenario or something about which I should be seriously concerned.

I also felt something novel for me since this entire odyssey had begun nearly one year before: I felt fear.

I sat on a couch in the apartment and tried to be a clinician again. *How* did he get infected? Several possibilities, each one more implausible, presented themselves:

1. He had become infected as part of a brand-new outbreak totally unrelated to the previous one, and this was just a weird coincidence of timing. At first, this seemed to simply have "bullshit" written all over it. West Africa had *one* documented case of Ebola prior to the 2014 outbreak—just two spillover events from animal to human since the discovery of Ebola. Now we were to believe that a *third* one would start so soon on the heels of the other? However, *if* Ebola spreads through the bat population in epidemics, it could mean that there might be more copies of the virus in *them* as well, leading to more chances for a bat-human species jump, and this one just happened to take. It was like having more aces in a deck of cards in a game of poker: Sooner or later, someone was going draw one.

2. There was a nonhuman primate animal that became infected and in turn infected the young man. Chimps and gorillas and other primates become sick from Ebola just like we do; maybe there was such an animal involved here? Biologically, this was plausible. Demographically, I was dubious, because Margibi County isn't deep into the jungle where such animals could be found. If a case had popped up in, say, Maryland County, on the border of Ivory Coast, I might buy the theory. Just south of the town of Harbel in Margibi County, there is an island on which a chimpanzee

colony lives, but there hadn't been any talk of a chimpanzee outbreak, and he would still have to have gone there, so I doubted this explanation.

3. There had been a "quiet" chain of transmission that had escaped the notice of health authorities. This seemed to me to be exceedingly unlikely. By June 2015, you couldn't walk into the remotest village in Liberia without tripping over someone who worked for the CDC or the WHO or one of dozens of aid organizations. The contact tracing system even at the end of the outbreak revealed that an impressive display of resources had been directed at finding every possible case. I wouldn't be surprised at all that a case or two might go unnoticed by the surveillance teams during the worst of the crisis in August or September. However, for this scenario to be possible, people would have to have been infecting other people for three straight months, all without anyone ever knowing about it.

4. The virus had *attenuated*—that is, caused milder symptoms that would not be thought of as Ebola—in several people, causing a subclinical chain of transmission, until it hit this young man, and the full force of the virus's pathology returned. This seemed a stretch.

5. There was a reservoir for the virus that we weren't aware of. We had always thought the main reservoir was bats, but what if *other* mammals could become infected and pass it along as well? Cows were rare in Liberia, but dogs were not. Millions of people back in the States had gone temporarily nutty about the dog-can-transmit-Ebola angle when Nina Pham, one of Thomas Eric Duncan's nurses who had become infected, had to have her Cavalier King Charles Spaniel, a preciously cute animal named Bentley, put into quarantine while she recovered. The CDC had to include a page on its website addressing this question. My attitude

had been that this was what comes of a scientifically illiterate society coping with such news. Mosquitoes don't transmit AIDS for the same reason that dogs can't pass Ebola: The virus is just not adapted to live in that organism. We would have been hearing about a sick dog epidemic in West Africa during this outbreak because the opportunities for cross-species transmission between humans and their furry friends were far too great, but there was never once a report of such a problem. We humans just happen to be the unlucky mammals whose molecular biology is welcoming to the virus, and dogs aren't. But would this new case make me reconsider this stance?

I contemplated each of these scenarios in order and dismissed all of them with a shake of the head as if something intellectually icky had been placed on my mental plate. They all seemed outlandish. Over the next few days at least three people had become infected, making it a true outbreak—and making me take a deep breath before I plunged into the work at JFK each morning with the air of *Oh, what the hell* that had made the ETU work go so smoothly, but this time there was no PPE nearby and no spray team cruising the halls.

By this point the international media was starting to report what I was hearing through the back-channel gossip: The concern was about a dog. The three infected people were reported to have eaten a dog together and fell ill soon after. Lest you recoil about the dog consumption, understand that Liberia is a protein-starved nation. A hamburger is an expensive luxury, and a steak, decadent; the red meat that gets served on roadside stands looks more like roasted beef jerky and gets sold for the price of a few sodas. What meat that does get consumed is overwhelmingly chicken, as the birds are fairly easy to raise and don't tax the land resources. So dogs, of which there is an abundant feral population, often get snatched by hungry villagers and turned into food.

The authorities in Liberia were taking the dog hypothesis seriously. My friend Christine Wassuna, who was running one of the Biosafety Level 4 laboratories in central Monrovia, said that they had found where the dog's corpse was buried and would be exhuming it for PCR testing. I was floored by this news, as it seemed to be grasping at straws. There were actual, responsible scientists who thought that *dogs* could be the reservoir? That the virus could hide out and just happen to infect humans? I was incredulous.

Reservoir, I thought. *Where does the virus hide out?* I wondered.

And then it hit me, and I felt stupid for taking as long as I did to realize the answer that had been staring me in the face all along.

Liberia had actually had a near miss with declaring the outbreak over much earlier than May 9. The problem was that, as the epidemic wound down, they got to zero only to find new cases pop up a few days later. The intervals between these cases got longer and longer, however, and eventually the forty-two-day clock started in earnest in early March. Then on March 20, after two weeks of Liberia seeing no new cases, a woman in Monrovia named Ruth Tugbah fell ill. The tests for Ebola were positive, and she would die of the disease in the following days, having again started a new chain of infection that led to a few hospitalizations but, mercifully, no deaths beyond her own.

As part of the contact tracing process, Tugbah was noted to have a boyfriend who had survived his own bout with Ebola, for he had been discharged from an ETU months before. A sample of his semen was obtained and tested for the presence of the genetic material—which is to say, the test just looked for pieces of the nucleic acid of Ebola rather than a complete, intact virus, because that test requires more elaborate scientific infrastructure than Liberia had to offer. Still, a positive test would be suggestive, and it was, the sample having been provided 175 days after the onset of his symptoms, which was 74 days longer than the virus had ever been known to persist in a human.

Ruth Tugbah's sad story couldn't be considered definitive proof of anything, but it certainly suggested that Ebola now had to be thought of not only as a zoonosis—that is, a disease humans obtain by being exposed to animals to which the microorganism is evolutionarily adapted—but also as a sexually transmitted disease. Because the virus persisted in semen but not in vaginal fluids (as considerable testing had shown), the sexual transmission was unidirectional: Men could infect women, but not the other way around.

There were hardly dozens of data points to make ironclad the conclusion that Ebola "lived" in semen much longer than anyone had previously thought, but what data points *did* exist were highly suggestive. The index case in the new Nedowein cluster still had no known cause, but sexual transmission made a great deal of sense.

The problem with this theory didn't lie in its intellectual and scientific consistency or its Occam's razor–like economy. As far as I was concerned, barring some startling new revelation, it was right. The *problem* was having sub-Saharan Africans acknowledge that men having sex with men actually took place on the continent and wasn't *just* practiced by morally perverse, white-skinned Westerners.

Ironically, at almost precisely the same time the story of the Nedowein cluster was reaching the outside world, a newsworthy event was taking place in Washington that would have almost as much of an impact as the new cases of Ebola were having back in the States. On June 26, in a case known as *Obergefell v. Hodges*, the U.S. Supreme Court in a 5-to-4 vote declared that same-sex couples had the constitutional right to marry. I felt a great deal of pride upon hearing the news just as I was traveling through the airport to catch a plane to Liberia. Sprinkled in between my dread about the Nedowein cluster was pure euphoria that the United States—*my* country— had made human decency front-page news. God bless you, Anthony Kennedy.

The reaction among my African friends was far more subdued. I had become part of a new Facebook community after working in Bong County, so now I periodically viewed the feeds of these friends, and many of them reacted to the news of the SCOTUS decision with bewilderment. Aside from their inability to comprehend how a nation governed at least in part by decent Christians could resort to such a policy, many had an especially difficult time understanding the *Obergefell* decision in relation to President Obama, who is as revered in Africa for being the first African-American to hold that office as he is by African-Americans back home. They thought, somehow, that this was *Obama's* policy rather than that of a different branch of government, as unaware of the separation of powers as a typical American would be of the complicated political power distribution in Iran. Robert

Mugabe, the ninety-one-year-old longtime leader of Zimbabwe, almost became crazed after the decision. "I've just concluded, since President Obama endorses the same-sex marriage, advocates homosexual people and enjoys an attractive countenance—thus if it becomes necessary, I shall travel to Washington, D.C., get down on my knee and ask his hand," he said in mock, well, something. The fact that the attractively countenanced president wasn't technically responsible for this, even if he did support it, made little difference.

Obergefell served to remind those of us working in Africa (or at least it reminded me) that whatever goodwill had been earned by bringing Ebola to heel, there were still deep cultural fissures where misunderstandings could quickly escalate to hostilities, and not all would be sweetness and light in the months to come. Not long after the decision, a Facebook post circulated among several of my African friends, taking direct aim at not merely gay marriage but even the most casual tolerance of the "gay lifestyle," or call it what you will:

LETTER TO WHITE MEN . . .

Dear white men, U asked us to wear coats under
hot sun, we did;

~

U said we should speak your language, we have
obediently ignored ours.

~

U asked us to always tie a rope around our necks
like goats, we have obeyed without questioning.

~

U asked our ladies to wear dead people's hair
instead of the natural hair God gave to them, they
have obeyed.

~

U said we should marry just one woman in the
midst of plenty black angels, we reluctantly
agreed.

~

You asked us to use rubber in order to control
our birth rate, we agreed. . . .

~

Now U want our MEN to sleep with fellow MEN &
WOMEN with fellow WOMEN so that God would
punish us like Sodom and Gomora?
we say No!!
We don't agree with U this time! Proudly African,
we say a huge NO to GAY relationships and
LESBIAN.

~

If U say NO to HOMOSEXUALS & LESBIANS type
NO!!!. And Share with your friends. . . .

~

Dont forget to Share with others

[Sic.]

"No," would be the next line of the feed, entered by someone.

"NO," came another line, and so on, the feed populating with enough "No" posts to seem as if someone had just pressed *Enter* on the keyboard and kept their finger on the button. If I had seen these kinds of sentiments expressed by my Facebook acquaintances in the States, I would simply have defriended them without a second thought. But it was more complicated here.

The reaction to the *Obergefell* decision did illustrate how cultural biases can affect scientific decisions. At the very least, sexual transmission was the *most likely* explanation of the Nedowein cluster, and that had real implications for the future. There were thousands of survivors, male survivors, whose semen was incubating a lethal virus. As with AIDS in the 1980s, if safe-sex practices weren't emphasized to *all* groups, new chains of transmission could start, and the epidemic would drag on like a brush fire, possibly for months, possibly for *years*, as the virus managed to find a new home in which to accommodate itself until it could strike again. But emphasizing this to all groups meant that acknowledging such groups even existed, and no African government was in any hurry to bestow any legitimacy on these sexual practices. *If this is how they could contract Ebola*, you can almost hear the reasoning go, *then they* deserve *to die*. The fact that others might also contract the disease and die just by being in the vicinity of such people didn't enter into the calculus.

Nedowein, though, quietly receded into a whisper. The story had barely registered back in the United States, but even here, it seemed to last not much past mid-July, as no further cases came to light. The dog story didn't pan out but seemed to be the last explanation left on the table, since none of the public servants were going to explain that the index case had probably acquired the infection as a result of having sex. The episode had ended without any celebrations this time, with everyone hoping that this was the last they would hear from Ebola ever again. The forty-two-day clock, which now seemed to be an increasingly strained way of concluding the outbreak was over, began again, but the nation wasn't collectively crossing off each calendar day as it had done before in April. When no further cases surfaced, people at JFK assumed the worst would not happen. I was less sanguine.

During this period, a patient had come to the Blue Room (since painted white) under murky circumstances from Grand Gedeh County, the area on the northeast edge of the country bordering Ivory Coast. He was lying there, moaning in bed, with a fever of 104 degrees, and my intern seemed untroubled by the fact that he couldn't explain to me in any detail what had happened to the man or how he had slipped through the screens, given that he could easily have been considered a potential case. Normally I'm an encouraging teacher, but this time I had sharp words for one of the trainees and it forced me, as the attending physician in Dr. Njoh's absence, into the unpleasant dilemma as to whether I was going to examine this patient without any PPE, since there was none to be had as far as I understood. It's a story for another day; the fact that I'm alive and writing these words, having never developed Ebola, should indicate that the man, who died later that night, wasn't infected. But I had Phil Ireland call his contacts at the Ministry of Health to run a confirmatory test just to be sure.

I spent the last two weeks of July with two primary goals: to enjoy my residents to the fullest extent possible, since I did not know when

I would see them next; and to play the role of decadent American tourist and scour the city's nicer bars in search of Monrovia's best drink. The final Saturday before I left, I managed to find what I was looking for. It was a margarita, at a bar called Tides, in a section of the city that I had never seen before, on the far side of the city center on UN Drive. The bar was in a second-story walk-up and looked out north onto the Atlantic Ocean; the destitute West Point neighborhood that had seen such exceptional misery one year before could be seen to the right. There was only a sliver of moon in the sky, and so the night was dark. Tides has a patio that opens right out onto the ocean, and the wind was blowing hard that night. I caught up with Trish Henwood, who also had come back to train Liberian doctors to use ultrasound machines, and I also chatted with various others who were there to help out. I drank three of these margaritas—it really is the best drink in Monrovia—in fairly short order, and eventually wobbled my way to the patio and just stared out at the ocean and up at the sky.

Trish, two other companions living at the Congo Town apartment, and I rode back home at midnight. We drove east on an unusually empty Tubman Boulevard, which only hours before was packed to the point that the five-mile distance to Tides took more than an hour to reach. It was like the entire population of Monrovia had disappeared in a puff—all the more amazing because I have seen Monrovia not teeming with people only once before, and that was at 3:30 a.m. after walking a friend home in the Sinkor neighborhood near JFK.

The car was quiet. We sat and listened to the BBC news on the radio. The length of the drive was occupied by an extended report of the Pluto flyby of NASA's *New Horizons* spacecraft. The story had been taking place over the past few days, but I wasn't able to fully appreciate it, since I hadn't seen any of the new pictures of Pluto, given the limited bandwidth of my temperamental mobile Wi-Fi hot spot.

Even so, as I sat there listening to the radio program, I couldn't help but feel a sense of wonderment at the magnificence of the event. This icy chunk of rock that circles the sun at an unimaginably long distance from our home had become linked to us in a new and utterly profound way. I was traveling on a road in Monrovia, a place that seemed no less distant to me than Pluto itself only two years before, hearing the voice of a reporter in London talk about a piece of metal built by my fellow Americans that was chirping out electronic signals to us just before it left the solar system on its own grand journey. It was humbling. It was wonderful. It inspired awe, true awe.

Earlier that day, I had stopped by JFK to check in on my resident, a woman named Joyce Bartekwa, who was taking call that day. A resident's on-call shift in Liberia is old-school: They start work one morning and work all the way into the following afternoon, without ever catching sleep and having hardly a moment to sit down, and they do this on average once every three or four nights for a year. Joyce was one of Liberia's most remarkable success stories, and so I had hoped to drop by to shower upon her every ounce of encouragement I could before leaving the country. She had started out her career as a nurse but had managed to make her way to Dogliotti to get her medical education, and she was now on the verge of advanced training. By my estimates, she was every bit as good, and frankly better, than many residents back in the States.

I didn't find her. I moved about the Critical Care Unit on the first floor and saw a seventeen-year-old who had been admitted in terrible respiratory distress two days before. We knew from looking at the X-ray that she had an enlarged heart and her lungs had too much fluid, both inside and outside. I couldn't tell you the cause, for without the resources to order the proper tests, all I could do was guess. Joyce had put a needle in the pocket of fluid outside her lung, draining the fluid off in order to give the lungs room to expand and bring more oxygen to her body. When I happened to wander in that afternoon, the patient had smiled for the first time.

I do not know what became of that young woman. Her symptoms improved from the drainage, so she no longer required care, and hospitalizations are exorbitant affairs for the average Liberian family, so it was time to go home the following day. I have no illusions about her long-term prognosis; whatever made that heart so big and unable to pump was unlikely to reverse itself, and few of the medications that could stave off the worst effects of the heart failure would be affordable to her family. The tattered Liberian health-care system wasn't capable of working *that* kind of miracle, and wouldn't be anytime soon. But at that moment when I encountered her, she was thriving and happy to feel better. That night, as we drove home, the improvement in her status, however temporary it may have been, filled me with a certain hope, not only for her, but somehow for Liberia as well. Driving along Tubman Boulevard, going from the city center through Sinkor and past JFK, I spotted a Coca-Cola billboard advertisement that I hadn't noticed before. Its message was one of pure optimism, simple in its presentation. It merely showed a man about my age, emerging from a car door, looking straight into the camera with a content appearance. "I'm confident of better days ahead," read the caption.

It is not my nature to feel such confidence, but perhaps that night I was as well.

EPILOGUE: SUNSET, SUNRISE

We bury people for dignity. Their dignity, and ours.

—Bruce Borowsky

On January 14, 2016, the World Health Organization issued a press release declaring the West African Ebola outbreak to be over. Technically, it marked the first time since Emile Ouamouno had fallen ill that the forty-two-day clock had run its course in all three countries and no cases could be found.

In the United States, it was a small news item, little noticed except by the global health community or those who had become Ebola junkies. The front-page news had been dominated for weeks by the increasingly divisive battle for the Republican nomination, the tenor of which had been determined in part by some of the anxieties that the outbreak itself had unleashed. Even though the announcement hadn't generated much of a splash, it did allow the WHO to declare some kind of a victory, finally affixing a stop date to the unprecedented epidemic, allowing the world to say in one collective sigh, "It's over."

The virus, however, wasted no time issuing a sharp rebuke to the WHO for even considering this feel-good moment. The following day a new case cropped up in the Port Loko District of Sierra Leone; the young woman who had been diagnosed with the infection, named Tunis Yaha, was already dead. The staff of the WHO had, in fact, predicted this. The press release was careful in its wording, stating even in the headline that so-called flare-ups were likely to occur. Ten of these flare-ups had been recorded thus far. Vigilance, the press release noted, would need to be maintained well into the future. But since they knew other cases might well emerge, that only raised the question of why anyone would "declare" a cessation of the outbreak at all. Because of the sheer bad luck of the press release's timing, coming as it did within hours of the announcement of one of these flare-ups, the WHO appeared foolish at a time when it desperately needed to shore up its image. Of course, shoring up its image was the whole reason for the press release in the first place. It was a gamble that did not pay off in terms of public relations.

In a related effort to prove that it was not asleep at the wheel of global health, and perhaps feeling the sting from the miscalculation of the Ebola announcement, two weeks later the WHO declared a public health emergency surrounding what until then had been a little-known virus called Zika. Zika is a mosquito-borne illness belonging to a family known as *flaviviruses,* whose relatives included dengue, yellow fever, and more distantly, hepatitis C; my early postdoctoral research had been on dengue, so I knew flaviviruses pretty well, and even I had never heard of it. Now, however, two clinical syndromes had been spotted in Brazil that might be linked to the virus, leading public health authorities to investigate further. The first syndrome was a neurological condition known as Guillan-Barré syndrome: Clinically, it behaved as though a person was getting a rapidly progressive version of multiple sclerosis, and it had the potential to be lethal. The second syndrome, which garnered much more attention as 2016 began, was the appalling condition of microcephaly, in which a baby's brain and head do not develop completely. Severe cases showed babies with faces but no forehead at all, and the skull would just drop down after the eyebrows to the back of the neck. Our innate facial-recognition software, a biological program that functions deep within the most primitive centers of our cognition, goes haywire at the sight of such a child.

The early epidemiologic research on Zika suggested a link between the two, but by the time of the public health emergency declaration, the fact that Zika *caused* these conditions had not yet been firmly established. The conclusions about Zika's danger certainly seemed rushed, given that public health officials work hand in hand with scientists, and science is an inherently conservative field, cautious in its suppositions and rarely in a hurry to announce hard conclusions. Had the Zika outbreak been killing indiscriminately, like Ebola had done, then arguably caution needed to take a backseat. But Zika, whatever its putative harms, affected very few people and could not be supposed, even under worst-case scenarios, to threaten tens of thousands of people or bring the world economy to a halt.

As I write these words in March 2016, the current estimate is that Zika might lead to microcephaly in one live birth per one thousand. That statistic is not far from the incidence of Fetal Alcohol Syndrome in the United States, a condition with equally devastating consequences for the baby and, because it damages the developing brain, for much the same reasons. Yet one would be hard pressed to find the same level of disquiet about Fetal Alcohol Syndrome in the press, even though this condition can be entirely prevented by a sharp reduction in the alcohol intake of heavy-drinking pregnant women. By contrast, individuals themselves living in endemic areas can do effectively nothing to prevent Zika, and public health measures such as mosquito control could very likely have unintended consequences that could be just as bad or worse than the Zika problem ever could produce on its own.

It is certainly possible that events in the months or years to come will vindicate the WHO for its choice to label the Zika epidemic a public health emergency, and I will be as chastened as I hope Gregory Härtl currently is. Härtl, you will recall, is the WHO official who had engaged in the Twitter war with MSF, accusing them of exaggeration, insinuating that they were fomenting panic in the early hours of the Ebola outbreak. Maybe Zika will really be all that, and my dismissal of it as a truly serious health threat on a par with TB, HIV, and drug-resistant bacteria, among several other issues, will be seen in the sharp and unforgiving light of hindsight as another misstep by an arrogant doctor infatuated with his own judgment. The point I'm trying to make, however, is that what *can't* be disputed is Zika's provisional status as a threat. The global health community, as well as the international media, is *already* reacting, and reacting emphatically, to Zika's menace, but at least at this moment, the scope and the magnitude of this epidemic is far from clear.

How to account for Zika's current infamy, which might ultimately be seen as an overreaction? I think one need look no further than the debacle of the Ebola-is-over declaration. The phenomenon of Zika as a cultural and scientific force can be understood as a direct effect of the Ebola outbreak.

And it is but one such effect. World travel restrictions to the outbreak nations are another effect. International agribusiness and transcontinental trade in material commodities have both been affected by the outbreak. The current political landscape of the United States—which at the time of this writing in mid-2016 is highly fluid and dynamic, and routinely includes frankly disturbing rhetoric that now passes for respectable opinion among the leaders of one major political party along with tens of millions of its voters—has been influenced mightily by the events that unfolded in remote African villages throughout 2014 and much of 2015. One doesn't have to search too hard to find these effects, both direct and indirect, of the West African outbreak.

But the most important effect of the Ebola outbreak is, of course, the dead.

By the time the WHO issued its final situation report prior to declaring the outbreak over, the tally was staggering. Officially, there had been 28,601 cumulative cases—that's the kind of fixed, reified number that will be committed to memory by people fascinated by and drawn to Ebola and the disaster-porn titillation it can induce. Yet "cumulative cases" is a deceptively simple epidemiologic phrase reflecting the difficulties of tracking the epidemic given the numerous impediments facing the workers. It includes confirmed cases—those with a positive blood test—but also takes into account those who probably had Ebola but never came to formal medical attention, either because they had avoided ETUs or because they were dead already. Of the final tally, just over half fit into this category.

Similarly, the final death count stood at 11,300. Both the number of cases and the number of dead are universally agreed-upon undercounts, though by how much nobody can be certain. "The majority of these cases and deaths were reported between August and December 2014," notes the WHO situation report, and given that we know the virus had been running rampant in May, June, and July of that year before the international organizations had put many boots on the ground, thousands more must have been infected and succumbed.

No matter the exact number, by the time August 2014 had rolled around, so many deaths were taking place in Monrovia that there was not enough space and time to bury all the dead. The Sirleaf administration was forced to make the unenviable decision to cremate the bodies. Until then, Ebola skepticism still largely ruled the day among the populace, but the cremations caused a seismic shift in perception. Since burial is a deeply sacred rite in Liberian society, not even the most cynical Liberian would resort to a policy as extreme as mass cremation unless something truly unprecedented was taking place. And, moreover, that it posed a genuine threat to everyone. "It started to sink in when the cremations began," Phil Ireland told me in July 2015. One of the medical students who had been working at JFK had contracted the disease and had now died. Phil, by that point, had survived his infection, and along with some of his colleagues they placed the young man in a body bag and took him to one of the burial sites on the edge of the city. There, instead of hearing the quiet of the cemetery, they were confronted with the sounds of a crematorium running at full tilt. When the skulls exploded from the pressure, there was a grenade-like sound. "It was so chilling. Sends something down your spine when you hear it," Phil said to me as he shook his head and tried to rid himself of the memory.

In Bong County, we were much luckier. Time and space allowed us develop a proper cemetery, and all of the dead from the ETU were buried there. You got to the cemetery by walking the peripheral road next to the compound and then veering to the left down the hill where the jungle takes you back into its arms and the gravel, fencing, and blue tarp suddenly seem a distant memory. The trees stand about ten meters high and have vines that cascade down them. The clearing for the bodies is a little bigger than a basketball court. The gravesites are lined up in neat rows. The birds and insects assert themselves here, sometimes loudly, but even with this noise there's a profound silence that hovers over it. I think it is one of the most beautiful places that I have ever been on earth. I also think it is one of the most horrifying.

There are about five rows of graves, with the earliest victims buried in the first row, moving outward in time as the outbreak continued. I start to know the people behind the names at the end of the first row, and I stop knowing them midway through the fourth. Their names are marked on wooden markers about the size of a car's license plate, and I can see them in my head. Winner Thomas. Moses Gboi. Freeman Sirleaf. Joe Bongo. Ballah Kollie. Robert Yini. Mamie Flomo. Willie Rancy. Yattah Singbeh. Dorcas David. Solomon Zonnah. There are other names there as well, people whose stories I do not know, who had died in the two weeks before I arrived and the two months afterward. Aaron Tokpah. Kammah Paye. Fatu Cyphus. Roland Sackie. Matthew Tarweh. Baby Kerkula. By the time the Bong County ETU had closed its doors, nearly 150 of these graves were occupied. Not all had died from Ebola. If a patient died in the ETU but their test returned negative, they still had to be buried there, because of the concerns that the body might have copies of the virus as a result of having been inside the Hot Zone. But most of the patients, at least one hundred of them, had died from the virus.

A group of day laborers was hired to do the work of digging the graves. Although I only rarely saw them since I was pretty busy up the hill, when I came down I could see how physically demanding the work was. They required thick leather gloves to hold the wooden shovels and spades necessary to go two meters into the thick and muddy African soil. The repetitive motion caused so much wear on the gloves that they had to be replaced every few days. I promised myself that I would go down at some point to help out, but the weeks passed quickly, and then I found myself headed for home, and one of my major regrets from that time is that I never did assist in this simple yet challenging task, both for their dignity, and mine.

John Jameson was one of the members of the grave-digging team. Ben Solomon of *The New York Times* interviewed him for a seven-minute clip called "Inside the Ebola Ward." It was a masterpiece of journalism in Bong County, with Ben's video accompanying Sheri Fink's words and Daniel Berehulak's photographs as the definitive account of one small corner in the Ebola battle. Two others were featured in the piece: Garmai Cyrus of the psychosocial team and Colin Bucks of the medical staff. Jameson, however, was given the last word in the interview, an editorial decision on Ben's part that proved prescient, Garmai's and Colin's eloquence notwithstanding.

"We won't forget about Ebola," Jameson said. "I'm working as a gravedigger. I'm not a doctor or a nurse. Instead of me spending the day doing nothing, I decided to join in the process to fight against Ebola. Our brothers and sisters, they are all dying. Day and night. Every day. They brought a baby here when the baby died. Four days old baby. So they could bury the baby close by her mother. No mercy from Ebola.

"I have a family. I have two children. When my children grow up, they will see in magazines, in books, and they will see some pictures about Ebola. They will know, 'Oh our dad [was] here. I think he was fighting through the process during the times of Ebola.' They should be proud.

"Ebola is affecting the world seriously," Jameson concluded. "If I go and sit aside and just be looking at it, you know what Ebola will do? It will damage so many people in this world. So when I'm working here, I'm helping to save the world."

It is because of men and women like John Jameson that the world still stands.

The baby to which Jameson referred was, of course, the baby that had been born to the woman whom I so hastily evaluated without adequate protection in the first week of October, whose name was Diana Flomo. As most of us had predicted, though without any satisfaction, the baby, who probably had Ebola, did not have long to live. To the best of my knowledge, that chain of death ended there, and no one else was infected.

Stu Sia had been the person in charge of marking the graves. It is his handwriting that I can see on the markers in my mind's eye. The strange quality of seeing your handwriting coming back to you in unanticipated moments has always fascinated me. My handwriting from this time can be found in the pages of our admission ledger, but Stu's is a more public remnant of those few months. The initial lettering was done with a Sharpie because of a lack of black paint, an improvisation that was later corrected so the names could persist for posterity. Though what the jungle will do to some simple wooden markers, or how quickly it will do it, is unclear.

In addition to the names of the dead, which are introduced by the phrase, "In Loving Memory," the grave markers have one additional piece of information: the birth and death dates. Many older Liberians do not know their actual birthdates, nor do many who were born during the Civil War, since the accurate recording of time was a low priority then. Without knowing this, your eye might be caught by the shocking number of people who were born on January 1, but it is just a quirky by-product of those times. Unlike graves in the States, where these dates are usually provided by the sterile descriptors of "born" and "died," Liberians have opted for a more poetic way to proclaim a person's entrance into and exit from this world. *Sunrise* is your beginning. *Sunset*, your end.

Bendu Howard is a name that you will *not* find in that cemetery, as her sunset, I hope, is still far off in the future. A sixteen-year-old, Bendu fought off the virus, and in her convalescence discovered she had an appetite for caring for others. At the time she was nearing complete health, there were many children in the confirmed ward, and Bendu had started following the nursing and psychosocial staff around to learn about ways in which she could help. Before any of us had processed it, we were training Bendu. By the time her viral load was negative, she had made the unfathomable request to stay on in the unit and help out for a few days. When I heard about the request, I just blinked in astonishment, and I was hardly the only one.

The few days passed, and then when she was ready to return home, she asked if she could come back to work for us. If she really was immune, she reasoned, she would be an asset in the confirmed ward because she could stay in all day without PPE and help in the daily tasks. So each morning she came to work, passed through into the Hot Zone, and then emerged at the end of a shift through the decontamination shower just as every patient did on discharge. When I last saw her, she had declared to me that her life's calling was to be a nurse, an idea that took shape as a consequence of being in the presence of the very finest that profession has ever produced.

There were other sunrises that took place in defiance of Ebola's deadly menace. As the worst of the outbreak had passed and the streets of Monrovia were returning to normal by late 2014, there were news reports of an upsurge in weddings. In mid-2015, one of the more unexpected weddings took place, one to which the IMC staff had become connected. Two of the staff working in the operation's headquarters in Monrovia, one a Liberian and the other an expat, had fallen in love. Had the outbreak never happened, they never would have met. I did not know the happy couple myself, but I followed the event on my IMC friends' Facebook feeds. The pictures included several of the people I knew, no longer appearing grimy and wearing the cheap clothing or scrubs in which I had become accustomed to seeing them, but decked out in formal finery, all beaming.

The burials that took place that terrible year were designed to provide a sense of dignified closure, even those burials, like the ones in Bong County, that were finished within a minute and performed with few words and often no tears. But the weddings that returned to Liberia, Sierra Leone, and Guinea were the ceremonial bookends to the Ebola outbreak—communal assertions that, whatever setbacks lay ahead, happiness and contentment would still triumph. There were more sunrises to be witnessed.

Acknowledgments

While I wrote the words, this book could not have been possible without the help of the following people, through their intelligence, their warmth, and their willingness to give.

There are many people I met during my training at Fort McClellan in Anniston, Alabama, to whom I am indebted for their generosity of spirit. An abbreviated list includes Martha Mock, Tony Fiore, and Satish Pillai of the CDC; Rupa Narra of the CDC's Epidemic Intelligence Service; Nahid Bhadelia of Boston University; Major Matthew Chambers of the U.S. Army; Emily Veltus of MSF; Commander James Lawler of the U.S. Navy; Lieutenant Colonel Tom Wilson and Lieutenant Colonel William E. Thoms of the U.S. Air Force; the PIH posse of Anany Prosper, Paul Pierre, and Joia Mukherjee; Dan Kelly of the University of California, San Francisco; Preetha Iyengar of Save the Children; and Pam Falk. Then there is the ultimate badass, Lieutenant Commander Elizabeth Lybarger DeGrange of the U.S. Public Health Service, without whom the experience of Camp Ebola would certainly have been less vivid.

There is a long list of IMC staff who each have incredible stories; their dedication and spirit inspired and humbled me when I worked there in October and November 2014 and when I returned in February 2015. One group in particular merits special thanks: the expat nursing staff. The lion's share of the work fell to the nurses, who not only risked their lives on a daily basis with frequent blood draws and IV line placements, but coordinated the work of the national staff nurses and nursing aides, all while tending to upwards of fifty patients, clad in full PPE, working in the searing heat for up to three hours a stretch. Thanks, therefore, to Rosa Nin-Gonzales, Pero Tabby, Patrick Githinji, Bridget Mulrooney, Audrey Rangel, Elvis Ogweno, Kelly Suter, Megan Vitek, Amaia Artázcoz, Rakel Vives Font, and a very special thanks to my guardian angel, Nora Hellman, whose timely words in a dimly lit office one morning at Cuttington University in February 2015 literally helped me cling to life when the darkness nearly consumed me.

The remainder of the IMC crew with whom I had the honor of working will always hold a special place in my heart. Sean Casey and Pranav Shetty were all one could ask for as they ran the ETU. I came to think of Sean and Pranav as the Jordan-Pippen of international medical relief—though I won't speculate, at least publicly, as to which was Jordan and which Pippen. Others on the IMC crew, all of whom deserve more than just being a name in a list, alas, include Hilarie Cranmer, Margaret Traub, Adam Levine, Colin Bucks, Trish Henwood, Steve Whiteley, Kwan Kew Lai, Stuart Sia, Fredericka Feuchte, Sambhavi Cheemalapati, Jean-Francois Baptiste, Yves-Pierre Beauchemin, Godfrey Oryem, Sam Siakor, Garmai Cyrus, "President" Thomas Jefferson, Vasco Wuokolo, A. Welehyou Duo, Amanda Karpeh, Julius Sevelee, Sophie Bellorh Jarpah, Yarmah Cooper, Love Fassama, Augustin Mulbah, Bendu Howard, Comfort Harris, Marco Morelli, Eoin "Sláinte" Ó Riain, Katie Mullins, Olivia Roberts, Simon Cowie, Maia Baldauf, Linda Shipton, Samer Attar, Paul Douglas Waggoner, Joshua Wilkie, David Imo Mwita, and last but not least, Dziwe Ntaba. As I write their names, I think of the stories they told me, of the horrors and the triumphs and the hilarities they encountered in their work, and it feels shameful just to list their names without telling readers more. My apologies to them all.

Without the members of the U.S. Navy who had been deployed to Liberia, the entire experience of the Bong County ETU would have been remarkably more stressful. Because of their ferocious competence, a fast turnaround time that provided absolutely reliable results prevented many dilemmas from ever happening. Thanks go out to them and their leader, Lieutenant Commander Ben Espinosa. Talk about things I never thought I'd say, but what the hell: *Go Navy!*

Others that were there along the way: Daniel Berehulak, whose genial nature never failed to make my soul feel lighter; Ben Solomon; Rick Kopelman; the amazing Ayan Zado; Cristina Santamaria and her always-buoyant missives; Karen Wong of the CDC; Rene Vega, a doctor who could not be better suited for a group named Heart to Heart; Gus Kuldau, for graciously tolerating my appallingly rude tantrum on Facebook; Nisha Makan, with whom I had conversations about infrastructure and development that were far too short; Jason Odhner; Laura Chambers-Kersh; Gregg Lucksinger; Laura Milligan; Lauren Sattely Snow; Hunter Keys; Jennifer Dienstag Levine; Marra Gad; Kidist Tarekegn; Ignace Nzayisenga; Sia Kamarra; and Roseda Marshall, the president of the Liberian College of Physicians and Surgeons. A special thanks to Sheri Fink for being there from nearly the beginning.

Many people from my home institution of UMass deserve shout-outs. Most important is the Tackle Ebola group, whose work was funded by the Paul G. Allen Family Foundation and includes Trish McQuilkin, Ann Moorman, Jeff Bailey, Katherine Luzuriaga, Christine Wassuna, and Salimata Bangoura. Jennifer Berryman, the Vice Chancellor for Communications at the UMass Medical School, was incredibly kind throughout my many comings and goings. My department chair, Robert Finberg, along with Chancellor Michael Collins, gave real support after I had returned from my first stint. Deb Poliquin treated me with much-needed nonchalance at a time when a good many people thought of me as something akin to being radioactive. Rick Forster provided behind-the-scenes moral support in his typically levelheaded manner, proving his status as a man of exceptional quality. Nancy Skehan just sat and listened to me for a few hours one night as I tried to readjust to the reality of being back in Massachusetts days after I left the ETU. Jackie St. Martin gave me Saint Anthony to watch over me during the outbreak, and he watches over me still, though likely with reservations. Thanks to all of them.

Likewise, I was blessed to have had a fantastic set of correspondents from UMass throughout my deployments in Liberia in 2014 and 2015. Their good cheer made e-mail a special treat and served as my mental home away from home while I worked in the ETU, on the campus of Ebola University at Cuttington, or at JFK in Monrovia. Thanks therefore to David Clive, Sara Jacques, Chris Bielick, Keith Boundy, Katey Walsh, Tara Bouton, Sunkaru Touray, Suzanne Sprague, Adam Hodes, Justin Lui, Tony Ogunsa, Shu Yang, Vitaly Belyshev, Anne Barnard, Kim Cullen, Emily Bouley, and Jennifer Perez. Also thanks to my internal medicine clerks who insisted that we continue didactics from Monrovia via Skype: Valerie Valant, Caroline Bancroft, Sarah Fulco, Mary Cavanaugh, Jasmine Khubchandani, Justin Vaida, and Sarah McGowan.

I would also like to thank some non-UMass members of the ACCEL group, a consortium of academic institutions devoted to on-going work in Liberia. There is Lise Rehwaldt, an ob-gyn long based in Liberia working at Phebe; my Liberian karaoke partner Tina Thomas; Alexandra Vinograd; Kathleen Rowe; A. K. Raja Rao; and Gregory Engel, who has been getting the residency program back on its feet after losing so many critical players. Also thanks to Ian Yeung of the National Institutes of Health in Bethesda for his kindness, scholarship, and clinical acumen.

Bravo to all the members of the staff at JFK Hospital, whose bravery knows no bounds. I would especially like to thank Joyce Bartekwa, Zoeban Parteh, Yassa Barclay, and Ian Wachekwa for their enthusiasm and thoughtfulness, as well as Joseph Njoh, JFK's sole internist at the time of my return in 2015. A great thanks is due to Phil Ireland, who not only endured what even an atheist would regard as hell but came through the experience seemingly spiritually unscathed, still ready and willing to answer the call to help heal his fellow Liberians and patients in general. Hippocrates is smiling somewhere, I'm sure of it.

I am grateful to Pastor O'Malley Moore Segbee and the congregation of Grace Baptist Church in Gbarnga for their gracious hospitality in taking me into their fold for one day. Pastor Segbee passed away during the writing of this book; I hope that my words about him and that day have proven worthy of his leadership during the outbreak. Similarly, Dennis Khakie exhibited heroism in going before his congregation as an upbeat survivor, setting an example for courage in the face of terror. Dennis, too, has since passed away; may his name be a blessing.

Thanks to the pros: Andy Ross for maintaining faith in his slush-pile writer; George Witte for his editorial work and for seeing value in the project; Sara Thwaite, my fellow Buckeye, for timely and helpful replies; Carrie Watterson for continuing our collaboration; Meg Drislane, Tracey Guest, Rebecca Lang, and the rest of the St. Martin's crew.

Thanks to the people who read portions of the manuscript and gave helpful feedback, a pat on the shoulder, or both. Jana Broadhurst was the first person to listen to the proto-thoughts that would eventually develop into this book one night in Anniston, Alabama; I very much appreciate her feedback, which allowed some ideas to take root. Isaac Peace Hazard, Barrie Wheeler, and Amit Segal propped me up at various points during the writing of the manuscript. Bruce Borowsky and Bess Welden (along with her wonderful husband, David Hilton) all provided special help with their typical brilliance, especially as I made my final push in finishing the manuscript during some cold days in Maine in March 2016. Mark Meyers, as he has done since a tender age, served as my sounding board from beginning to end and in doing so kept my deeply neurotic but intermittently productive core on track, patiently indulging all my trepidations and making the world seem not quite as severe a place as I frequently assume it to be.

With characteristic fortitude, Miriam Tuchman unflappably protected her family while the world watched Liberia and the rest of West Africa with bated breath. No set of words can fully convey my appreciation for her sacrifices.

A final thanks to my children, Erez and Ariella, for being my Polaris, even when the rest of the night sky went to black.

Bibliography

Achebe, Chinua. "An Image of Africa: Racism in Conrad's *Heart of Darkness*." In *Hopes and Impediments: Selected Essays, 1965–1987*, pp. 251-261. Portsmouth, N.H.: Heinemann Educational Books, 1988.

Allen, Samantha. "Back from Liberia, UMass Memorial Doctor Will Not Treat Patients for 21 Days." *Worcester Telegram & Gazette*, November 14, 2014.

Associated Press. "Liberian Official: 7 More Deaths Linked to Ebola." June 17, 2014.

———. "Doctors Without Borders: Ebola 'Out of Control.'" June 20, 2014.

———. "Ebola Cases Rise in Africa as Doctors Sound Alarm." June 23, 2014.

———. "Ebola Kills Liberian Doctor, 2 Americans Infected." July 27, 2014.

———. "Liberian Couples Marry, a Sign of Less Ebola Fear." November 18, 2014.

Barbash, Fred. "Disneyland Measles Outbreak Strikes in Anti-vaccination Hotbed of California." *Washington Post*, January 22, 2015.

Berehulak, Daniel. "Portraits: Braving Ebola." *New York Times*, October 31, 2014.

British Broadcasting Corporation. "Liberia Ebola Epidemic 'Over,' Ending West African Outbreak." January 14, 2016.

Brittain, Amy. "The Fear of Ebola Led to Slayings—and a Whole Village Was Punished." *Washington Post*, February 28, 2015.

Cheng, Christine. "Sirleaf: A Controversial Laureate?" *Al Jazeera English* online, October 12, 2011. http://www.aljazeera.com/indepth/opinion/2011/10/201110127284188210.html, accessed July 2016.

Ciment, James. *Another America: The Story of Liberia and the Former Slaves Who Ruled It*. New York: Hill and Wang, 2013.

Cooper, Helene. *The House at Sugar Beach: In Search of a Lost African Childhood*. New York: Simon & Schuster, 2008.

Cooper, Helene, Shear, Michael, and Grady, Denise. "US to Commit Up to 3,000 Troops to Fight Ebola in West Africa." *New York Times*, September 15, 2014.

Cowell, Alan. "Liberian Leader Reported to Fire Officials for Defying Ebola Order." *New York Times*, August 26, 2014.

Davis, Rebecca. "Panic in the Parking Lot: A Hospital Sees Its First Ebola Case." *National Public Radio*, October 14, 2014.

Deen, Gibrilla, et al. "Ebola RNA Persistence in Semen of Ebola Virus Disease Survivors—Preliminary Report." *New England Journal of Medicine*, October 14, 2015, DOI: 10.1056/NEJMoa1511410.

Fink, Sheri. "3 Liberian Health Workers with Ebola Receive Scarce Drug After Appeals to the US." *New York Times*, August 16, 2014.

———. "Life, Death, and Grim Routine Fill the Day at a Liberian Ebola Clinic." *New York Times*, October 7, 2014.

———. "Heart-Rending Test in Ebola Zone: A Baby." *New York Times*, October 9, 2014.

———. "Wish to Do More in Ebola Fight Meets Reality in Liberia." *New York Times*, October 27, 2014.

———. "In Liberia, a Very Good or a Very Bad Sign: Empty Hospital Beds." *New York Times*, October 28, 2014.

———. "Ebola's Mystery: One Boy Lives, Another Dies." *New York Times*, November 9, 2014.

———. "Exposure Concerns Grow in Liberia After Diagnosis of First Ebola Case in Weeks." *New York Times*, March 24, 2015.

Garrett, Laurie. *The Coming Plague: Newly Emerging Diseases in a World Out of Balance.* New York: Macmillan, 1994.

———. "Heartless but Effective: I've Seen 'Cordon Sanitaire' Work Against Ebola." *New Republic*, August 14, 2014.

Gholipur, Bahar. "How Ebola Got Its Name." *Huffington Post*, October 10, 2014. http://www.huffingtonpost.com/2014/10/13/ebola -name_n_5976600.html, accessed July 2016.

Giahyue, James Harding. "Liberia Declared Ebola-Free, Signaling End to West African Epidemic." *Reuters*, January 14, 2016.

Goah, Bernard Gbayee. "Ellen Johnson Sirleaf Should Not Be Allowed in the USA!" *Front Page Africa*, May 1, 2014.

Grady, Denise. "Health Agency's New Assessment of Epidemic Is More Dire Still." *New York Times*, September 22, 2014.

———. "Ebola Cases Could Reach 1.4 Million Within Four Months, CDC Estimates." *New York Times*, September 23, 2014.

Grady, Denise, and Fink, Sheri. "Tracing Ebola's Breakout to an African 2-Year-Old." *New York Times*, August 9, 2014.

Guardian. "New Ebola Death in Sierra Leone as WHO Says Epidemic Over." January 15, 2016.

Hall, John. "Robert Mugabe 'Proposes to Barack Obama': Zimbabwe's Leader Says He Will Travel to the White House, 'Get Down on One Knee and Ask His Hand' as He Mocks US Legalisation of Gay Marriage." *Daily Mail UK online*, June 30, 2015. http://www .dailymail.co.uk/news/article-3144219/Robert-Mugabe-proposes -Barack-Obama-Zimbabwe-s-leader-says-travel-White-House -one-knee-ask-hand-mocks-legalisation-gay-marriage.html, accessed July 2016.

Hickox, Kaci. "Her Story: UTA Grad Isolated at New Jersey Hospital in Ebola Quarantine." *Dallas Morning News*, October 25, 2014.

Hildebrandt, Amber. "Ebola Outbreak: Why Liberia's Quarantine in West Point Slum Will Fail." *CBC News World*, August 25, 2014.

Hochschild, Adam. *King Leopold's Ghost: A Story of Greed, Terror, and Heroism in Colonial Africa.* Boston: Houghton Mifflin, 1998.

Jacobson, Gary. "Revenue Off 25 Percent, ER Visits Down by Half at

Presbyterian Dallas during Ebola Crisis." *Dallas Morning News*, October 22, 2014.

Johnson, Steven. *How We Got to Now: Six Innovations That Made the Modern World*. New York: Riverhead Books, 2014.

Kaplan, Karen. "Vaccine Refusal Helped Fuel Disneyland Measles Outbreak, Study Says." *Los Angeles Times*, March 16, 2015.

Kiley, M. P., et al. "Filoviridae: A Taxonomic Home for Marburg and Ebola Viruses?" *Intervirology* 18 (1982): 24–32.

Kreuels, Benno, et al. "A Severe Case of Severe Ebola Virus Infection Complicated by Gram-Negative Septicemia." *New England Journal of Medicine* 371, no. 25 (2014): 2394–401.

Leendertz, F., et al. "Assessing the Evidence Supporting Fruit Bats as the Primary Reservoirs for Ebola Viruses." *Ecohealth* 13, no. 1 (March 2016): 18–25.

Light, Nannette, and Fancher, Julie. "Reunion between Nina Pham, Dog Bentley Must Wait." *Dallas Morning News*, October 25, 2014.

Loftis, Randy Lee, Mervosh, Sarah, and Ramirez, Marc. "Ebola Crisis Is Testing Presbyterian Hospital Dallas." *Dallas Morning News*, October 18, 2014.

MacDougall, Claire. "Liberia Reports New Cases of Ebola." *New York Times*, July 2, 2015.

Mate, Suzanne, et al. "Molecular Evidence of Sexual Transmission of Ebola Virus." *New England Journal of Medicine* 373, no. 25 (2015): 2448–54.

McNeil, Donald. "Ebola, Killing Scores in Guinea, Threatens Nearby Nations." *New York Times*, March 24, 2014.

———. "Ebola Doctors Are Divided on IV Therapy in Africa." *New York Times*, January 1, 2015.

Miller, T. Christian, and Jones, Jonathan. "Firestone and the Warlord: The Untold Story of Firestone, Charles Taylor, and the Tragedy of Liberia." *ProPublica*, November 18, 2014.

Moore, John. "Battling Ebola in Liberia." *New York Times*, August 16, 2014.

Nossiter, Adam. "Ebola Reaches Capital of Guinea, Stirring Fears." *New York Times*, April 1, 2014.

Nyenswah, Tolbert, et al. "Community Quarantine to Interrupt Ebola Virus Transmission—Mawah Village, Bong County, Liberia, August–October, 2014." *Morbidity and Mortality Weekly Report* 64, no. 7 (2015): 179–82.

O'Carroll, Lisa. "Ebola Epidemic: Sierra Leone Quarantines a Million People." *Guardian*, September 25, 2014.

Onishi, Norimitsu. "Liberian Boy Dies after Being Shot During Clash over Ebola Quarantine." *New York Times*, August 21, 2014.

Phillip, Abby. "Eight Dead in Attack on Ebola Team in Guinea: 'Killed in Cold Blood.'" *Washington Post*, September 18, 2014.

Piot, Peter. *No Time to Lose: A Life in Pursuit of Deadly Viruses*. New York: W. W. Norton, 2012.

Preston, Richard. *The Hot Zone: A Terrifying True Story*. New York: Anchor, 1995.

Quammen, David. *Ebola: The Natural and Human History of a Deadly Virus*. New York: W. W. Norton, 2014.

Reuters. "Mystery Hemorrhagic Fever Kills 23 in Guinea." March 19, 2014.

———. "Guinea Confirms Fever Is Ebola, Has Killed Up to 59." March 22, 2014.

———. "Liberian Health Authorities Confirm Two Cases of Ebola: WHO." March 30, 2014.

———. "Five Dead as Sierra Leone Records First Ebola Outbreak." May 26, 2014.

———. "Ebola Outbreak Is Largest Ever." July 1, 2014.

Roberts, Michelle. "Zika-Linked Condition: WHO Declares Global Emergency." *BBC News*, February 1, 2016.

Sack, Kevin. "Downfall for Hospital Where Ebola Spread." *New York Times*, October 15, 2014.

Sack, Kevin, Fink, Sheri, Belluck, Pam, and Nossiter, Adam. "How Ebola Roared Back." *New York Times*, December 29, 2014.

Saéz, Almudena Marí, et al. "Investigating the Zoonotic Origin of the West African Ebola Epidemic." *EMBO Molecular Medicine* 7, no. 1 (January 2015): 17–23.

Searcey, Dionne, and Fink, Sheri. "Day After Victory over Ebola, Sierra Leone Reports a Death." *New York Times*, January 15, 2016.

Solomon, Ben. "Inside the Ebola Ward." *New York Times*, October 23, 2014.

Stylianou, Nassos. "How World's Worst Ebola Outbreak Began with One Boy's Death." *BBC News Africa*, November 27, 2014.

Takahashi, Saki, et al. "Reduced Vaccination and the Risk of Measles and Other Childhood Infections Post-Ebola." *Science* 347, no. 6227 (2015): 1240–42.

VICE News. "Butt Naked in Liberia." 2013. http://www.vice.com /video/butt-naked-in-liberia, accessed March 2016. The original VICE series featuring Joshua Blahyi was aired in 2010 under the title "The VICE Guide to Liberia": http://www.vice.com/video/the -vice-guide-to-liberia-1.

Whitcomb, Dan. "Update 1—Disneyland Seeks to Reassure Public amid Measles Outbreak." *Reuters*, January 22, 2015.

Wilonsky, Robert. "Congressional Committee Releases Timeline Detailing How Presbyterian Treated Ebola Patient Thomas Eric Duncan." *Dallas Morning News*, October 25, 2014.

World Health Organization. Ebola Situation Report. All reports archived at http://www.who.int/csr/disease/ebola/situation-reports /archive/en/. In particular, the situation reports from October 10, 2014, November 26, 2014, July 8, 2015, and January 3, 2016, feature prominently in the events described in the book.

———. "Latest Ebola Outbreak Over in Liberia; West Africa Is at Zero, but New Flare-ups Are Likely to Occur." January 14, 2016.

Wordsworth, Dot. "How Ebola Got Its Name, and Why It Isn't 'Yambuku Fever.'" *Spectator*, October 25, 2014.

Index